THE REMINISCENCES OF
Rear Admiral Ernest M. Eller
U.S. Navy (Retired) – Volume III

INTERVIEWED BY
John T. Mason Jr. and Paul Stillwell

U.S. Naval Institute • Annapolis, Maryland

Copyright © 2016

Preface

This third and concluding volume of Admiral Eller's memoir provides convincing evidence of the versatility that is called for in a Navy unrestricted line officer. Among other things, his skills included use of oral and written communication on behalf of the service, diplomatic and strategic ability in dealing with overseas nations, and seamanship and tactical ability on board ship. What also comes through repeatedly is Eller's proactive nature in getting things going—ranging from trips throughout the Middle East to kick-starting many worthwhile projects concerned with naval history.

Throughout the narrative, the admiral demonstrated his loyalty to nation and service. Because of his abilities as an observer and writer, he was able to provide detailed word pictures on the many places his travels took him on behalf of the United States. He covered the bitter Defense Department unification battle that overtook Washington in the late 1940s, the vital role of Middle East oil in supporting United Nations naval forces in the Korean War, the role of Navy ships as ambassadors, and the fight against Communism during a difficult period in the long-lasting Cold War. He worked with five men who at various times served as Chiefs of Naval Operations: Chester Nimitz, Louis Denfeld, Forrest Sherman, Robert Carney, and Arleigh Burke. He also provided profiles of a host of foreign leaders.

My predecessor, Dr. John T. Mason Jr., conducted the bulk of the interviews in this volume. When I took over from Dr. Mason in the early 1980s, Admiral Eller intended that there be one final interview to discuss the many facets of his leadership in the preservation and writing of naval history. I had the pleasure of conducting that interview. I found him to be a thoroughgoing gentleman. As the head of the Naval History Division, he was clearly energetic. He not only served as honcho for a wide variety of projects, but also he raised funds and performed hands-on work in many cases of gathering materials, editing manuscripts, and providing answers to the many questions that came to his office. The Navy Museum in the Washington Navy Yard stands as a tangible legacy of his stewardship.

Once the interviews were transcribed, the admiral went over every page with pencil in hand to make changes and additions to improve the finished product. I have done only minor tweaking, so the pages that follow comprise the story as Admiral Eller wanted it preserved. Joanne Patmore, who was previously part of the Naval Institute's oral history staff, retyped the interviews to incorporate the admiral's changes in a smooth version. Jonathan Hoppe of the Naval Institute converted Joanne's computer files to modern software. I have inserted a number of footnotes for further edification of readers, and I corrected spellings in several instances, a particular challenge in the sections that deal with personalities and geography in the Middle East Force. Regrettably, this volume took much longer than expected to reach publication. The admiral's son, Peter Eller, provided impetus and a donation to facilitate completion of the job.

Thanks go to Janis Jorgensen, Susan Corrado, and Eric Mills of the Naval Institute staff who have been involved in the printing and binding of the finished product. In completing the volume, the Naval Institute expresses its gratitude to the Tawani Foundation and the Pritzker Military Library of Chicago for their generous financial support of the oral history program that produced this memoir.

>   Paul Stillwell
>   U.S. Naval Institute
>   November 2016

The U.S. Naval Institute Oral History Program

Researchers and authors have been drawing on the Naval Institute's Oral History Program since 1969, the year it was established by Dr. John T. Mason Jr. He and his successor, author and historian Paul Stillwell, sought to capture, preserve, and disseminate a permanent record of the stories of significant figures in U.S. naval history. Under the leadership of Vice Adm. Peter H. Daly, U.S. Navy (Ret.), CEO of the Institute, the program has expanded, with increasing numbers of historians conducting more interviews.

These oral histories are carefully fact-checked and reviewed by both historians and interview subjects before they are made available. The Naval Institute is known for this high level of editorial intervention and polishing. The reader is reminded, as with all oral history interviews, that this is a record of the spoken word.

The Naval Institute wishes to acknowledge the many donors who make this program possible, in particular the generous support of the Tawani Foundation of Chicago and Jack C. Taylor of St. Louis.

REAR ADMIRAL ERNEST McNEILL ELLER
UNITED STATES NAVY (RET.)

Ernest McNeill Eller was born in Marion, Virginia, on 23 January 1903, the son of Edward E. and Elizabeth McNeill Eller. He attended the North Wilkesboro High School, North Wilkesboro, North Carolina, and North Carolina State College at Raleigh before entering the U.S. Naval Academy in 1921. As a midshipman he was managing editor of *The Log*, president of the Trident Society, and editor of *The Trident*. Graduated and commissioned ensign on 4 June 1925, he was subsequently promoted to the rank of captain in 1944, to date from 20 July 1943, and served in the temporary rank of commodore from 30 September 1946 until 1 December 1947. On 1 April 1954, he was transferred to the retired list of the U.S. Navy and was advanced to the rank of rear admiral.

After graduation from the Naval Academy in 1925, he served in the USS *Utah* (BB-31) until 14 June 1926, when he reported to the Naval Torpedo Station, Newport, Rhode Island, for instruction. On 3 January 1927 he joined the USS *Texas* (BB-35) and served on board that battleship until 28 May 1927. Following instruction in submarines at the Submarine Base, New London, Connecticut, he served successively from February 1928 to April 1932 in the USS *S-33* (SS-138) and the USS *Utah*. During his tour of duty with the latter, she underwent conversion from a battleship (BB-31) to a target ship (AG-16). For the next three years, he had duty at the Naval Academy, in the Department of English and History and in the Executive Department.

During his next period of sea duty, he organized and conducted the Fleet Machine Gun School in the USS *Utah*, in which he served until May 1938. He then returned to the Naval Academy for duty in the Department of English and History and the Department of Ordnance and Gunnery. From September 1940 until May 1941, he served as assistant naval attaché in London, England, and as an observer in the British Fleet for radar, antiaircraft, and other war developments.

After brief duty in the Fleet Training Division of the Navy Department and the Bureau of Ordnance, developing antiaircraft training and weapons, he was ordered to the USS *Saratoga* (CV-3) and served as her gunnery officer until May 1942. He was on board that aircraft carrier when she made a high-speed run from San Diego, California, to Pearl Harbor, Hawaii, with urgently needed plane and pilot replacements immediately after the Japanese attack on Pearl Harbor. He was also on board when the *Saratoga* was torpedoed in January 1942, while on an operational foray into the Marshall and Midway Island areas.

He served for the next three years on the staff of the Commander in Chief U.S. Pacific Fleet, as assistant gunnery and antisubmarine training officer. In addition, he analyzed actions and wrote CinCPac's war reports during the first part of this tour of duty. He was awarded the Legion of Merit with Combat V. The citation follows in part: "For exceptionally meritorious conduct . . . while attached to the staff of the Commander in Chief, United States Pacific Fleet and Pacific Ocean Areas, during operations against enemy Japanese forces in the Pacific War area from May 1942 to April 1945. Analyzing war reports and developing, expanding and supervising all types of training, particularly anti-aircraft, anti-submarine, amphibious and shore bombardment, [he] participated in the landings on Makin and Okinawa and in other combat operations which led to improved methods and development of new weapons. In his constant attention to improvements in weapons and armament of his ships and in his supervision of Fleet ammunition supply, he rendered vital service in developing and maintaining the combat readiness of the fleet . . . "

During the summer and fall of 1945, he commanded the attack transport *Clay* (APA-39), participating in three occupation moves into Japan and China. From late in December 1945 until March 1946, he served as district public information officer, Twelfth Naval District, San Francisco, California. He reported in April 1946 to the Office of Public Information, Navy Department, Washington, D.C., to serve as Deputy Director and on 31 July 1946, assumed the duties of Director of Public Information. He was promoted to the temporary rank of commodore on 30 September 1946.

Selected to attend the course at the National War College, Washington, D.C., which convened on 30 August 1948, he completed the course in June 1949 for duty in the Staff Planning Section of the Joint Staff, Joint Chiefs of Staff. In this duty he accompanied the Joint Chiefs of Staff to the member countries of the North Atlantic Treaty Organization (NATO), establishing plans for the military structure of that organization. A year later, at the outbreak of the Korean War, he became Commander Middle East Force, in the Persian Gulf-Indian Ocean area. He assumed command of the USS *Albany* (CA-123) on 14 May 1951, and in April 1952 he was assigned to the Office of the Chief of Naval Operations, International Affairs Division. Later in 1953 he was hospitalized and on 1 April 1954 was transferred to the retired list of the Navy.

On 15 September 1956, Admiral Eller was recalled to active duty as Director of Naval History and Curator of the Navy Department, Washington, D.C., and served as such until relieved of active duty on 23 January 1970.

In addition to the Legion of Merit with Combat V, Rear Admiral Eller earned the American Defense Service Medal, Fleet Clasp; Asiatic-Pacific Campaign Medal; the Navy Occupation Service Medal, Asia and Europe Clasps; the China Service Medal; and the National Defense Service Medal with bronze star.

He received a master of arts degree in psychology at George Washington University, Washington, D.C., in 1934. In addition to gunnery technical manuals and various articles in non-professional magazines, he wrote extensively for the U.S. Naval Institute *Proceedings*. His essays won the Naval Institute's General Prize Essay Contest in 1932, 1942, and 1950, and he was selected for honorable mention in other years.

Admiral Eller married the former Agnes Fogle Pfohl of Winston-Salem, North Carolina, and they were the parents of two sons, Peter and John Eller. The admiral died at his home in Annapolis, Maryland, on 30 July 1992. He was 89 years old at the time.

CHRONOLOGY OF NAVAL SERVICE

23 January 1903	Born in Marion, Virginia
23 June 1921	Midshipman, U.S. Naval Academy
4 June 1925	Ensign
4 June 1928	Lieutenant (junior grade)
1 July 1934	Lieutenant
1 July 1939	Lieutenant Commander
15 December 1942	Commander
30 August 1944	Captain
30 September 1946	Commodore
1 December 1947	Appointment as commodore terminated; reverted to permanent rank of captain
31 March 1954	Released from active duty
1 April 1954	Transferred to the temporary disability retired list and advanced to rear admiral due to performance of duty in combat
15 September 1956	Reported for active duty
1 May 1957	Placed on retired list by reason of permanent disability and continued on active duty
23 January 1970	Relieved of active duty

SHIPS AND STATIONS

Jun 1925–Sep 1925	Navy Yard, Boston, Massachusetts Instruction
Sep 1925–Jun 1926	USS *Utah* (BB-31) Junior Division Officer
Jun 1926–Dec 1926	Naval Torpedo Station, Newport, Rhode Island Instruction
Dec 1926–May 1927	USS *Texas* (BB-35) Watch and Division Officer
May 1927–Dec 1927	Submarine Base, New London, Connecticut Instruction
Dec 1927–Jul 1929	USS *S-33* (SS-138) Navigator
Jul 1929–Sep 1929	USS *Chaumont* (AP-5) Passenger

Sep 1929–Apr 1930	Naval Hospital, Washington, D.C. Patient
Apr 1930–Apr 1932	USS *Utah* (BB-31/AG-16) Gunnery Officer
Apr 1932–Jun 1932	Edgewood Arsenal, Maryland Faculty
June 1932–May 1935	U.S. Naval Academy, Annapolis, Maryland Faculty
May 1935–May 1938	USS *Utah* (AG-16) Gunnery Officer
May 1938–Sep 1940	U.S. Naval Academy, Annapolis, Maryland Faculty
May 1941–Oct 1941	American Embassy, London, England Assistant Naval Attaché
Oct 1941–Nov 1941	Bureau of Ordnance, Washington, D.C. Fire Control Research
Nov 1941–Apr 1942	USS *Saratoga* (CV-3) Gunnery Officer
Apr 1942–May 1945	Commander in Chief Pacific Fleet Staff Assistant Gunnery and Training Officer
May 1945–Jun 1945	Bureau of Naval Personnel, Washington, D.C.
Jun 1945–Dec 1945	USS *Clay* (APA-39) Commanding Officer
Dec 1945–Apr 1946	Headquarters, 12th Naval District Public Information Officer
Apr 1946–Aug 1946	Office of Public Information, Navy Department, Washington, D.C. Deputy Director
Aug 1946–Aug 1948	Office of Public Information, Navy Department,

	Washington, D.C. Director
Aug 1948–Jun 1949	National War College, Washington, D.C. Student
Jun 1949–Jul 1950	Joint Staff, Office of the Joint Chiefs of Staff, Washington, D.C. Strategic Plans Group
Aug 1950–Apr 1951	Middle East Force Commander
Apr 1951–Mar 1952	USS *Albany* (CA-123) Commanding Officer
Mar 1952–Mar 1954	Office of the Chief of Naval Operations, Washington, D.C. Assistant Director, International Affairs Division
Sep 1956–Jan 1970	Office of the Chief of Naval Operations, Washington, D.C. Director of Naval History and Curator

Deed of Gift

The U.S. Naval Institute is hereby authorized to make available in any format it chooses, from bound-book hard copy to electronic/digital Internet access and as part of videorecordings, the audio recordings, transcripts, and videorecordings of the oral-history interview series conducted for Volume 3 concerning the life and career of Rear Admiral Ernest M. Eller, U.S. Navy (Retired). Disposition, repositories, and access shall be at the discretion of the Naval Institute.

Admiral Eller's legal representative, the undersigned, does hereby release and assign to the U.S. Naval Institute the rights and title to these interviews, with the exception that the undersigned and family retain the right to use the material for personal, noncommercial purposes. The copyright in the oral, transcribed, and videorecorded versions shall be held by the U.S. Naval Institute. All recordings, transcriptions, and videorecordings of the interviews shall remain the property of the U.S. Naval Institute.

Signed and sealed this 3rd day of August 2016.

Signed name _Peter M. P. Eller_

Printed name Peter M. P. Eller

291 Wood Road • Annapolis, MD 21402-5034

*The United States Naval Institute
gratefully acknowledges*

Dwight and Joan Allgood

Peter and Karen Eller

John Eller

*for their generous assistance in underwriting
the completion of the oral history of*

***Rear Admiral Ernest M. Eller
U.S. Navy (Retired)***

Interview Number 14 with Rear Admiral Ernest M. Eller, U.S. Navy (Retired)
Place: Annapolis, Maryland
Date: Wednesday, 19 December 1978

John T. Mason, Jr.: Well, Judge, this morning you want to add a few details to your tour of duty as the Director of Public Information in the Navy at Washington. You want to add them at this point, sir?

Admiral Eller: Yes, sir. We had a number of special events, and I thought I might mention some of the highlights. One was in February 1947, when *Cusk* fired a Loon.[1] This was the first United States submarine-launched guided missile. We were using German technology as well as our own. We continued with this surface-to-surface missile, which is now the rage, for about six years. *Tunny* launched about six years later the Regulus I, which was a great improvement over anything that we'd had previously.[2]

John T. Mason Jr.: But the Loon was the first of these?

Admiral Eller: The Loon was the first, though of limited range, which I've forgotten, perhaps 30 to 60 miles. It and its successor were very splendid additions to the submarine. But at that time we began to develop the Polaris missile, and we abandoned it.[3]

John T. Mason, Jr.: What was the propulsion for it?

---

1. The first launch of a missile from a submarine was a Loon fired from the USS *Cusk* (SS-348) off Point Mugu on 12 February 1947. For details see the Naval Institute oral history of Vice Admiral Eugene P. Wilkinson, USN. Loon was the U.S. Navy's version of the German V-1 self-propelled bomb. It was initially intended as a ship-to-shore bombardment weapon. Later it was used as a platform for general missile development in the areas of propulsion, guidance, control, and launching techniques.
2. The USS *Tunny* (SSG-282) test-fired the first submarine-launched Regulus I missile on 15 July 1953.
3. The first version of the submarine-launched Polaris ballistic missile, the A-1, was 28 feet long, 4 feet in diameter, and weighed about 30,000 pounds. It had a range of 1,200 nautical miles. The missile entered fleet service in 1960 in the nuclear-powered submarine *George Washington* (SSBN-598).

Admiral Eller: Rocket propulsion. It was both submarine launched and a surface-to-surface missile. It was really just a subsonic low-flying airplane. When we got the Polaris, we thought we had the great pacifier of the world, and we didn't need the surface-to-surface missile. The Russians still didn't have the large fleet that they soon built.

One of our major occupations was trying to get people into the Naval Reserve. We saw we were losing our active Navy through the severe reduction in budget. Our regular services were being cut back drastically. So we organized national Naval Reserve drives and set up a Naval Reserve section in my office to coordinate with BuPers and the Recruiting Division and with practically all parts of the Navy that had anything to do with outside activities.[4]

This was organized very much like a national campaign for recruiting in the war. We contacted all of the units in the country of the different civic organizations, starting with national headquarters; veterans groups; the Boy Scouts; the Girl Scouts, women's clubs'; men's clubs; and service clubs. Also we organized in each district to reach every community. This took up a tremendous amount of time for our staff. We were trying to raise a million men, and we raised, I suppose, about 800,000.

John T. Mason Jr.: This was particularly difficult, was it not, because in that period of time the thought prevailed that war was over—war was a thing of the past?

Admiral Eller: War was no longer a threat. The atomic bomb had made normal war impossible. In fact, the whole country was mesmerized with this idea. It was so far beyond anything that we'd ever had in power of weapons that it stunned the country into irrationality.

John T. Mason Jr.: What techniques did you employ to overcome this euphoria, so to speak?

---

4. BuPers – Bureau of Naval Personnel.

Admiral Eller: It was very difficult. Our techniques were to appeal to citizens' patriotism if they were needed. Even in atomic war, there would be the necessity for people to serve, to clean up, to occupy, and for ships to sail the seas. Also, in the reserves you could serve your country on the side and still carry on your civilian occupation.

John T. Mason Jr.: I suppose you were aided somewhat, were you not, by the fact that the draft was in business?

Admiral Eller: Yes. That encouraged people to join, of course. But the draft wasn't being exercised very much, as I remember.

John T. Mason Jr.: No, but it was there as a potential. It was on the books.

Admiral Eller: It was on the books but not needed. The services were being cut back. We appealed to their patriotism should they be willing to serve in some way.

John T. Mason Jr.: I would think a large percentage were men who had served in World War II.

Admiral Eller: This was largely true, and what we were trying to do was get people to go ahead and continue their service, because we knew that they were well trained. Of course, this had tremendous payoff in the Korean War. If we hadn't had these trained men and hadn't had our ships mothballed, we would have been in a terrible situation. We fought it, as you know, on a shoestring and almost lost it at the start—at least almost lost Korea. If we hadn't had this reservoir of trained men, we'd have been in a perilous situation. We don't have it now, unhappily.

John T. Mason Jr.: How did you succeed in getting funds for this reserve program with the attitude prevailing in the Department of Defense? Secretary Johnson was, I believe, in on this.[5]

Admiral Eller: No, he wasn't.

John T. Mason Jr.: Oh, he wasn't in? Forrestal was still the Secretary?

Admiral Eller: Yes. Forrestal was very understanding.[6] Of course, it didn't take a great deal of funds, because we had the existing organization. It was largely a matter of travel funds for speakers and literature. We merely used the organization we had when we set up the special section in my office, made up of people who were on duty somewhere else, maybe in BuPers or in recruiting or in my office. They were sent into this section for temporary duty, an ad hoc arrangement.

John T. Mason Jr.: It's been said often that the reserve is kind of a pet of the Congress. Was this in evidence when you asked for funds?

Admiral Eller: It was always easier to get money for reserves or for anything related to reserves. But generally nowadays, and I believe so then, the Navy budget went in as a whole. Each part might have to be defended by the bureau concerned. So it was always easier to defend it. But the total actual allocation came from the Navy Department to begin with. The real fight to get money in the Navy budget came from trying to divide the pie at that time in the Navy Department. The budget process went on for a year. It was one of the most interesting things I had to do in the job.

---

5. Louis A. Johnson served as Secretary of Defense from April 1949 until September 1950. He cut back substantially on defense expenditures, a program that had to be reversed with the beginning of the Korean War in June 1950. He was removed as SecDef a few months after the war started.
6. James V. Forrestal served as Secretary of Defense from 17 September 1947 to 27 March 1949.

There was a minor celebration as part of this drive on 6 July 1947, the 200th anniversary of John Paul Jones's birth.[7] Of course, this gave us the opportunity to give wide publicity to his achievements and to the meaning of the Navy in the Revolution and to the basic traditions that John Paul Jones established. We used the celebration to stir up patriotism and encourage men to come into the reserves. During it there was an amusing incident. In the Naval Station San Diego station paper, there was an article: "Descendent of John Paul Jones Here on Station."

"Jones's sons and sons and sons and on down the line are represented by John Paul Jones, seaman second class, storekeeper striker. He remembered his father telling that his ancestor, the famous sea fighter—"

Well, Jones had no legitimate sons. He never married.

Years later, when I had Naval History, I saw a Navy Day item from the Ninth Naval District headlined, "John Paul Jones in the Navy Today." The reporter noted that Jones was hesitant to talk about his ancestor. By then he had learned.

I'll mention another missile spectacular, of which we had a number, which we used to publicize the Navy. This was the firing from *Midway* of the V-2 on 6 July 1947, which was the development of the German buzz bomb.[8]

John T. Mason Jr.: Yes.

Admiral Eller: We arranged a great spectacular. We had many of the high officials on board *Midway* from the Navy and other services and civilians.

This was a 28,000-pound missile, mostly rocket propulsion. It had a terrific blast from which to protect the deck. It was a prefect launch, and everybody was cheering on deck and congratulating the Navy. Then at about six miles it exploded. Just six seconds

---

7. John Paul Jones (1747–1792) was the young country's first great naval officer and a hero of the Revolutionary War. He is probably best known for his successful command of the USS *Bonhomme Richard* in her victory of HMS *Serapis* in 1779.

8. The *Midway* (CVB-41) was a new aircraft carrier, having been commissioned in 1945. For details of the test, see the Naval Institute oral history of Rear Admiral Robert W. McNitt, USN (Ret.). The V-2 was a liquid-fuel rocket, 46 feet long and weighing 13 tons. It carried a one-ton warhead. The German V-2 offensive against the Allies began in September 1944 and ended in March 1945.

actually. So if it had exploded a few seconds earlier, it would have been disaster.

John T. Mason Jr.: Dan Gallery had a role in that, did he not?

Admiral Eller: I think he did. I don't know whether he was the skipper of the USS *Midway* then or—

John T. Mason Jr.: No, he was, I think, in the department in the bureau.[9]

Admiral Eller: One of the things that I had learned from the experts was if anything goes wrong, don't try to hide it. Of course, this was something you couldn't have hidden, because of the crowd of observers. I don't think we had any press on board. It was supposed to be secret enough. But the many officials that were there would have talked about it. So we immediately put out the story, telling the full details, and there were no repercussions.

A little later than this, after Sullivan took over the Secretaryship from Forrestal in late 1947, we turned back to Marjorie Post Davies the yacht *Sea Cloud* that the Navy had used during the war.[10] So she invited the Secretary and me as public information officer, and Agnes. In fact, I think Admiral Holloway, Sullivan, and myself and our families were invited on board.[11] Marjorie Post was then married to Ambassador Joe Davies. There was no question who was running the ship. They had a full crew, of course, but she gave the commands. We spent overnight cruising the Chesapeake Bay, up the Severn and down the bay. One of the things that struck me was that the bathroom in our cabin had gold fixtures.

---

9. Rear Admiral Daniel V. Gallery, USN, served from 1946 to 1949 as Assistant for Guided Missiles in the Office of the Chief of Naval Operations. His oral history is in the Naval Institute collection.
10. James V. Forrestal served as Secretary of the Navy from 19 May 1944 to 17 September 1947. John L. Sullivan served as Secretary from 18 September 1947 to 24 May 1949. From 1942 to 1943 the Coast Guard leased the yacht as a weather ship. In 1943 she became the Navy's USS *Sea Cloud* (IX-99), though still with a Coast Guard crew. The yacht was returned in 1944 to Joseph E. Davies, former U.S. ambassador to the Soviet Union and Belgium. Mrs. Davies, the former Marjorie Merriweather Post, was heiress to a cereal fortune and a noted philanthropist.
11. Rear Admiral James L. Holloway Jr., USN. The oral history of Holloway, who retired as a four-star admiral, is in the Columbia University collection.

In connection with this cruise, there was a fly-by-night reporter from the *World-Telegram* in New York. He wrote an account that shows, again, how much error goes into the press and is believed by people. He said that there were two different citations prepared for the yacht's service in the war. He said that Forrestal had one prepared, and then because of the slow movement within the bureau Mrs. Davies didn't receive the citation. The reason for our being on the ship was to present this citation and hear the words of praise to the ship and vice versa to the Navy for returning it.

This writer, whose name is Farrell, further said that Mrs. Davies not having received the first citation, asked Sullivan, who was then Secretary, to prepare one, and he did. Also that Forrestal was on board and at the time of presentation read the Sullivan citation instead of the one prepared for him. Well, he wasn't on board, and there was only one citation. So Farrell wrote this little gossip column just to get attention.

John T. Mason Jr.: Out of whole cloth.

Admiral Eller: Yes. Like most faulty news, there was some fact, in that there was a presentation.

One of the best things we did, and one of the most effective things the Navy can do, was a civilian orientation cruise run out of our office. These one-day training cruises on the training carrier at Pensacola, are still being carried on. From a central point we would pick up leading men in communities—educators, press, bankers, industrialists, ministers. They were flown to Pensacola by Naval Reserve planes on training duty. The cruises themselves were part of the pilot training course. Consequently, there was no extra cost to the Navy from that standpoint, and men paid their own mess fees.

This was uniformly beneficial to them in understanding how the Navy operated, particularly aircraft carriers, which were under attack, of course, what it meant to have the sea power.

One man who had been an Army flier in World War I said, "It was the most thrilling experience in my life next to getting married."

We had a great number of conferences, speeches, and meetings which myself or someone else in the office had to attend. I usually went to the Secretary and CNO's press conferences. In fact, I made arrangements for them. And either myself or one of the people in the office went to the general conferences each week or each morning so that we could sit in and know what was going on and be informed in advance of what was happening. I had to make a number of trips to speak at training command stations, the public relations seminars, and to civic groups.

Then we prepared press releases. I have a very nice one here for Admiral Nimitz that I might read into the record. Admiral Nimitz would sometimes change these, but he didn't change this one on the fifth anniversary of Guadalcanal:[12]

"Five years ago today the ships of the United States Navy under a sky umbrella of Navy planes, landed the First Marine Division on the jungle beaches of Guadalcanal and Tulagi. The heartbreaking task of reconquering the vast areas of the Pacific was under way. No one could foresee how many lives and how many years would be consumed by this gigantic campaign to win the final victory and peace that seemed almost beyond the reach of mortal men.

"The Marines who fought in the mud at Tenaru River and flew from the hot dust of Henderson Field, along with the sailors who went into the water between Lunga Beach and Savo Island knew that they were the vanguard of mighty forces to come. But they knew in their hearts that this fight had to be won, or victory would be set back years, and thousands of Americans might die in future battles. The fighting men of this integrated sea-air-land spearhead braved the unknown, won victory over great odds, and laid the foundation for our final entry into Tokyo Bay. The distinction of having fought at Guadalcanal will forever set these men apart."

This got very wide usage, as did all of our anniversaries for which we tried to produce something like this.

The last thing I'll mention or practically the last on Public Information, is that I was assigned collateral duty as deputy on the Joint Research and Development Board. This had been quiescent for a time after the war, then in the fall of 1946 started meeting

---

12. Fleet Admiral Chester Nimitz, USN, served as Chief of Naval Operations from 15 December 1945 to 15 December 1947. On 7 August 1942, U.S. Marines invaded the islands of Guadalcanal and Tulagi in the Solomons chain as part of the first U.S. counteroffensive in the Pacific War.

again. Vannevar Bush was chairman, a very capable administrator, but an empire builder and an autocrat who ran things with an iron hand, like Marjorie Post Davies.[13]

Other members were the Secretary or Assistant Secretary of the Army and of the Navy. Patterson came to one meeting for the Army.[14] And John Nicholas Brown, who was our Assistant Secretary of the Navy for Air, Research and Development, and Personnel, went for the first time with me along.[15] Thereafter he rarely went. I always attended as his deputy for the next year.

The officers for the Army and Army Air were first Lieutenant General Jake Devers, who impressed me as a very sound fighting soldier, calm and hard to unbalance.[16] I liked him very much. Then General Pete Aurand, who was similar but less calm.[17] Then Major General "Nuts" McAuliffe of the Battle of the Bulge fame.[18] He was volatile and determined but easy to deal with. I became fond of all three of them. Curtis LeMay was the air representative.[19] He was always hard to deal with. I'd known him at Guam in our mining campaign. He was tough and unsmiling, always chewed his cigar. He was hard driving, and he would never give up on anything. He had few words, but when he said them he meant them.

We took up subjects like ordnance development and guided missiles—new areas and directions we were going into. At that time I think the Navy was well ahead of anyone else, perhaps anybody in the world except what the Germans had had in guided missiles. And we were involved in radar and aircraft developments, including the beginning of blind landings, instrument landings. I flew on one of those with Black Jack Reeves, who headed NATS, Naval Air Transport Service.[20] Flying from Washington to Alameda, we made one

---

13. Dr. Vannevar Bush (1890–1974) was an American electrical engineer who served as director of the Office of Scientific Research and Development from 1941 to 1946.
14. Robert P. Patterson served as Secretary of War from 1945 to 1947 under President Harry S. Truman.
15. John Nicholas Brown, who served in the Navy in World War I, was later Assistant Secretary of the Navy for Air from 1946 to 1949.
16. General Jacob L. Devers, USA.
17. Major General Henry S. Aurand, USA.
18. Major General Anthony C, McAuliffe, USA. In September 1944, while in temporary command of the 101st Airborne Division, McAuliffe found his unit surrounded by the enemy at Bastogne, Belgium. When two German officers approached for his immediate surrender, the general's famous reply, "Nuts," boosted the morale of his men, who rallied helped break the last great German offensive of the war.
19. Lieutenant General Curtis LeMay, USAF, Deputy Chief of Staff for Research and Development.
20. Rear Admiral John W. Reeves Jr., USN, Commander Naval Air Transport Service.

of the first instrument landings there in broad daylight so the pilot could see clearly. It was very interesting to see the development from the beginning.

John T. Mason Jr.: Was this committee a forerunner of WESEG?[21]

Admiral Eller: I don't know. About a year later, when unification went into effect, the deputy on the committee was to become a full-time job. It should have been a full-time job all along, but now it would be. SecNav had to decide whether I would stay in it or go and stay with Public Information. Against my wishes the decision was made that I would stay in Public Information.

Another item that the board took up a great deal was atomic energy. Early in the war, NRL, Naval Research Laboratory, had been in on the first atomic energy development. The Navy had really started it in this country. The Navy work was absorbed by the Manhattan Project a year or so after Pearl Harbor.[22] NRL had early proposed a nuclear submarine. This was set aside during the war while all effort concentrated on the A bomb. But late in the war, or just after the war was over, Dr. Abelson of NRL brought forth a proposal of development of the submarine that was feasible if we could get the atomic energy then.[23]

Admiral Mills took it up to the Secretary and Admiral Nimitz. This I know from Admiral Nimitz himself.

John T. Mason Jr.: Is this Earle Mills?[24]

Admiral Eller: Earle Mills, Nimitz, and Sherman, who was then OP-03 for strategic plans and probably others, had discussed it.[25] They said, "Go ahead with it." I don't think any of

---

21. WESEG – Weapon System Evaluation Group.
22. Manhattan District derived from an Army Corps of Engineers term connected with the U.S. program to create an atomic bomb in World War II. The overall effort is often referred to as the Manhattan Project.
23. Philip H. Abelson in 1940 he received a Nobel Prize in physics. He worked on the Manhattan Project while at the Naval Research Laboratory during World War II. After the war he was involved in the development of naval nuclear power.
24. Vice Admiral Earle W. Mills, USN, served as Chief of the Bureau of Ships from November 1946 to February 1949.
25. Vice Admiral Forrest P. Sherman, USN, Deputy Chief of Naval Operations (Operations).

them had the idea that it would develop as rapidly as it did. But this was the decision, and Mills sent Rickover to Oak Ridge to be the Navy representative.[26]

This took a little battle in the Joint Chiefs of Staff to get the Navy back into atomic energy at all, because the Air Force wanted to keep all of the nuclear energy we were producing for the atomic bomb. Then, of course, at the same time the Navy started trying to get the nuclear bomb in a smaller missile. This was so violently opposed that it didn't go across, although we began to work on it and to develop it nevertheless, as I know from flying to Los Alamos. Was it Hayward who was there?

John T. Mason Jr.: Chick Hayward was there.[27]

Admiral Eller: He was there working on it. We were working then on the development. Of course, the first bomb could have been, had they known enough about it, much smaller because the explosive part was developed around the 12-inch or 14-inch shell with Parsons being the key man behind it.[28]

I was rather close to ordnance, having been working with it before and all during the war and being very much interested in all the new developments. So I was at the opening of White Oak Laboratory, and I was with Noble on a number of trips.[29] One of them was particularly interesting. We flew to Inyokern and Morris Dam.[30] We were developing the

---

26. Captain Hyman G. Rickover, USN, was considered the father of the nuclear Navy. He ran the U.S. Navy's nuclear-power program for many years, from 1948 until he eventually left active duty in 1982 with the rank of four-star admiral on the retired list.
Oak Ridge National Laboratory, Oak Ridge, Tennessee, which has long been involved in research and development in the field of nuclear energy.
27. Captain John T. Hayward served in 1948 as director of plans and operations for the Armed Forces Sandia Base, Albuquerque, New Mexico. working with nuclear weapons and coordinating with the Los Alamos Scientific Laboratory. See John T. Hayward and C.W. Borklund, *Bluejacket Admiral: the Navy Career of Chick Hayward* (Annapolis, MD: Naval Institute Press; Newport, RI: Naval War College Foundation, 2000).
28. Captain William S. Parsons, USN, was involved in the development of the atomic bomb in New Mexico. During the mission of 6 August 1945, Parsons was the weaponeer on board the B-29 named "Enola Gay" that dropped the bomb on Hiroshima, Japan. See Al Christman, *Target Hiroshima: Deak Parsons and the Creation of the Atomic Bomb* (Annapolis: Naval Institute Press, 1998).
29. Naval Ordnance Laboratory, Silver Spring (White Oak), Maryland. Rear Admiral Albert G. Noble, USN, was Chief of the Bureau of Ordnance, 1947–50.
30. Inyokern – Naval Ordnance Test Station, China Lake, California. Morris Dam was part of the California Institute of Technology, Pasadena, California.

Terrier at Inyokern.[31] This was either the second or third launching, containing revisions that had to be made, because it was a slow development. At the same time it was far ahead of any other missile. We saw two firings there. Then we went to Morris Dam, where we were developing an advanced torpedo. With us was a group from the American Ordnance Association—the committee on ordnance and guided missiles—to show them what was being developed.

The American Ordnance Association grew from the old Army Ordnance Association, which may have had an earlier name. The Army Ordnance Association was held together by Colonel James Walsh.[32] He had got out after World War I and made a lot of money or married money. He devoted all of his time that he could spare from his business to guiding the Army Ordnance Association through lean years, he and Colonel Leo Codd, the executive director.[33] Both were magnificent men. I was extremely fond of them.

They came to see me in Public Information about 1947 and said they were trying to change the association to take in more than Army ordnance. They wanted to bring in all aspects of ordnance development, and could we get the Navy to go into it? It seemed to me a good thing for the nation, because they were going to bring into it all of the industries and people who were working on ordnance developments. So I talked to Forrestal and to the Bureau of Ordnance. I think George Hussey might have been chief of the bureau then.[34] They were amenable, so we helped to get it started. From then on, Walsh and Codd were always ready to do anything they could to get me into the act.

On this particular trip they, as well as Noble, had asked me to go along. Coming back is one of the times that I think the Lord acted to save my life. We were crossing the Rockies, up as high as we could go, and still we ran into a terrific storm. The plane wasn't filled. I guess we had a dozen or so people in it. I was sitting by the window, behind a man who weighed about 300 pounds, of tremendous size. The plane was being shaken this way

---

31. The Terrier, a radar-beam-riding surface-to-air missile, began in the late 1940s as an outgrowth of the Talos supersonic test vehicle. It entered the fleet in the mid–1950s and was used until the 1970s.
32. Colonel James L. Walsh, USA (Ret.), graduated with the U.S. Military Academy class of 1909; among his classmates were future generals George Patton and Jacob Devers.
33. Colonel Leo A. Codd, USA, who served the Army Ordnance Association in various capacities from 1929 to 1963.
34. Rear Admiral George F. Hussey, Jr., USN, served as Chief of the Bureau of Ordnance from December 1943 to September 1947. He was promoted to vice admiral as of December 1945.

and that, and I wasn't feeling too well. So I moved over to the next seat to be ready to go to the head if I had to. About that time, we went up several hundred feet, then suddenly reversed and came crashing down again. And this 300-pound man, seat and all, just tore back into the seat that I had been sitting in two or three minutes before. It was as close an escape to death as I've ever experienced.

John T. Mason Jr.: Was he injured?

Admiral Eller: He was hurt some, but not seriously. He was in the seat, strapped in, of course.

John T. Mason Jr.: The whole seat came out?

Admiral Eller: The whole thing was ripped out and came back like a projectile.

That year, 1947, and this ends Public Information, was one of the most momentous, and perhaps the worst for the future of the Navy in our history. As I mentioned at the time, Forrestal changed and accepted the National Security Act, unification; he had it blocked. He was persuaded by the President and others to take the job. He then left the Navy Department, and our troubles really began under the new organization.[35]

My office coordinated the arrangements for his departure. We had a farewell in his office, with Sullivan taking over, of course. Besides his staff, we had the bureau chiefs, the deputy chiefs, Admiral Nimitz, the Vice Chief of Naval Operations, and department heads of offices like myself.

We let out all hands about 15 minutes early all through the Navy Department

---

35. The National Security Act of 1947 became effective on 18 September of that year. It provided for the unification of the services under the aegis of a single National Military Establishment, which later became the Department of Defense. Previously the Secretaries of War and Navy had been Cabinet officials. Now there were three different departments at sub-Cabinet level: Army, Navy, and Air Force. As part of the act the former U.S. Army Air Forces became a separate service, the U.S. Air Force. Forrestal became the first Secretary of Defense.

and lined the halls with people from his office in old Main Navy down to the street.[36] At Constitution Avenue we had admirals for side boys as he came out the door. All of Constitution Avenue was crowded with workers from the Navy Department and also, I guess, from the War Department. We gave a great cheer to him as he left. He was the finest public servant in that era that I had any contact with or knew anything about.

He took with him the nucleus of his staff from the Navy Department, including McNeil, the comptroller, later an admiral in the reserves—a completely sensible, balanced, and dedicated man.[37] And Captain Dick Glass, who was Senator Glass's nephew.[38] I think Dick was, more or less, his chief of staff.

Then in December Admiral Nimitz was relieved by Admiral Denfeld.[39] There were three good contestants at the time: Denfeld from BuPers; Admiral Duke Ramsey, the Vice Chief; and Spike Blandy, who was then CinCLant, I think.[40] Leahy favored Denfeld because of his ability to deal with Congress, and he was capable and liked and shrewd in Washington politics.[41] He didn't do so well in the Joint Chiefs. Aviators were pushing for Ramsey, who was a fine gentleman. I don't know whether you have anything from him or not.

John T. Mason Jr.: No.

Admiral Eller: He was a splendid gentleman. And anybody that knew Blandy was pushing for him. I think he was the smartest and most capable man that we had then. It might have

---

36. Main Navy was the popular name for the old Navy Department building at 17th Street and Constitution Avenue in Washington, D.C. The adjacent Munitions Building was long occupied by the War Department. In 1943, with the opening of the Pentagon, the Army moved out and transferred the Munitions Building to the Navy.
37. Wilfred J. McNeil, Fiscal Director, Navy Department, 1945–47; special assistant to the Secretary of Defense, 1947; Assistant Secretary of Defense and Comptroller, Department of Defense, 1949–59.
38. Captain Richard P. Glass, USN. Carter Glass, a Democrat from Virginia, served in the U.S. House of Representative 1902–18; as Secretary of the Treasury, 1918–20; and in the Senate, 1920–46.
39. Admiral Louis E. Denfeld, USN, served as Chief of Naval Operations from 15 December 1947 to 2 November 1949.
40. Admiral DeWitt C. Ramsey, USN, served as Vice Chief of Naval Operations from 15 January 1946 to 3 January 1948. Admiral William H. P. Blandy, USN, served as Commander in Chief Atlantic Command and Commander in Chief Atlantic Fleet from 3 February 1947 to 1 February 1950.
41. Admiral William D. Leahy, USN, served as chief of staff to the President (in his capacity as Commander in Chief of the Armed Forces) from July 1942 to March 1949. Leahy was promoted to the five-star rank of fleet admiral in December 1944.

changed the picture had he been in on the Joint Chiefs.

Then in the fall of 1948, since Forrestal was gone, I was released to the third class of the National War College. I'd spoken there in May 1947 to the first class, at Admiral Hill's invitation, on Public Information, its importance, and how to direct it.[42] So now I was going there to find out what they were doing.

Paul Stillwell: Was Hill still there?

Admiral Eller: He was there for the first three classes. He left with our class. You know Hill. We all know him, so I won't give my impressions of him as a fine leader.

His deputy was general Lemnitzer.[43] He was a smart man in some ways, but he often put on a front and bluffed when he didn't know anything. I don't know whether he was lazy mentally or not. He was hearty and likeable, but he tended to bluff. I saw that a few times. He later, of course, became—

John T. Mason Jr.: Chairman of the Joint Chiefs.

Admiral Eller: Chairman of the Joint Chiefs and then SACEur, the Chief of the Allied Command in Europe.[44]

Al Gruenther was director of the Joint Staff at the time, but he was down at the college quite a bit.[45] I got to know him pretty well during my year there. I don't know why he came, but you would see him around. He had preceded Lemnitzer. I think he was the first deputy there, wasn't he, under Hill? Gruenther was as smart or maybe even smarter than Lemnitzer, and he was shrewd, energetic. He did his homework and knew his job.

He was a very astute maneuverer in the Army hierarchy. In fact I think the Army

---

42. Vice Admiral Harry W. Hill, USN, was Commandant of the National War College from 1946 to 1949.
43. Major General Lyman L. Lemnitzer, USA, Deputy Commandant of the National War College, 1947–49. Lemnitzer later served as Chief of Staff of the Army, 1959–60, and as Chairman of the Joint Chiefs of Staff, 1960–62.
44. General Lemnitzer served as NATO's Supreme Allied Commander Europe from 1963 to 1969.
45. Major General Alfred M. Gruenther, USA, served as Director of the Joint Staff from August 1947 to September 1949. Before that he was Deputy Commandant of the National War College, 1946–47.

General Staff trained officers that way and only kept those who were clever and maneuvered. He had grown up through the General Staff. He also was a very sharp—they say one of the best—bridge players in the United States. He played frequently with his superiors. I believe that Eisenhower liked to play with him.[46]

John T. Mason Jr.: Yes, he did.

Admiral Eller: He was friendly and cheerful, the same as Lemnitzer. I liked both of them from a personal standpoint.

From the State Department, as the civilian deputy to Admiral Hill, we had Elbridge Durbrow, whom we called Durby.[47] He was a levelheaded career man, not one of those that became wanderers in the far blue yonder. He was subsequently ambassador in a couple of countries, somewhere in Southeast Asia I believe.

John T. Mason Jr.: Yes, he was. I believe he was at Saigon, wasn't he?

Admiral Eller: I believe so. Now he's active in conservation organizations like the American Security Council and other groups.

I won't try to go into the course, because you have that from Admiral Hill and others, but I will touch on some of the highlights—for me anyhow.[48]

It was worthwhile to have the time to read and study, but I had always been doing that anyhow on strategic, political matters. So that part of it was just what I'd been doing. But we did hear from a vast number of leaders of the country in their fields, ranging from the President through Carey, a labor leader.[49] I think we had Lewis.[50] We had ministers. We had a Zionist, who was a hair-raising man. We had some crackpot State Department speakers and some very sound ones. We had all the Defense hierarchy. So it was interesting

---

46. General of the Army Dwight D. Eisenhower, USA, served as Army Chief of Staff from 19 November 1945 to 7 February 1948.
47. Elbridge Durbrow was an American Foreign Service Officer who was Deputy Chief of Mission in the Soviet Union in the late 1940s and subsequently U.S. Ambassador to South Vietnam, 1957–61.
48. Admiral Hill's oral history is in the Columbia University collection.
49. James B. Carey, national secretary-treasurer, Congress of Industrial Organizations.
50. John L. Lewis served as president of the United Mine Workers of America from 1920 to 1960.

to see those people and to talk with them. Sometimes you had a chance to talk with them before and after.

The general feeling that ran through all these speeches, because they related them whenever they could to Defense, was that the atomic bomb had ended all war. We had it. Nobody else had it. This was a mirage, a will-of-the-wisp of twisted wishful thinking that they were following.

John T. Mason Jr.: And they didn't expect anybody else to get it.

Admiral Eller: They didn't expect anybody else to get it for years—if ever. In fact, all through 1948 and the first half of 1949, right up almost to graduation, they said so, speakers like President Truman, Secretary Johnson, who relieved Forrestal in March 1949, I believe.[51] Others were General Bradley, Vandenberg, and Dean Acheson.[52] They all said that we had the atomic bomb, and nobody else could have it in a long time. Soviet Russia wouldn't be able to get it for 20 or 25 years.

John T. Mason Jr.: Was that because they lacked the industrial capacity?

Admiral Eller: Supposedly. Also because they lacked the scientific development beforehand which we had had in the Manhattan Project. And, of course, within months from the last of these speeches, Russia exploded an atomic bomb.[53] This shows how you can allow yourself to dream and so influence your thinking that you get away from reason and common sense.

It was the party line, too, as far as those in government were concerned. This was something that distressed me at the time, and it has distressed me since. Once there is a party line, then everybody has to follow it. Thus you give the impression to the country

---

51. Harry S. Truman served as President of the United States from 12 April 1945 to 20 January 1953.
52. General Omar N. Bradley, USA, served as Chairman of the Joint Chiefs of Staff from 16 August 1949 to 14 August 1953. In 1950 he was promoted to five-star rank, general of the Army. General Hoyt S. Vandenberg, USAF, was Air Force Chief of Staff from 30 April 1948 to 29 June 1953. Dean G. Acheson served as Secretary of State from 21 January 1949 to 20 January 1953.
53. The Soviets first successfully exploded an atomic bomb on 29 August 1949 at a test site in Kazakhstan.

that this is truth. Of course, that was what Truman demanded. He wouldn't have anybody who wouldn't follow the party line. So it was the party line expressed by everybody. We were omnipotent with the bomb, and thus navies were now obsolete, one of the fallacies that derived from wishful thinking. The Navy was obsolete. We didn't need it. All you needed were airplanes and bombs and maybe some Army afterwards for the occupation force.

John T. Mason Jr.: But not the Marines.

Admiral Eller: Never the Marines. And you didn't need the Navy except for convoy, transport, and you didn't need that much since we had the atomic bomb. So everything now was the bomb and the Air Force.

All the while they were talking this nonsense, there was a series of international crises that should have brought leaders to their senses. It was obvious that Russia wasn't stopping in her pressure outward. The first crises were in the Middle East, where they continue today. Iran had been divided into spheres of influence during the war by the Soviets and the Western allies. As I recall, Iran had been divided into spheres of influence between Russia and England far earlier, at the time of the first Shah, father of the present one.[54]

Anyhow, it was divided up again during World War II. The Soviet sphere, including the Alborz Mountains above Tehran, took all the northern part. Britain and the United States took the southern part. It was agreed that after the war, on a certain date, they would leave; I believe it was March 1946. Britain and the United States pulled out their forces. The Soviets not only hung back but at the same time set up a puppet republic, Azerbaijan, in northwest Iran. They sent in, first, undercover troops and, of course, ample munitions to the guerrillas. There are always guerrillas available if you look for them and supply them and incite them.

---

54. At the time of this interview, in December 1978, Mohammed Reza Pahlavi, had been Shah of Iran since 1941, when his father Reza Kahn, abdicated. In January 1979 the Shah was forced to leave the country in the face of violent protests by conservative Moslems. Religious leader Ayatollah Ruhollah Khomeini established a government that has remained in effect despite his death in 1989.

The Shah sent troops against the supposed rebels and was beginning to win. Then the Soviets sent in tanks and reinforcements for their occupying troops. This was a very ticklish situation. At the same time, they were pressing on Turkey and demanding rights of equal control of the Dardanelles—in other words, permanent control. Also they had stirred up revolt of Communists in Greece, supplying and instigating them in civil war. The whole area was in turmoil. So at that time Forrestal, pushed by Nimitz and Sherman, although I don't think he had to be pushed much, went to the President and suggested that we send back the body of the Turkish ambassador, who had died in the fall, in *Missouri*. Of course, the USS *Missouri* appealed to the President, and this was done.[55]

The fact that she was coming was heralded simply as a peaceful gesture, just to bring back the ambassador. But in the area it was received with a great deal of joy. As a Greek writer said, "The vast power of the United States comes not here for aggression, but to serve peace, justice, right, and equality. A Turkish one said, "You came to knock at the sea gates of Turkey, whereas the enemy is knocking at the land gates. The United States came to bring peace and liberty, against the Russians coming to take over."

In the next two or three months everything began to quiet down. Iran, partly through clever maneuvering by the Shah (the Persians are very subtle and quite clever in maneuvering) agreed to give the Russians oil concessions in the north if they would take out their troops.

In the United Nations a motion was introduced to censure Russia for violating the agreement on evacuating Iran. General Razmara, a very capable man, was defeating the rebels in Azerbaijan.[56] So Russia finally pulled out her troops, and the issue was settled. But the oil rights didn't get to Russia, because the Majlis refused to ratify it, which I expect was already agreed in advance.

---

55. The battleship *Missouri* (BB-63) and her escorts visited Istanbul, Turkey, from 5 to 9 April 1946. The mission was to deliver the body of Mehmet Munir Ertegun, who was Turkish Ambassador to the United States at the time of his death on 11 November 1944. His body was then stored in a crypt at the Arlington National Cemetery until after the war, when the *Missouri* delivered it to Istanbul. This visit helped pave the way for the establishment of the U.S. Sixth Fleet a few years later. Truman's daughter Margaret had christened the battleship in 1944.
56. General Haj Ali Razmara was an Iranian military leader. He later was Iran's Prime Minister, from 26 June 1950 until his assassination on 7 March 1951.

In Turkey the pressure slackened off for a while. And in Greece the elections soundly rejected Communists. *Missouri*, after she had visited Greece, came back to the States.

John T. Mason Jr.: So the tides receded?

Admiral Eller: The tides receded, but only temporarily, because the Soviets never do stop pushing.

"Mighty Mo" had scarcely gotten home when a new crisis arose with new pressure both on Turkey and Greece and Italy. The Kremlin was trying to stir up Communists and also sending in arms.

At this time, Forrestal, with Sherman and Nimitz pushing again, got Truman to send over a stronger force, a carrier and a cruiser and a number of destroyers. I think the carrier was *Franklin D. Roosevelt*, another ship Truman could accept easily.[57] What Sherman and Nimitz were trying to do, and Forrestal, too, was to establish a permanent force in the Med that, by its presence, would support peace. This was the forerunner of the Sixth Fleet.[58]

In the spring of 1947, just about the time that all of this was happening, Truman promulgated the Truman Doctrine, which was to support Greece and Turkey economically and with military aid. This was one of the great decisions he made. Had he made all decisions as wisely, he would have been one of our greatest Presidents. The doctrine was a big help to free people everywhere, but it was really to help stabilize the Eastern Mediterranean and to support peoples resisted subjugation by armed minorities, which is still the major Soviet method. Of course, to do this we needed the free use of the seas, and that demanded a strong Navy, but this fact seemed to go out of the minds of Truman and most of his advisors.

I saw Truman close a few times. Twice in Public Information when he made one of his speeches at the National Press Club. I was in a small group with him before and after

---

57. *Franklin D. Roosevelt* (CVB-42), a *Midway*-class aircraft carrier, was commissioned 27 October 1945. Her first deployment to the Mediterranean lasted from August to October 1946.
58. Vice Admiral Forrest P. Sherman, USN, served from 7 February 1948 to 14 November 1949 as the first Commander Sixth Task Fleet. In 1950, after Sherman had left, the name was changed to Sixth Fleet.

the speech. He was delightful in a social group. He sat down and played the piano and talked to you just as if you were part of the family. He was jovial, hearty, hail-fellow-well-met, and just as pleasant to be with as you could think.

When Admiral Nimitz was detached, I went with him to the Oval Room in the White House. There was only a handful of people, the other chiefs of the services and their deputies. Truman was as kind and delightful to the admiral as you could think a person could be. He gave him a signed photograph saying, "From El Presidente." It was informal and pleasing. Had you not known anything about him other than that, you could have thought that he was your closest friend.

At the war college and in many of the Joint Chiefs of Staff decisions, he showed a different characteristic entirely. As I said, he was determined that everybody would follow the party line.

He took spoofing very readily. I saw this at the Gridiron Club, at the White House Correspondents' Association meetings and at another organization. One whole meeting of the White House Correspondents Association was a drama made up around criticizing Truman in a clever and delightful way. He took all that evening with apparent great pleasure and then played "The Missouri Waltz" on the piano afterwards.

But when anyone tried to buck him in his decisions, he was hardheaded and ruthless. If he had always been right, it would have been wonderful. But he could be badly wrong. To my mind he made three or four great errors that have hurt the country immensely. The first one was the failure to understand sea power and his emphasis on the atomic bomb. Although he had used the Navy effectively through this period of 1946 to 1948 and had seen its achievements during the war, he still was deluded by the atomic bomb. He was still going to do away with the Navy entirely.

I related earlier how our top speakers at the National War College were all shown to be wrong about the atomic bomb, because that had become the party line. This party line unanimity also extended to closed minds to our country's need for strength on the sea. Because of Truman's rationalization about the bomb, he determined to cut the Navy drastically, especially naval aviation and the Marines. Bradley always spurred him on. He spoke twice at the National War College. Then later I got to know him fairly closely.

He was a pleasant man, too, like Truman, but very ambitious and narrow-visioned. He abominated the Marines.

John T. Mason Jr.: Was that the source of Truman's dislike of the Marines?

Admiral Eller: It could be. Of course, officers in the old Army had been somewhat mortified by the great praise the Marines had gained at Belleau Wood.[59] I think this had aroused in narrow-minded people hostility that they never forgot.

The Marines were noted for their gallantry and were adored by the country. The Army had to take a much larger group of people who couldn't have the same morale and prestige that the Marines had developed.

At one of his speeches, again Bradley proved dramatically wrong. He said that we would never again have amphibious landings like those in the Pacific, that all we needed from the Marines was a small police force. As for the Navy, we didn't need the carriers with no navy to oppose them. The only possible need for a Navy was for convoy and transport to take the Army overseas if required.

Of course, one of the worst errors that Truman made was to appoint Johnson as Secretary of Defense. I didn't see much of Johnson besides hearing him at the war college. He was an ambitious, intelligent in some ways, clever man who was maneuvering for political office. He had been Assistant Secretary of War at one time during the war, I think, and had done a good job in the war in whatever his duties were.

But Truman brought him in, I believe, to push out Forrestal and to crush the Navy, to bring it into line. As he said, "Knock their heads together." Johnson knew nothing about the Navy. He had no broad strategic conceptions. He was there to get ahead in the world as a politician and to follow out his boss's orders and therefore gain favor. I think he was partly instrumental in pushing out Forrestal early and also in breaking his spirit. I believe Forrestal was going to finish up the year in May 1949, but he was forced to resign the first of March 1949.

59. Belleau Wood, near Chateau Thierry, France, was the scene of a notable World War I battle, 6 June 1918.

Truman's emphasis on yes men was a disaster to the country. Another major error—and maybe this is one that he couldn't have prevented—was the establishment of Israel, of his really pushing it.[60] This, of course, started with the Balfour Declaration back in 1917.[61] The error started then, and it might never have been corrected, but Truman was being pushed by Jewish people—not all of them. There is an organization now that I receive literature from that strongly opposes Zionism.

John T. Mason Jr.: But the Zionists were in the saddle, were they not?

Admiral Eller: Yes, and they still are, because they fight with ferocity and with no holds barred and are very vicious in their attacks. A Zionist leader came down from New York to speak to us at the college. He may have been head of the Zionist organization. He was as dictatorial as he could be when anyone asked him a question. In fact, I asked one: "What is going to happen to the Arabs?" He tore into me as if I were trying to kill him. Truman undoubtedly had this kind of pressure, and he had a Jewish press in the major papers, that are largely Jewish controlled.

There should have been a place for the Israelites, for the persecuted ones of Europe. Of course, this was another pressure, because England had tried to stop immigration when the Jewish population reached about half of the Arab population in Palestine.

I don't think there were more than a handful of Jews in Palestine at the turn of the century. After the Balfour Declaration, they began to pour in and had reached several hundred thousand by the time World War II had ended. Then after World War II, the inflow from Europe, especially Germany, became a flood, which England tried to check. I remember a number of incidents during the period in which refugee ships would be stopped, and others would slip by. Britain prepared a camp for them on Cyprus. They

---

60. On 14 April 1948, in Tel Aviv, David Ben-Gurion declared the State of Israel in Palestine. Ben-Gurion became the new nation's first Prime Minister. On behalf of the United States, President Harry S. Truman recognized the new nation that same day.
61. The Balfour Declaration was a letter dated 2 November 1917 from British Foreign Minister Arthur J. Balfour to Walter Rothschild, a leader of the British Jewish community. The declaration pledged British support for a Zionist homeland, provided that the rights of the non-Jewish communities in Palestine were respected.

would slip out of there.

The Arabs, of course, were very hostile to the flood of immigrants, because they had owned the land by then for about 1,500 years. It's just as holy to them as it is to the Jews. As you know, the Moslems accept the Old Testament completely, and they accept the New Testament to a point, considering Christ as a prophet.

John T. Mason Jr.: Yes, a prophet in a series of prophets.

Admiral Eller: Yes, for them Mohammed was the last and greatest.

So Truman was pushed by these forces, and maybe he couldn't have done anything else, but he didn't have to be precipitous when they established Israel in 1948. He and the U.S.S.R. both rushed to acknowledge them, on the same day. I'm not sure whether Russia was doing this deliberately to get the United States involved deeply. But it wasn't very long—a few months or a couple of years—until the Soviets turned to the other side and began to support the Arabs. They reversed themselves completely. They saw where their benefit was. First, there are many more Arabs than Israelites. Second, the Soviets held to their understanding of the strategic importance of the Middle East, and of the developing oil.

Oil was discovered there long before World War II, but had not been developed to amount to anything during the war except in Iraq and, to a lesser degree, in Persia but not in the Arabian Peninsula. It was just beginning to develop as a really important influence, and some leaders were beginning to understand the potential of it when I went there in 1950.

I guess Truman was forced into accepting Israel, but he might have been a little wiser and slower and not antagonized the Moslem people so much. This is a sore point that is going to be with us for a long time. That part of the world has been a trouble spot for much of history.

John T. Mason Jr.: A crossroads.

Admiral Eller: Jews were living quite happily in most of the Arab countries. I saw them in Turkey and elsewhere, even after Israel was established. Turkey had accepted the different religions and the different nationalities quite freely. Iraq also had many Jews, and Egypt had a large number.

Another 1948 crisis was the Berlin blockade.[62] The first moves started in April 1948, developed into a full blockade by June, and lasted nearly a year. We had a number of speakers on this issue at the college. It was a very touchy situation where war seemed imminent at any time, but the atomic bomb wasn't going to be useful. This still didn't bring our top people to their senses.

While we ourselves were occupied with only the current crisis in Europe or the Middle East, the Soviets were looking at the world as a whole. They pushed in all directions, including China. Truman's China policy was another very grave and deep error. Advised by many of his principal subordinates, he abandoned Chiang Kai-shek.[63]

John T. Mason Jr.: General Marshall was one of the—[64]

Admiral Eller: Marshall was, yes; this is something that diminished Marshal in my estimation. He was sent to China by Truman to try to make Chiang Kai-shek form a coalition government with the Communists.

Chiang Kai-shek had thrown them out of China after World War I, having experienced their duplicity. He was a great man who was very tough and wise in his perceptions. He knew that if they got into the government that they would destroy him and destroy democracy that he was trying to create in China. He had a Herculean job because of the warlord system that had lasted in China for centuries and of a country weakened by generations of conflict. This empire of hundreds of millions of people has

---

62. On 1 April 1948 the Soviet Union began a land blockade of the Allied sectors of Berlin, preventing overland transport from West Germany. U.S. and British airplanes then began an airlift that flew food and coal into the city until the blockade was lifted on 30 September 1949.
63. Generalissimo Chiang Kai-shek served as President of Nationalist China on the mainland from 1943 to 1949 and as President of the Republic of China on Taiwan from 1950 until his death in 1975.
64. General of the Army George C. Marshall, USA, retired as Army Chief of Staff in November 1945 and was shortly dispatched on a special mission to China to try to end fighting between the Chinese Nationalists and Communists. After initial success, his efforts failed. He was subsequently Secretary of State from 1947 to 1949.

been at war or in unrest and trouble for a century from the 1850s, as the decline of the Manchu Empire took place.

China is the only nation that I know that has gone through a series of rises to greatness and declines, and rises again. She was in a deep decline. Then early in this century, Sun Yat-sen, with Chiang as his young assistant, tried to form a democracy to get rid of the warlords and create a unified China.[65] And they were making progress when the Japanese, in the 1930s, saw that Chang Kai-shek was developing China into a unified power. Sun Yat-sen was then dead. So Japan invaded, set up a puppet in Manchuria, and supported the northern warlords.

China had been at war when World War II came. The Japanese expanded their invading forces. At the same time Mao and Chou En-lai expanded their Communist forces.[66] All through the war they were maneuvering to take over after the war and fought very little against the Japanese, from my understanding, but as much as they could against Chiang Kai-shek.

So here was a country that had been in turmoil and trouble for so long that people were sick of war, more than we were of Vietnam, for example. They were ready to swallow false promises. Of course. Chiang Kai-shek had corrupt men in his government. I don't know if they were much more so than some of ours, unhappily. So that he was damned by Vinegar Joe Stilwell in particular and by some State Department men who were out there.[67] At the college we heard this party line repeatedly, that Chiang Kai-shek was corrupt and that the Communists were coming in with an agrarian revolution that was for the people and not for Communism. This was the administration's party line that speakers advocated, right through the year.

Two speakers I remember from the State Department in particular. One was John Carter Vincent, who was a brother of the wife of one of our admirals whom we knew

---

65. Sun Yat-sen (1866–1925), often considered the father of the Chinese Revolution, planned the overthrow of the Manchus and established the Kuomintang, the Chinese Nationalist Party, in 1912.
66. Mao Tse-tung was head of the Communist Party in the People's Republic of China from the time the Communists seized power in 1949 until his death in 1976. Chou En-lai became Premier and Foreign Minister of China when the Communists won control of the nation in 1949.
67. Lieutenant General Joseph W. Stilwell, USA, was commander of American forces in the China-Burma, India area and Chiang Kai-shek's chief of staff fro 1942 to 1944, when irreconcilable differences with the Chinese leader led to his reassignment to Washington.

very well.[68] We had met him. The other was a man named Davies.[69] Both of them were strongly pro-Mao, not as Communists but from the fact that he represented honest agrarian revolutionists, and both of them were bitterly against Chiang. Davies was like a wild man. He was a fanatic.

Then the Army was generally against Chiang. Stilwell, of course, hadn't gotten along with him; he didn't get along with many people. Chiang Kai-shek had finally asked for him to be relieved. I think that if we had had somebody out there like Al Wedemeyer from the start, we would have had a different understanding of China.[70]

During the year at the college, in addition to hearing speakers and making team studies—some short, some long—each of us had the opportunity to make major studies. I made three in all. One was on China. I took the opposite side of the government party line, because I believed then, and still believe now, that because of the problems Chiang Kai-shek faced we had to have patience with him and help him as much as we could. So I expressed this, very much as I am saying now, but in more detail. I was against Marshall's trip from the standpoint of what he was trying to do, not from the standpoint of his trip, but trying to bring the Communists into the government because they would take over.

Then sometime during the year 1948–1949 we made the decision to abandon Chiang Kai-shek and to pull out the Marines from North China whom Wedemeyer had been able to keep there in 1945, against the advice of General Stratemeyer.[71] We also quit sending aid. We announced this publicly, which was as great a harm as the end of aid itself, because it showed the people of China and the world that we had abandoned him. Consequently, of course, it wasn't very long until the Communists drove in and pushed Chiang Kai-shek out,

---

68. John Carter Vincent had a long connection with Chinese affairs, having spent time both in China and in the State Department's Division of Far Eastern Affairs. His sister Margaret was married to Rear Admiral Allan E. Smith, USN.
69. John P. Davies of the State Department's Policy Planning Staff.
70. Lieutenant General Albert C. Wedemeyer, USA, served in China from October 1944 to September 1946. He was chief of staff to Chiang Kai-shek and commander of U.S. forces in China.
71. Lieutenant General George E. Stratemeyer, USAF, had commanded Army Air Forces in the China Theater and later was Commander Far Eastern Air Force, 1949–51.

and he went into Taiwan. And now we've made another disastrous move in abandoning Taiwan.[72]

I would guess that 95% of the class held opposite views to mine. That included practically all of the Army officers, except for two who didn't go along with the party line, one of them a very smart engineer. And many of the Navy, unhappily, followed the information in the press, which then often emphasized one side of this issue, slanting it.

In addition to our political and military studies and discussions, we also took up other aspects like labor unions and Communism. From the beginning I've distrusted Communism, especially after the experiences in Russia during the early yeas and what happened to the people. So I made two of my major studies on how the Communists take over a respected organization. They have a system that's infallible unless people try to be aware of it and alert the other members of the organization. If they can control the offices of secretary, treasurer, and public information, then they control the organization. Most people only believe what they hear. Most don't have time to read and study. And if you have the money, you can divert that to where you want it to go.

Communists would bring their people into an organization, or they would find people there already with a one-track or warped mind, a radical who failed to look at the whole picture. These would be used as puppets and tools. My report was based upon a study of labor unions that Communists had taken over. Two or three of our labor unions were taken over during the war. They were thrown out of one, I think by Cary, who was thought of as a Communist. He was really being used by the Communists and didn't realize it. When he woke up to the true facts, he then tried to push them out and ultimately succeeded. His story of how they took over is typical.

The union will call, say, an annual meeting or a special meeting for elections. The Communists will have a core of people planted who know what they want. They will argue against men they don't want and drag out the meeting. Those present in the labor union have to get up early and go to work the next morning. So one by one they drift out. I know I drift out of some meetings the same way. I get sick and tired of long-winded,

---

72. The United States officially recognized the People's Republic of China (mainland) on 15 December 1978 and severed diplomatic ties with the Republic of China (Taiwan), though both countries maintain quasi-official representation with each other.

often foolish, arguments and leave. So members drift out; finally, when enough are gone, leaving a Communist-dominated majority, then they elect the president, usually a well-meaning, fine man, respected by everyone. He becomes the figurehead behind which the Communists operate. The vice president may be similar. But the secretary is one of their faction, and also the treasurer and the public information officers. From that point they have taken over the organization, because most people don't work in it.

By similar means Communists have taken over many types of organizations, including religious ones. In fact, I'm sure they've taken over the World Council of Churches, although most of the people are well meaning, highly respected, and devout people. And I have a feeling they have taken over the National Council of Churches, or at least have such power that they control the way it operates.

In my second major Communist paper I looked at the world situation from the standpoint of the Kremlin, then dressed as a Russian for the presentation. This was a team project with two or three of us working on it. I dressed as a member of the Comintern and gave my speech.

John T. Mason Jr.: These papers were given to the whole class?

Admiral Eller: These two were. I gave my Comintern speech as if to the ruling group in the secrecy of the Kremlin. It covered what they were obviously doing already, of course. All I had to do was to cite what was going on around the world. The basic facts that I concentrated on were how they worked from within. Every country has its evil men, its radicals, the dissatisfied. Many of them are ready to follow any leader who promises them a beautiful tomorrow or promises prestige and power. The Soviets were going to work their way through the world this way if they could, and they would try to destroy the United States from within.

John T. Mason Jr.: How were these received?

Admiral Eller: Both of them, I think, were received with the same sort of views that the listeners had before. You don't quickly change people's views. They generally liked the second one, especially because of the delivery.

John T. Mason Jr.: The props.

Admiral Eller: The props. But I don't think the presentation changed people's opinions very much. Perhaps it gave them a more balanced understanding.

We had a field trip to Panama. General Matthew Ridgway was the Army commander based there with military responsibility for all of Latin America, Central America, and South America.[73] His staff made a presentation covering the area. Then he summarized it and was open for questions. I don't think I've known a more capable man than General Ridgway. I was highly impressed with him. He was intelligent, incisive, very knowledgeable. He, like Turner, knew more about the facets of the different parts of the job than his staff. He also had a broad vision, encompassing the whole range of possibilities, far beyond the tunnels that many other people look into.

Our naval district with maritime responsibility for the area was also based in Panama. The public information officer had worked for me when I had Public Information. He got in touch with me and asked if I would like to meet General Remón, who was head of the National Guard.[74] Whoever controlled the Guardia controlled Panama.

So he arranged to meet the general in a place where he always came along about 9:00 in the evening. This was a little bar on a side street in Panama. I talked with him there for about an hour on the situation in Panama itself and Latin America. He was an avowed friend of the United States and a very sincere man, I think. In time he was assassinated or pushed out, or perhaps drank himself to death. During our meeting he would drink a glass of spirits and then push it out on the bar, and they would fill it and hand it back to him with no question. He was running the country.

---

73. Lieutenant General Matthew B. Ridgway, USA, Commander in Chief Caribbean Command, 1948–49.
74. José Antonio Remón Cantera became chief of the national police in 1947. He was involved in coups and later served as President of Panama from 1 October 1952 until his assassination on 2 January 1955.

It was interesting to hear his views on the problems in Panama. He was convinced that Panama couldn't be a democracy. It had to be run in its present stage of development by somebody in authority. Much of the population is illiterate; most would have no idea what to vote for. The true friend of the country was the United States.

The current President was the head of the Guardia and came to power by taking over from the previous President and then having himself elected.

John T. Mason Jr.: And now he has stepped down as President, but he retains head of the Guardia.

Admiral Eller: Yes, so there's no change—just like the secretary of the Communist Party.

Another interesting experience there was a visit to the San Blas Islands. I knew the commander of our naval aviation in Panama, and I asked him for a plane to fly some of us to the islands. There are usually pilots needing training flights. So he arranged it, and we took along two or three others, including Dave Tyree in my class and Rudolph Winnacker, one of our professors.[75] The college staff consisted of officers from the services, men from the State Department, and a handful of civilian professors unassociated with government departments.

John T. Mason Jr.: Of national repute too.

Admiral Eller: Yes, I guess so. Rudolph Winnacker was one.

Life on the island was really almost like going back 2,000 years. Most of the Indians lived in dirt-floored huts with thatched roofs. The kids ran around naked. The women wove, and the men went to Panama and worked, I think, in the canal ports, coming home on weekends or periodically. They lived simply, off of fish, I think, and fruits from the jungle. I don't think they worked hard. It was very interesting to see them and realize

---

75. Captain David M. Tyree, USN, was a Naval Academy classmate of Eller. Rudolph A. Winnacker later served as the first Chief Historian of the Office of the Secretary of Defense, holding that position from 1949 to 1973.

how these people who lived so near were as far from civilization as the tribes of darkest Africa. Much of Panama, I understand from those who know it well, is like this out in the jungles and the countryside.

John T. Mason Jr.: All Indian, yes.

Admiral Eller: Shifting to another facet of the trip. John Crommelin was in the class.[76] He was an aviator, the eldest of five brothers who graduated from the academy, one in my class.[77] He created a furor on Capitol Hill later in the year and gave me a preview in Panama.[78]

Much of my time in Public Information had been in fighting the powerful forces seeking to do away with the Navy. The country had to be aware of the continuing need for the Navy. In fact, practically everything we did was directed toward that end. A major part of it stressed the need for carriers and for naval air, which there was so much effort to destroy. Even at the college I continued this effort and did a great deal of letter writing in connection with it. John knew this and wanted me to walk with him out in the country. For most of an afternoon he unburdened his worries about the future of the Navy and country, and what he would like to do to wake the nation up. He was already considering risking his career, as he had risked and almost given his life in the war. He was worried and frustrated to desperation.

I happened to run across a letter I had forgotten that I wrote to DeWitt Wallace of *The Reader's Digest*.[79] I might mention a little out of this: "The Air Force was able, because of the enthusiasm of the country for the atomic bomb, to use some of the most dishonest and untrue writers in the country."

There was a very skillful writer named Huie, whom I got to know in Public

---

76. Captain John G. Crommelin, USN.
77. Henry Crommelin graduated 18th in the class of 1925; he retired in 1959 with the rank of vice admiral.
78. Captain Crommelin leaked documents that indicated plans to have naval aviation absorbed into the new Air Force. The Navy's reaction was known as the "revolt of the admirals." See Edward P. Stafford, "Saving Carrier Aviation—1949 Style," *U.S. Naval Institute Proceedings*, January 1990, pages 44–51.
79. Wallace was founder and publisher of the popular periodical.

Information through trying to correct him on some of his writings.[80] But he didn't write for correctness; he wrote to try to prove a point and left out the truth, if necessary. I had read *The Reader's Digest* from its infancy. In fact, I subscribed for Agnes a life subscription in the early 1930s for $25.00—the cheapest investment I've made. So I knew and loved *The Reader's Digest* and admired its efforts for accuracy.

The editors were taken in by Huie. I think the Air Force sent Huie to them and told them he was a good writer. Here was a man that would give them an honest picture of the difficulties facing the country and of the need for aviation to be the supreme force in our military strength. So they had Huie write this series of articles. I've forgotten what they were all about, but one was about the bombing that I mentioned of the *Utah* in the 1930s.

John T. Mason Jr.: Yes, when she was an experimental ship.

Admiral Eller: This exercise had taken place, and the Army Air was to find us offshore and to bomb us and sink us, in which they succeeded, according to Huie, but the Navy covered up. Just to summarize, they didn't find us in the time period allotted, which was 24 hours, I believe, as we operated 200-300 miles offshore. They didn't find us, and the operation was called off. So we were steaming peacefully back to port, and all of a sudden appeared a group that had been high-level bombers but now were down low at 2,000-4,000 feet. We looked at them and were laughing and saying, "Hell, we fooled you boys. You didn't find us." And all of a sudden we saw their bomb bays open. We said, "Well, they are just simulating." The next thing we knew, the bombs were coming down, and we hit the deck, all of us. Happily, none of them hit. And that was the story of the operation.

---

80. William Bradford Huie wrote a series of articles that appeared in *The Reader's Digest* in December 1948 and the early months of 1949. In part he recycled material, including the discussion of the 1937 bombing of the *Utah* (AG-16) that had appeared in his book *The Case Against the Admirals: Why We Must Have a Unified Command* (New York: E. P. Dutton, 1946).

Huie wrote just the opposite account. When I read the article, I wrote to Barclay Acheson, a friend of mine next to DeWitt Wallace, a marvelous man, and I complained.[81] On his suggestion, I wrote Wallace:

"I refrain from commenting on Huie's many errors and misstatements in these articles. I continue to refrain from discussing most of these, although I am convinced that you have taken a stand that will damage American thinking in action for years to come. But I cannot pass one group of erroneous statements concerning myself and the ship in which I served. In the late 1930s I had the gunnery school in USS *Utah*, which the Navy wisely used to develop both this and antiaircraft tactics and gunnery and air attack tactics. We occupied much of our time working with our naval aviators and some time with our Army aviators. Both groups were then able and zealous Americans. In addition to my antiaircraft duties, I dealt with aviation unit commanders and supervised the observance of bomb-marking parties at some hazard to ourselves from falling bombs, from which we got accurate data to help in the solution of both the air attack and the antiair problems.

"In those days and long before most of us in the Navy were convinced that the Navy could be efficient in serving the country only by scientific integration of all available weapons into the triad of sea power, on, under, and above the sea, in the air above it.

"In my job I was intimately connected with the details of the USS *Utah* episode intemperately fictionalized in your April issue. I wrote most of the report on the operation, a factual evaluation, as we naturally made all of our reports of similar operations. I therefore resent this printed account, not only as a reflection of the integrity of the Navy, which I rejoice to say has a high and honorable code, but upon my own honesty and loyalty. The account given in your April article is so distorted it becomes a malicious old wives' tale. Every pertinent incident of the operation and the results were opposite to those set forth in your pages. Indeed, this one episode justifies my conclusion of other inaccuracies I have observed in this series that is one of the most dangerously slanted group of articles in our modern press."

Now, I don't know, but I think this had some effect because—

---

81. Barclay Acheson was director of international editions, part of the top management of *The Reader's Digest*. His sister was married to DeWitt Wallace, and the three were the magazine's founders.

John T. Mason Jr.: What kind of reply did you get from Mr. Wallace?

Admiral Eller: I don't know. I just found this letter. My papers are all mixed up and so voluminous. I happened to run into this last night.

I think, unhappily, the major result of my tours in Public Information and the National War College was the conclusion that a large proportion of the national leaders had a deplorable lack of foresight and were little men not good for the country.

John T. Mason Jr.: That's a pretty devastating conclusion.

Admiral Eller: It is, a large proportion of them. Now, Forrestal was an outstanding exception in the Cabinet. There were other good men, not as good as he, but there were others. Forrestal was honest; he tried to know the facts. He knew more about any part of the world's situation than anybody else in a Cabinet meeting. Forrestal was a driver. He drove himself as hard as anybody else and also had a perceptive mind. He saw, from the beginning, I'm afraid, that unification was going to be a disaster. But there were too many like Johnson and Matthews who worked for their own ends and not the future of the Navy.[82] Now, those two are the worst that I had any real close contact with. Both of them were just an unhappy type of man to put in the jobs that they had.

John T. Mason Jr.: And, well, analyze the circumstances under which they came. It was almost purely political, was it not?

Admiral Eller: Yes, it was political. In fact, Truman brought Johnson in to push out Forrestal, to knock heads together and get a strong authoritative Secretary of Defense, which Forrestal resisted and wouldn't have taken the job had it been on that basis. Then Truman brought in Matthews, somebody out in the Middle West who said he had never seen anything larger than a rowboat, and told him to get the Navy in line. Matthews devotedly followed the call of the President—working for his own ends, I think.

---

82. Francis P. Matthews served as Secretary of the Navy from 25 May 1949 to 30 July 1951.

Then their lack of understanding of history and international affairs, and, therefore, the meaning of the sea and sea power. If you study history and study what has happened in the world in the last century, you can see that without control of the seas we wouldn't have freedom today. You go all through history and see that the ultimate issue in any global conflict, or any overseas conflict, has to be the seas; the Navy has to be fundamental in it. And the shipping, to move men and cargo, has to be fundamental. But this was all pushed aside by the atomic bomb mirage.

Unhappily, my next duty after the National War College reinforced this conclusion. I wanted to go to sea and thought that I ought to, but I was ordered to the staff of the Joint Chiefs of Staff after graduating from the war college in late June or early July. I resisted it, but I was sent in order to pay for going to the war college.

John T. Mason Jr.: You had an obligation at that point?

Admiral Eller: Yes. I think one of the reasons was that Gruenther wanted to use me. I didn't know it at the time, but I think he did.

John T. Mason Jr.: Who was the Chairman of the Joint Chiefs?

Admiral Eller: The senior one in the Joint Chiefs was Bradley. There were only the three: Bradley, Denfeld, and Vandenberg. Bradley made general at the end of the war or late in the war, and Denfeld had become a full admiral and then become CNO with the departure of Admiral Nimitz in 1947. So Bradley was senior, even though Denfeld was older.[83]

I was sent to the Joint Chiefs Strategic Plans Division. We had teams, one or two officers from each service who would work on war plans of the future or problems of the present preparing position papers that we developed for the Joint Chiefs. We haggled over

---

83. General Omar N. Bradley, USA, born 12 February 1893, date of four-star rank on 12 March 1945. Denfeld was born 13 April 1891; his date of rank as four-star admiral was 7 January 1946.

position papers, and it was like dealing with the Communists, because you had to fight every word and phrase to be sure that it meant precisely what you thought and couldn't be interpreted otherwise. It was a dreary type of work, and I never did like it. One was often dealing in problems as if they existed in limbo without other situations involving them.

John T. Mason Jr.: You mean without taking into consideration the economics and all the rest?

Admiral Eller: Well, yes, and really not taking into account the real forces that we needed in order to do what we intended to do. We would prepare the plan there and get it agreed upon within the section. Then we would send it up to the services. They would pick it over and be sure that it said just what they wanted, and it would come back down again, and we would go over it again. We would send it back, and it would come back, and finally it would go to the Chiefs. They would accept it or reject it. But it was treading water as far as I was concerned.

At that time NATO was developing.[84] Truman had issued the Truman Doctrine and then the Marshall Plan. Both of these—the Marshall Plan and the Truman Doctrine—were truly great decisions and extremely beneficial to the world and to us thereby.[85]

Then the Berlin Blockade had come. This had shown Europe and us that they needed more economic aid and economic development. So the organization of NATO was started. This had been agreed upon. I think our Senate finally passed or accepted it in July 1949, soon after I joined the Joint Chiefs staff.

Now it was decided to send the Joint Chiefs to Europe to set up the military side of NATO. Gruenther had sometime earlier talked to me about who should go with them, what type of persons he would take along. It ended up that two went along with the Joint

---

[84]. NATO – North Atlantic Treaty Organization, which was established in 1949 as a multi-national means of coordinating defense against a potential attack from the Soviet Union.
[85]. The Truman Doctrine, described earlier in the interview, involved halting the spread of Communism in Europe. At the Harvard University commencement in 1947, Secretary of State George C. Marshall made an address in which he outlined a plan for the economic rebuilding of war-ravaged Europe. Congress passed the European Recovery Act, and the program of American support came to be known as the Marshall Plan.

Chiefs and Gruenther: an Army colonel, Bill Bayer, and myself as the Navy worker.[86] The President loaned his plane. Gruenther was very skillful in maneuvering. He negotiated a very high per diem so that we lived like kings in the plane. It opened my eyes when I got on board and saw all this fancy food that you normally see in the Waldorf.

John T. Mason Jr.: What was this, a Constellation?

Admiral Eller: It was Air Force Number One plane. It bore a name as the President's plane.[87] It was set up luxuriously with bunks, places to play cards, and lounging rooms. It was an emperor's plane.

So we took off, I think from the north end of National Airport from the MATS base.[88] There was a great crowd of people to see us off. It would have been natural for the President to be there, and I think he was. This was good publicity trying to draw the Western world together into a unified defense against the Soviets, who were still pushing outward in China and elsewhere.

I had a briefing from Red Yeager, Admiral Denfeld's senior aide.[89] Red had been with him a good while and knew his habits. He told me what I soon found out, that Denfeld was a very simple and unassuming man. He wasn't demanding at all. He was quite humble in many ways, considering the positions he had held. He drank very little, but he always liked to have a Scotch or two at bedtime to relax after the day's occupations. So Red gave me a little handbag loaded with bottles of miniature Scotch.

John T. Mason Jr.: One swig.

Admiral Eller: Each one was a drink. We were going to be gone a couple of weeks. Also, Admiral Denfeld didn't like to carry money. He didn't like to be bothered. So I would handle the finances and then give him a report of expenses at the end of the trip. Of course,

---

86. Colonel William L. Bayer, USA.
87. The aircraft, a DC-6, was named *Independence* in honor of President Truman's hometown in Missouri.
88. MATS – Military Air Transport Service. The ten-day trip began on 29 July 1949.
89. Captain Howard A. Yeager, USN.

we didn't have any real expenses, because we were taken care of everywhere, unless we wanted to buy something on the side. We didn't have much time to do anything else, for that matter.

We landed in London first and held our first conference with the British Chiefs. Then I began to realize who was running the show. Bradley did most of the talking. Vandenberg did a little interjection now and then. And Denfeld said practically nothing.

I felt unhappy about it, because, practically neglecting the Navy, Bradley started off telling the British Chiefs, outlining what our plans were in general. Everything was going smoothly. Then he said, pointing to a larger map in the conference room, "Now, we cannot set our defense line east of Tunis and Sicily."

Well, the British Chiefs nearly fell out of their chairs, having lived all their lives trying to hold Cairo and the Suez Canal and the Middle East and India. They nearly collapsed.

There was a furious interchange of conversation, "You can't mean this!"

Bradley said, "Yes."

Then Vandenberg said, "Yes, we can't fly planes there. We don't have the planes."

This was based upon not what we were doing, but what we could do with the forces that were being cut in the services. And Denfeld kept quiet. I guess he knew that Bradley had the President's directive and Johnson's directive. He felt he could do nothing about it. So we had quite a hassle over that. Bradley held firm. This was just what we could do. The British finally, reluctantly, accepted it unbelievingly, I'm sure, because we didn't hold to it. I then realized that Admiral Denfeld was very good in handling Congress, but with his hands tied he couldn't do much in the Joint Chiefs of Staff.

John T. Mason Jr.: He was just ineffective.

Admiral Eller: He couldn't do anything else, I guess. I was quite unhappy, and then I realized afterwards that he was stuck there. And the Navy was being cut more than anybody else. So we didn't have anything to go to the Eastern Med.

John T. Mason Jr.: I can imagine a few other CNOs, though, who would have spoken up regardless.

Admiral Eller: That's why I say Blandy might have forestalled this.

A little later I began to realize, increasingly on the trip, that Bradley, Admiral Denfeld, and Gruenther were all maneuvering for position.

The amendment to the National Security Act, with Johnson pushing it, had gone through Congress. It gave the Secretary of Defense more authority. It set up a formal Joint Chiefs of Staff with a separate Chairman of the group. What we had already was operating all right, but now the Chairman would have the authority. Then he would be going to the President and not the Chiefs of the other services.

John T. Mason Jr.: He was the spokesman.

Admiral Eller: He was the spokesman and could slant the views as he liked; the others were really kept silent. This is disastrous, because the President and Congress should receive information directly from the people who know. Then they can make the decision and not just someone who has been told by the President, maybe, to make this decision and come back and tell Congress and the President what he wanted to hear to begin with.

Another item that Yeager had given me was a pad of one-time code messages. That means you wrote your message in code, tore off the sheet, and then the next sheet had an entirely different code on it. Bradley, Gruenther, and Denfeld were frequently sending messages back to Washington. I wasn't given the privilege to look into them. But I could see that at least part of them were based on ambition. Bradley was maneuvering for appointment to the new position of Chairman. Gruenther was maneuvering for a position in the Department of the Army, which he got, and later he became head of the European Command, SACEur.[90] And Denfeld was recommended for reappointment.

---

90. SACEur – Supreme Allied Commander Europe, a NATO billet.

John T. Mason Jr.: Which he didn't get.

Admiral Eller: Yes, he did.[91]

John T. Mason Jr.: He did?

Admiral Eller: Which should have gone to Admiral Blandy, as the President had promised. I ran into Blandy in the corridor of Main Navy as he came back from the White House following the first decision two years earlier. He told me that the President had promised that he would have the next tour, but he wanted to give the first one to Denfeld because Leahy wanted him.

During our time in London, we met in our embassy and outlined plans with the Danish and Norwegian Chiefs of Staff. Of course, to them the northern part of Europe was what was important. We may have met with the Icelandic representatives, because they became members of NATO. But I can't remember.

After the meetings all day, as in each place, we went to official receptions, dinners. All the arguments with the British Chiefs seemed to be forgotten. Everything was harmonious, and nothing, naturally, was mentioned. The details of how the organization would be worked out were to be developed later on by a committee appointed from the various services. They would work out what is operating now.

In Paris we met with the French Joint Chiefs in their building. Then later with the Dutch, Belgian, and Portuguese Chiefs at the American Embassy. Each one had a separate hour. I have some of the names, but there is no use to put them in because they are elsewhere.

Admiral Denfeld had a superb room in the hotel. Bill Bayer and I were stuck in a hole in a back corridor. I don't remember the hotel, but it was a beautiful one. He had a room as big as our whole house.

John T. Mason Jr.: It was probably George the Fifth.

---

91. Denfeld was reappointed but then fired before he could fulfill the second two-year term.

Admiral Eller: It might have been. Admiral Denfeld brought me in after dinner. Then he began to open up for an hour and talked freely about what was happening. He was very unhappy about it, as, of course, was I. But his hands were tied. He drank his two Scotches and went to bed worrying, I think, as I did.

From there we went to Heidelberg and stayed in the old Schloss Hotel, right at the castle, a fine old hotel. It had been taken over by the Army as a guesthouse. It overlooked the Neckar River. The moon was full, or part full, a most beautiful situation. Denfeld and I had the Mark Twain suite. He had the big room and I the little. The bathtub was as big as I've ever seen, ten feet long, probably. It was huge.

There we conferred with General Clarence Huebner, commanding general of U.S. Forces in Europe.[92] As you remember, Germany was divided into three sectors: French, British, and American. Admiral Denfeld and I also met with John Wilkes, who had the naval contingent.[93] Then we visited the field activities of the Army in Southern Germany. The officers lived scrumptiously. Although not being brutal, like many occupiers, they took over the best parts of—

John T. Mason Jr.: The best housing.

Admiral Eller: The best housing. They lived in either a fine hotel or a great manor house. I remember going with Admiral Denfeld to the building to have a meal with them. They were living like kings. And the Navy didn't do much worse. The headquarters was not in Frankfurt or Cologne, but somewhere in between on the Rhine. The officers had a very fine house and were living off the fat of the land. I think they were unhappy to see the occupation end. There wasn't much use for the Navy then, though they still had LCVPs and LSMs and other landing craft used in crossing the Rhine and during the occupation in transferring supplies across.[94]

---

92. Lieutenant General Clarence R. Huebner, USA, Deputy Commander in Chief, U.S. European Command, 1947–50; Acting Military Governor of Germany, 1949.
93. Rear Admiral John Wilkes, USN.
94. LCVP – landing craft, vehicle and personnel; LSM – landing craft mechanized.

We went to see John J. McCloy, who had been recently appointed as American High Commissioner in Germany for the U.S. zone.[95] I think his office was in Frankfurt. It might have been in Bonn, but I believe it was Frankfurt. His office could have been, and may have been one of Hitler's offices. You had the impression of being dwarfed when you walked in. You entered through wide folding or sliding doors, and there, miles away it seemed, sat the high commissioner behind a huge desk. Hence, as you walked up you felt smaller and smaller as he was examining you. That was one of Hitler's tricks, bringing people into halter.

John T. Mason Jr.: Using psychology.

Admiral Eller: Yes. I liked McCloy, whom I saw later in New York. He was quite a fine representative.

Then we went to Vienna. We may have gone to Rome; I can't remember.

John T. Mason Jr.: What was the purpose of all these different areas that you went to?

Admiral Eller: The purpose was to tell them what we were trying to do and get their ideas on setting up the military organization of NATO that ultimately resulted. CinCLant, for example, also became SACLant with a joint staff from the different nations in NATO.[96]

John T. Mason Jr.: Was General Eisenhower on the scene yet?

Admiral Eller: No, he was not. He became the first SACEur after it was actually established.[97]

---

95. John J. McCloy, a lawyer and banker, served as American High Commissioner for Occupied Germany from 21 September 1949 to 1 August 1952.
96. CinCLant – Commander in Chief Atlantic; SACLant – Supreme Allied Commander Atlantic.
97. General of the Army Dwight D. Eisenhower, USA, had been Army Chief of Staff until relieved by Bradley in early 1948. Later he served as Supreme Allied Commander in Europe in 1951–52 when the military portion of the NATO was established.

The trip was to set up the general principles in meetings with the Joint Chiefs of other nations. From these a working group would develop the details on organization. Of course, there was a great deal of political maneuvering for the different positions.

John T. Mason Jr.: Yes, yes.

Admiral Eller: You've been told about them, no doubt.

Here is a photograph taken at one of our meetings, a very small group, as usual. Here's Admiral Denfeld. Look at the differences in the faces of Bradley and Vandenberg. A smile on Bradley's face, a sad look on Denfeld's. I'm next to Vandenberg.

We took notes, and Bayer and I were supposed to be the working group.

John T. Mason Jr.: This is Colonel Bayer, next to Bradley?

Admiral Eller: No, that's Gruenther.

John T. Mason Jr.: Oh, that's Gruenther.

Admiral Eller: Yes, Bayer must have been on the other side of the tables where the ones we were meeting with sat.

I found Admiral Ferrari's name card. So we met with the Italians somewhere, but I don't remember where.

Then we went to Vienna and stayed in the Bristol Hotel, a beautiful old hotel that was then pretty well run down. Vienna was a sad city. There was a dividing line right through the city, as in Berlin. I'm happy it didn't remain. On one side were the Soviets in their drab uniforms and their tanks. You couldn't cross this line, or you would get shot. It was the beginning of the Iron Curtain.

We met there, perhaps, with the Italians. Admiral Sherman flew up from the Mediterranean. He had the Sixth Fleet then. I think he flew up on his own. He should have been called up to confer with the Joint Chiefs, but he wasn't. I know that Admiral

Conolly was unhappy about his coming on his own, because on our way home via London he asked me what Sherman was doing in Vienna.[98] I couldn't tell him much. I think both of them were angling for appointment as CNO. I talked with Admiral Sherman quite a bit in Vienna.[99] He was interested in knowing what was going on in both—on our trip and back in Washington. He was, of course, an honest man, but an honest man in his ambition and sound in his thinking.

Vienna was sad. Besides the gloomy Soviet presence, the buildings were threadbare and run down. The people's clothes were worn. You could see that Austria had suffered badly during the war and during the occupation, with the Soviets grimly holding on to part of the country.

We did get a chance to go around some, more there than anywhere else. We went to some of the fine old palaces and museums and churches. Then a couple of us got up to the Vienna Woods. It was interesting to look across. A few miles away were Soviets in Hungary and Czechoslovakia. We were in a different land entirely. The one radiance that remained in Vienna was the beautiful music. You could still hear that in the restaurants and bands in the parks.

From Vienna we came home via London. We landed in Washington with great fanfare, met by all the government officials, the press, and a crowd of onlookers. It was quite a to-do. I wish I had kept some of my papers. I turned all of my secret papers in, including notes at conferences. These are just odd ones that I found. I don't even have any of the newspapers.

Soon after our return, Bradley was appointed Chairman of the Joint Chiefs of Staff since the amendments had made this possible.[100] Gruenther had got advanced in the Department of the Army. As I said, he became SACEur later, and Denfeld got reappointed.[101] I went back to planning in the Joint Chiefs of Staff, which was a dreary job, especially now that the campaign to reduce the Navy was intensifying. We had a separate Chairman of the

---

98. Admiral Richard L. Conolly, USN, served as Commander U.S. Naval Forces Europe from September 1946 to November 1946, when the title was changed to Commander U.S. Naval Forces Eastern Atlantic and Mediterranean. In April 1947 the title was changed again, to Commander in Chief U.S. Naval Forces Eastern Atlantic and Mediterranean (CinCNELM). He remained in the billet until December 1950.
99. Sherman and Eller had served together on Admiral Nimitz's staff during World War II.
100. Bradley's tenure as Army Chief of Staff ended on 15 August 1949, when he was succeeded by General J. Lawton Collins, USA. On 19 August Bradley became Chairman of the Joint Chiefs of Staff.
101. Gruenther was NATO's Supreme Allied Commander Europe from 11 July 1953 to 20 November 1956.

Joint Chiefs of Staff coming into office and anxious to slash the Navy. Congress began to get disturbed at what was happening, whether or not our services were being cut back too much. Carl Vinson was especially concerned about the Navy.[102]

So they had hearings on the Hill to determine what should be done—whether the different services were satisfied. These hearings were a little more moderate than some of the statements I'd heard at the war college until Bradley came out with his Fancy Dans."[103] Then the President repeated it.

How Radford survived is a miracle.[104] He presented the naval aviation view very solidly before Congress, said what was wrong with unification, and what was needed.

Then Denfeld presented the overall Navy view, but in a very restrained manner without stressing the flaws in the B-36 strategy, which our aviators were emphasizing.[105] It wasn't a suitable plane. It couldn't do what was claimed for it, and the carriers were needed for strategic warfare, as well as local overseas wars. Denfeld, at some time in his talk, said, "And I agree with all that Radford has said." As a result of this, the President became infuriated and fired Denfeld. This was in early November, I think.[106] Then Sherman was called in.[107]

Sherman and Norstad had been the influential ones in arranging the details for the unification act to begin with.[108] I think the President knew that he couldn't cut the Navy's

---

102. Carl Vinson of Georgia entered the House of Representatives in 1913 and was appointed to the Naval Affairs Committee in 1917. He became the ranking Democrat in 1923 and chairman in 1931. When the Armed Services committee was formed in 1947, Vinson became chairman and held that position, except for two short periods when Republicans held the House, until his retirement from Congress in 1965. The aircraft carrier *Carl Vinson* (CVN-70) is named for him.
103. In 1949, when senior naval officers protested the cancellation of the super carrier *United States* (CVA-58), Bradley described admirals as "fancy Dans who won't hit the line with all they have on every play unless they can call the signals."
104. Admiral Arthur W. Radford, USN, served as Vice Chief of Naval Operations from 3 January 1948 to 16 April 1949.
105. Consolidated Vultee, based in San Diego, built the Air Force's B-36 bomber, known as the Peacemaker. The B-36D model was equipped with four J-47 jet engines in under-wing nacelles and six piston engines that drove propellers. The jet engines enhanced the plane's maximum speed from 376 miles per hour to 435 miles per hour. It first flew in 1946 and subsequently was operational in the Strategic Air Command from 1948 through 1959.
106. Denfeld's tenure as Chief of Naval Operations ended on 1 November 1949.
107. Admiral Forrest P. Sherman, USN, served as Chief of Naval Operations from 2 November 1949 until his death on 22 July 1951.
108. Major General Lauris Norstad, USAAF, was Director of Plans and Operations, War Department General Staff.

throat too openly; that's how Radford got off. Truman brought in Sherman, who should work within the act he had helped shape, even though he might not be a tool.

While all this was happening, one Saturday in October I got a ruptured disc. I didn't know what it was at the time. I couldn't sleep; I couldn't sit; I couldn't stand; I couldn't lie down. I couldn't do anything without being in excruciating pain. I went to the office the next Monday and got worse. I nearly fainted early Tuesday morning while preparing to go again, so I went to the Naval Academy hospital. It turned out that I had a ruptured disk in the lower back. The leg was numb; you could stick pins in my foot, and I would never know it. I was laid up there and in Bethesda for about two months.[109] The only thing that helped was sitting in a hard chair and lying on the floor, sleeping on a board.

John T. Mason Jr.: Did you have an operation?

Admiral Eller: No. I saw two people here. I won't get into the story, but the second one was a wonderful doctor, the senior medical officer, Captain Creagh.[110] He said that he had operated on hundreds of them, and if you can tolerate it, don't have it. One of the ways to tolerate it is just to be inactive.

John T. Mason Jr.: And let it heal?

Admiral Eller: And let is subside. It expands and presses against the nerve.

John T. Mason Jr.: Yes.

Admiral Eller: Like any injury, it puffs out, and when it goes down, why, it will be better. I've never got over it, but nevertheless it did go down slowly.

During this time Sherman took office in early November and asked for me to be his flag secretary. We had known each other from Admiral Nimitz's staff. When he found out

---

109. National Naval Medical Center, Bethesda, Maryland.
110. Captain Gerard B. Creagh, Medical Corps, USN.

I was laid up, he needed somebody in a hurry, of course, so he put in, I think, Ira Nunn.[111] It may have been someone else. Ira was on his staff; Ira told me about it, in fact.

John T. Mason Jr.: Neil Dietrich was with him, wasn't he?[112]

Admiral Eller: Neil was. There was another one, not Woodford, but something like that. A very fine and capable group.[113]

Then I went back to planning again. I found out the best thing for me was to get hard boards in my car for the drive to Washington and to use a heating pad. I slept on a heating pad and board for months.

John T. Mason Jr.: That would tend to take the swelling down.

Admiral Eller: It increases the flow of blood and reduces the swelling.

I took the heating pad with me to the office. Riding in cars is one of the worst things that you can do for a disc, but I had to do it. I worked part time for a while, and then I finally got back into shape so that I was carrying on normally, although always with quite a bit of pain.

The work on the war plans was discouraging. It was all unreal. We were doing Alice in Wonderland planning without the strength to do what we wanted and should do to be world leaders, especially without strength at sea. We were engrossed in Europe and the Middle East, and let Asia go as if it weren't important, although most of the population of the world is there. To my mind the Chinese have no superiors in capabilities, except maybe in political management.

I was very unhappy about our loss of strength at sea, which was increasing steadily. I didn't foresee Korea, but I foresaw that we were going to lose Asia if we didn't do something about it.

---

111. Captain Ira H. Nunn, USN, served as Sherman's senior aide.
112. Captain Neil K. Dietrich, USN.
113. Captain C. Warren Wilkins, USN, was administrative aide to the CNO.

At this time an Army officer told me in confidence that he had seen the rough of a plan to cut the Navy to four carriers and the Marines to a handful. I didn't talk about it and couldn't talk about it, because it was top secret. Then, lo and behold, the plan came out that during fiscal 1950–51, on Secretary of Defense recommendation, the President was going to cut the Navy to four carriers and the Marines to six infantry regiments. In other words, make them just a police force and the Navy just a transport force. This was openly announced. Well, maybe not openly, it was made known for planning in the services, and the first steps were taken to implement it. This discouraged me. I saw that we were going to have real trouble ultimately. At the same time, I didn't know what to do about it and couldn't do anything in the job I was in.

In late May 1950, I thought about trying to get to sea, went to see Admiral Sherman and talked to him about it. He said that he was very much interested. An aviator had been ordered to command the Middle East Force, but he said he would send me there instead, promptly had the orders changed, and I got the orders.

At this time—I guess maybe that same month or May or early June—I went to Albuquerque and attended the short course in atomic energy. I saw the atomic bomb and how it was made, all of its ramifications. I also visited Los Alamos again and Sandia.[114] This was just a short break, but the training was very useful to me, having known something about it already.

John T. Mason Jr.: Just bring you up to date on it?

Admiral Eller: Yes. It was especially useful because of my knowledge of interests in the Navy's use of atomic energy.

We weren't allowed to take our families to the Middle East then. Agnes planned to accompany me to Europe with the boys and live there until maybe the situation would develop that I could bring them on to the Middle East. I had a few days' leave the last part

---

114. Los Alamos, New Mexico, was the site of research and development of nuclear weapons. Sandia was the site of another nuclear weapons development facility in New Mexico.

of June, and suddenly on a Sunday afternoon the whole world changed. It was 25 June when the North Koreans roared into South Korea.[115]

We had withdrawn our forces, and the Russians had withdrawn theirs, too, theoretically. But they had trained a strong North Korean Army and built up a huge air force and armed forces. Actually, as I read afterwards, they had announced in Moscow that Korea would be unified by the time elections were supposed to be held on 4 August. No one took any thought of that, I guess. I didn't. I didn't know about it at the time.

But I did know, and everyone knew, that they were building up their forces there, and we had withdrawn our troops, as they supposedly had theirs. We had left the South Koreans with just a militia and not much in the way of aircraft or tanks or anything else. And, unhappily, following the policy the Joint Chiefs of Staff had given in England and in other conferences, we had drawn a line in the Pacific. It was announced openly by Acheson and others that our perimeter of defense in the Far East was offshore in the islands.[116] This was an invitation to the Soviets to move in, of course. And they did, just as I was going to the Middle East. It seemed that this might be the start of World War III, as it was in a sense. The Soviets have not ceased to keep the world in turmoil. So we cancelled Agnes's going to Europe, and I went alone to the eastward, expecting trouble.

---

115. The Korean War began on 25 June 1950, when six North Korean infantry division and three border constabulary brigades invaded South Korea. The troops were supported by approximately 100 Russian-made T-34 tanks. In New York that same day the United Nations Security Council adopted a resolution condemning the invasion.
116. On 12 January 1950 Secretary of State Dean Acheson made a speech at the National Press Club in Washington and talked of a U.S. "defense perimeter" that defined national interests. He did not identify Korea as being within that perimeter. When North Korea attacked South Korea in June 1950, Acheson urged President Truman that the United States should go to the defense of South Korea, which it did.

Interview Number 15 with Rear Admiral Ernest M. Eller, U.S. Navy (Retired)
Place: Annapolis, Maryland
Date: Tuesday, 15 May 1979

John T. Mason, Jr.: Well, today we begin a new and interesting chapter. You received your assignment in May of 1950 to command the Persian Gulf Force, the Middle East Force.

Admiral Eller: Right. I was deeply interested in the importance of the area and from youth had been fascinated by its history. After the appointment I spent all my spare time for weeks seeing as many people as I could in the State Department who knew anything about the area, and those in the Navy and the Army, and the oil people, both in Washington and in New York.

I was planning to take Agnes to Europe so that I could see her and the boys occasionally from there. But the Korean War burst at the end of June, and I was scheduled to leave in July, so they stayed home.

From New York I sailed in the transport *General Maurice Rose* and had the good fortune to have with me a friend from academy days, Captain Winston Folk, class of 1923, a very erudite and literate individual.[1] We were roommates on the cruise across. We got to Southampton in early August, thence to London, where I spent several days with Admiral Richard Conolly and his staff.

John T. Mason Jr.: CinCNELM, was he?

Admiral Eller: CinCNELM, and he had another had whose title I forgot.[2] His senior aide was Commander Elward Baldridge, whom I'd known since he was a child, son of Captain H. A. Baldridge, who became the first director of the museum here and really

---

1. Captain Winston P. Folk, USN.
2. Admiral Richard L. Conolly, USN, Commander in Chief U.S. Naval Forces Eastern Atlantic and Mediterranean (CinCNELM).

built it up.³ He was one of the great people I've known in the Navy. His career was shattered by a nervous breakdown. He confined himself almost to his home until Admiral Nimitz brought him back and set him up to start the museum here at the academy in the late 1930s.

John T. Mason Jr.: Whom were your relieving?

Admiral Eller: Captain William Rassieur, class of 1923.⁴
    In London I had extensive briefing from those on the staff who had the different duties relating to Admiral Conolly's widespread responsibilities. I was subordinate under him. His area ran to Calcutta; that part of it from Suez to Calcutta would be my responsibility. Admiral Conolly was deeply interested in my area. He had been to the Middle East a year or so before.⁵

John T. Mason Jr.: He had been to Arabia, hadn't he?

Admiral Eller: Yes, and had visited old King Ibn Saud.⁶ In fact, when I left one of the duties he gave me was to take a decorated shell case to Prince Manseur, the King's favorite son.
    Admiral Conolly was just leaving to go afloat in his flagship *Columbus*, but he spent most of an afternoon talking with me. He stood before his large wall map and pointed out critical areas of the Middle East, such as the Strait of Hormuz into the Persian Gulf, and that of the Bab-el-Mandeb between Aden and the African coast.⁷ He related the importance

---

3. Commander Elward F. Baldridge, USN. Captain Harry A. Baldridge, USN (Ret.), curator of the Naval Academy Museum.
4. Captain William T. Rassieur, USN, served as Commander Middle East Force from 6 March 1950 to 18 August 1950.
5. For details of Conolly's 1946 tour of the Middle East, see the Naval Institute oral history of Vice Admiral Herbert D. Riley, USN (Ret.).
6. Abdul-Aziz ibn Abdul-Rahman Al Saud, known in the West as Ibn Saud, founded the Kingdom of Saudi Arabia in 1932 and ruled as King from then until his death in 1953.
7. Bab-el-Mandeb is a strait between the Arabian Peninsula and the Horn of Africa.

of each of the countries as he saw it. To him, as it was to me, Persia and Iraq were really the keys to the Persian Gulf and, therefore, very vital in any planning to stop Soviet invasion into the Gulf.

All of us, I think, were afraid that World War III was about to start. As a consequence, we were greatly concerned over the oil in the Persian Gulf area. A quarter of the population of the world lives in that area, mostly Muslims and Hindus—the latter, of course, largely in India. Most of the world's petroleum is also there. It is the gateway to Africa and dominates the sea routes between the Mediterranean and the East.

After conferences with him and the staff, I left one evening by Pan Am plane for Cairo. I wanted to spend a day there with Captain Bill Headden, the naval attaché, because the Red Sea and the eastern coast of Egypt were also in my area.[8]

I stayed awake overnight, because I had never been near the Alps, and it was fascinating flying over them with a bright moon shining. We reached Rome sometime after midnight to refuel. And I had an interesting conversation there with a young Scottish boy—maybe 10 or 12—who was returning from home leave in Scotland on an oil company plane to the island of Bahrain, where his father was in the Bahrain Petroleum Company, called BAPCO for short.

I asked, "Are you sorry to leave Scotland?" This was the time of year that Scotland is most beautiful.

"No," he said, "we have a better home in Awali [the oil town]. My father gets better pay. We have good food and good schools. I'm happy to be growing up there."

Flying over the Mediterranean was stirring. I had never been east of Gibraltar or very far into the Mediterranean. Flying into the sun, we raised the dawn early over the windswept sea. I couldn't help but think about the empires of the past and the history that was made on the sea which shaped the history of the world. Here was born naval power that had helped bring and preserve freedom. All of the great empires of the world from about 500 B.C. have depended on sea power in the Mediterranean up until our modern times. So I stayed awake thinking of this and watching the uptorn sea below.

Then I saw a haze on the horizon, the coast of Egypt. It was like a gray mist at first, a gray cloud on the horizon. It gradually became darker, and you saw endless sand. Then, gradually, there emerged, like a great green snake, the Nile weaving through the sand.

---

8. Captain William R. Headden, USN.

There was no vegetation anywhere except along the banks of the Nile and where the canals spread out. Water was life. It was a spectacular sight that I'll never forget. As we came down to the airfield some distance outside of Cairo, the plane came down like a boiler. When we opened the door, it was like stepping into an inferno. This was in mid–August, the great heat.

I had sent most of my uniforms by ship earlier. But I wore blues, and I had brought with me my officer's raincoat, which I needed in London. In the hot landing, I forgot it and left it in the rack of the plane, which soon flew on for Arabia, India, and ultimately Tokyo. I was catching a later one that night. When I realized that I had left it, I told Headden, and he told Pan Am, and some months later I retrieved it in Cairo, following its round trip to Japan.

Headden, classmate and friend from academy days, drove me out into the country to the Suez Canal, showing me the way of life and problems. We had interviews with his friends: Egyptians, British, and American. He was briefing me all the time. He's a great talker, so I heard everything he knew about the area.

John T. Mason Jr.: Were they, even at that time, boiling over the establishment of Israel?

Admiral Eller: Yes, they were, but not as badly as later. Of course, they had been defeated in the war of 1948—the Arabs, more than the Egyptians. The Egyptians are not Arabs; they are a mixture of many people, though they are Moslems. The Arabs hate the Israelites just like poison from the days of Ishmael. I think they turn back to them.

We drove out to the pyramids and to the Sphinx and, as I said, talked to many knowledgeable people. I was quite interested in seeing, particularly, the canals from the Nile toward the Red Sea, where the population was working the soil. The area around the canals, being arable, with the water, supports much of Egypt's agriculture.

You could still see the old treadmills, men or women walking on the treadmills bringing water up out of the canals to the fields. The vegetables and grain were as green as if they had the richest soil in the world, and it was because the waters of the Nile are full of minerals and nutrients that come from the hills of Africa.

The women were scrubbing in the water and beating the clothes at the water's edge. Little children, beautiful with their big dark eyes, were splashing in it. The men and the donkeys and goats and some camels were drinking out of it. The Nile was life itself, to them the Mother Nile.

Most of the houses were built out of bulrushes and mud. When you passed, you could imagine Moses being retrieved from the bulrushes along one of these canals. In addition to the feluccas, which don't look any different than the drawings of them 2,000 years ago, I saw a royal barge sitting in a canal. King Farouk was still in power.[9]

The Egyptians I talked to were not happy with the British. They were having political difficulties with them. They wanted them out of the country entirely, and particularly everywhere except along the Suez Canal, where the main British forces were stationed. The British didn't trust the Egyptians. They thought very poorly of them as administrators and soldiers and had a certain arrogance toward them that caused the Egyptians' hostility to become even greater. I think this was the great fault of the British administration in the colonies. They looked down upon the people they were governing as inferiors, whereas in many cases these same people, their leaders, were as educated and capable as the British— perhaps not as many good administrators but as educated and capable.

In the evening we dined at one of the most beautiful hotels in the world, or so it seemed to me—the Semiramis. This was a semi-modern hotel sitting right over the Nile. The Nile runs through Cairo, weaves through as part of the city. Long after midnight, I caught a plane out.

Now, for the second night, I didn't sleep because of interest in looking down on the coast of the Red Sea, then over Saudi Arabia. Saudi Arabia has three great provinces. Hejaz, the western one, contains the diplomatic capital of Jeddah. This is also the port from which pilgrims enter, headed for Mecca or Medina if they have not come by caravan across Arabia.

The Hejaz is a narrow, sandy plain with very little vegetation on it, then a range of mountains that looks as if it has been up-torn by volcanic catastrophes. It made me think

---

9. Farouk I was the King of Egypt from 1936 until his abdication in 1952.

of Sodom and Gomorrah, because all of that range had been anciently volcanic. It also is almost completely barren.

Next you come to the central section of Saudi Arabia, the Nejd. Of course, when you spell an Arabian word, you're spelling the English sound rather than the way it's written.

John T. Mason Jr.: Yes, of course.

Admiral Eller: The Nejd is largely a wide, barren plateau, several thousand feet above sea level. As we crossed that, we came near Riyadh, the old King's capital, where he camped out almost as if he was in his tent in the desert.

At dawn we came to the great Dahana dunes. These are most impressive, as I would find out later when I crossed them by dune buggy. They must run 200 or 300 feet high, some of them large half moons, as the wind sweeps up the red-gold sand. It you look at the sand through a magnifier, it looks like many gleaming golden red sapphires.

At Dhahran, which was just as breathlessly hot as Cairo, I was met by Parker T. Hart, the consul general, who was under Ambassador Childs in Jeddah.[10] The ambassador stayed in the diplomatic capital of Jeddah, and Hart was charged with the eastern province of Hasa.

John T. Mason Jr.: That was the important oil center?

Admiral Eller: Yes, he was a young man in the State Department. But his performance in Hasa was so effective that he ultimately became ambassador to Saudi Arabia, and later on ambassador to Turkey.

He met me, and knowing that my plane was supposed to go right on after refueling in about an hour, we started talking. Then the pilot told me the plane had a defective engine, and they would be all day fixing it. So, fortuitously, I had the whole day in Dhahran and

---

10. J. Rives Childs was U.S. Ambassador to Saudi Arabia, 1949–50. Parker T. Hart later was ambassador from 1961 to 1965.

had a chance to talk extensively to Hart and to Floyd Ohlinger, acting head of ARAMCO, and his associates.[11]

I was able to get a good picture of what was going on. Their great concern—and mine, too, of course—was that if the war spread, we would have a problem, first, of trying to hold the oilfields. We had no power to hold them, so we would have to neutralize them. Plans were being developed to neutralize them by blowing up the wells and the refinery. Second, we had the problem of evacuating Americans. We probably had more Americans there in Saudi Arabia, in the oilfields and the refinery, constructing the Trans-Arabian pipeline, and in Bahrain, a few miles out in the gulf, than anywhere outside the United States or its possessions.

They were very much interested in strengthening Saudi Arabia's forces. Both Hart and Ohlinger had confidence in them, and I gained the same feeling later on. They were fine people. If we would give them the training and arms necessary, they would fight. Of course, they couldn't put up a prolonged resistance if the Soviets came in.

Late that evening, we took off for Bombay, where the *Greenwich Bay*, the flagship of the Middle East Force at the time, was visiting.[12] The commander of the Middle East Force, whom I was relieving, Captain Rassieur, was meeting me at the airport that afternoon. I was pretty sleepy then, having not slept for two nights. So even though I was fascinated with the new area and the flares of the oilfields lighting the night as we took off, I fell asleep.

About the time I got to sleep, the Egyptian steward on the plane woke me up and handed me a set of forms required for debarking at Bombay. He said, "If you'll fill these out, I won't have to wake you early in the morning." So I worked on them about half an hour or so. We were then well down the Persian Gulf with the mountains of Persia to port and the Trucial Coast States to the starboard.

I finished the debarking forms and went to sleep. I'd hardly got to sleep when he shook me again and said, "What do you want to eat?? I almost threw him out of the plane. So he let me alone for a while. A little while later, maybe half an hour or so, he shook me

---

11. Arabian American Oil Company.
12. USS *Greenwich Bay* (AVP-41) was a *Barnegat Bay*-class small seaplane tender. From 1949 to 1966 she served as Middle East Force flagship, mostly in rotation with two sister ships, the *Duxbury Bay* (AVP-38) and the *Valcour* (AVP-55).

again, and he asked, "What time do you want to be awakened at Bombay?" So I gave up and looked down on rugged Balochistan, which extends almost to Karachi.

We reached Bombay early the next morning. Rassieur and his aide, Lieutenant William Keen, had been there all night, because they kept getting word that the plane would be arriving momentarily. So they were sleepy too.

We went to the ship, but we didn't have much time, because Rassieur had arranged calls all that day to introduce me to officials. We would have three or four days in Bombay together. Then he would leave by the same plane I came in on—or the same route anyhow. The calls included some very interesting men. Clare Timberlake was the consul general in Bombay, having custody of the area for the ambassador in Delhi, Loy Henderson, whom I came to know later and was, I think, one of our greatest statesmen in the State Department.[13] He was a straight-thinking, clear-thinking, forceful man who had been sort of exiled, I think, to India before the State Department had the purge of Hiss and others like him—many of whom, unhappily, came back in.[14]

The mayor of Bombay was a Hindu. His city had a larger population than many small countries, around five million people in the city itself. Then the governor of Bombay presidency, or state, had a larger population than most countries in the world. I think its population then was over 40 million, and it's 50% more by now. The governor, Raja Maharaj Singh, impressed me as being a very able man.[15] He was a little man in stature but big in mind. He had the most fabulous memory I've ever encountered. He knew all the history of India, the dates and the events.

Later on, at a reception at the city hall, I was with him, and he went from table to table and greeted everybody by name. I commented on his good memory, and he said, "Yes, but most of it is useless. For example, I can remember every train schedule in England."

The governor had a veritable array of attendants dressed in white and red and gold. He was living just as the British had lived and like the maharajahs had lived. It was just a

---

13. Loy W. Henderson, a Foreign Service officer, was U.S. Ambassador to India, 1948–51.
14. Alger Hiss, a State Department official, was accused in 1948 of being a spy for the Soviet Union. He was convicted of perjury in 1950 and served three years and eight months in federal prison. The case was highly controversial.
15. Raja Maharaj Singh was governor of Bombay from 1948 to 1952; he was the first Indian to hold that post.

different name for the same type of rule—just as the Communist rulers in Russia are simply a different name for the ruling class of the Tsars.

He and other Indians I met were not particularly interested in our problems in Korea. The governor general was especially interested in the problems of his own state, of course—the large population, the amount of arable land, and the lack of food. That part of India is better off than other parts I saw, but the poverty was astounding. Lack of water is a great problem in India. You either get too little or too much. The monsoons bring the great rains.

One of the serious things that had happened after the British left was deforestation.[16] They were turning India into a desert, parts of it, by cutting down the trees.

John T. Mason Jr.: Using them for firewood.

Admiral Eller: Yes, many just for firewood.

John T. Mason Jr.: No restraint.

Admiral Eller: Then, of course, they had the national political problem of unification. The new nation had, I think, 15 or 20 languages and maybe 100 different dialects. There were really different people, like the Hindus, the Sikhs, the Gurkhas, the Moslems, the Tamils. English was the only common language, although the government was Hindi, the common language. They would get in trouble later over that, especially in the south with the Tamils.

The population problem was driven home to me going around the city. Bombay has some beautiful parks and some princely buildings—palaces almost—and some very fine commercial buildings. There are sections almost like Fifth Avenue in the quality and quantity of expensive goods. But most of the millions of people are packed together like

---

16. On 14 August 1947, a section of India was split off to become the new nation of Pakistan, an independent dominion in the British Commonwealth of Nations. India gained independence from Great Britain the following day.

sardines.

I had a driver named Fakhidi. He told me that he and his wife, his parents, his brother, and his brother's wife and two children lived in one room about 10 by 12, a little larger than this rug. Actually, they probably ate there and slept outside.

One night coming back from a reception, I saw thousands, hundreds of thousands, it seemed, of people still walking along in the white gowns men wear. And on the sidewalk a great number of these people were curled up asleep. The heat and the crowded quarters drove them to the sidewalks. I think some had no other home. It's a tremendous problem, and one can see what it has seemed so insoluble to rulers from generation to generation.

The British still headed the Army and Navy of India, both headquartered in Bombay. The commander of the Indian Navy was Admiral Geoffrey Barnard, who later came to this country as the head of a British mission.[17] He and the commander of the Indian Army saw a bleak future for India as a separate country. They were very pessimistic, as were English businessmen, who were sure that India would go communistic and fall apart economically. They were more pessimistic than the facts, but India did go downhill rapidly after the British left.

One of the two most interesting men I met there and saw much of later on was the sheriff of Bombay Presidency. He was a Muslim named Sir Fazal Rahimtoola.[18] He was cultured, educated in England, alert, with a very keen mind. In our conversations he said he had been mayor of Bombay. I expressed surprise that a Muslim would be the mayor of the Hindu city, especially after the bitter fratricidal war at the division of the country in 1947. It's estimated that millions of people were killed, both Hindus and Muslims. They went wild. They were like beasts almost in some of the cities. But he said the passions had calmed, and they realized that this was something of the moment. So I guess, shrewdly, the Indians had made him mayor of Bombay since Bombay still had a very large percent of Muslims in it.

---

17. Rear Admiral Geoffrey Barnard, RN, Commander Indian Navy Squadron, 1950–51.
18. He was sheriff of the Bombay Presidency in 1928, a one-year titular position, and held a number of other political posts over the years.

John T. Mason Jr.: It also has a lot of Parsis.

Admiral Eller: Parsis, yes. In fact, they drove me by their Tower of the Dead, where, as you know, they lay the bodies to be consumed by the sun and the birds of the air.

Like most Indians, he admired the British administration. I didn't hear anybody say anything against the administration. It was efficient; the public servants had integrity, and they were capable. But Indians didn't like them because of their aloofness and air of treating them as inferiors. He had been educated either at Cambridge or Oxford and was highly cultured but had not been accepted by the British.[19] He took me to the Willingdon Club, the principal club there. It was a distinction to belong to it. He said, "Now, when the English were here, I couldn't enter this club because I was an Indian." He said he knew India was going down and, "This is bad, but it's better to have freedom and to have a feeling of being equal to everyone than to have them here as our superiors."

After several days of these meetings and conversations, I saw Rassieur off on his plane, and Captain R. R. Briner, Rip Briner, the commanding officer, got the ship under way for Karachi, which was our next stop.[20] Briner was a very fine officer.

John T. Mason Jr.: What was *Greenwich Bay*?

Admiral Eller: She was an AVP, small seaplane tender. She was built as an AVP. Ships of her type were destroyer escort size or a little larger, with facilities on them for seaplane tending. She could and did tend seaplanes some. I had three flagships while there. Each came for about four months on station, which meant some six months away from the States. They would change every four months on station.

John T. Mason Jr.: Understandable.

Admiral Eller: *Greenwich Bay* had air conditioning to a degree. You couldn't have enough

---

19. Rahimtoola earned his bachelor's degree from St. Xavier's College and his law degree from Poona Law College, both in India.
20. Captain Richard R. Briner, USN, commanded the *Greenwich Bay* from October 1949 to November 1950.

air conditioning against the heat there. She was painted white to reflect the sun's heat. This helped, and we had ample awnings, which we used a great deal, and all the time for receptions on board. We always held our receptions on the forecastle. So if you were out in any kind of open water, it was comfortable topside, but it was hard to get enough air conditioning to be comfortable below deck.

Like his successors, Rip was an aviator. These were aviator make-you-learns for a big carrier.[21] I enjoyed him as a shipmate. We always went on receptions and calls together. Also some trips, though we usually didn't want to leave the ship at the same time.

Karachi was fascinating. It really could have been a frontier city. In the town you had a mixture of European and Pakistani clothing, not only those of the Punjab and the Sindh, which is the area around Karachi, but the Pathans, Pushtos from the mountain highlands. It was a striking sight. In 1950 there were not too many cars or trucks. Camels were the common dray movers—a camel hitched to a two-wheeled cart. These did much of the trucking of the city. You would see caravans coming in occasionally from the desert.

Sindh is essentially an arid area. It comes to life along the Indus River, which exits a number of miles below Karachi into the Arabian Sea. This is where the great agricultural area exists. As you go north from the Indus River, the land becomes more and more arid, and when you get to the province of Balochistan, which is not very far from Karachi, you're in nothing but nearly barren desert.[22]

An interesting sound in the city, both from the caravans coming in and from the camels hauling the dray carts, is the tinkle of their knee bells. These were ringing all the time in my ears, a beautiful tinkling music. They also had cattle-drawing carts, the humped Sindh cattle. I think its hump serves the same purpose as the camel's hump, to give them moisture in dry periods.

---

21. "Make-you-learn" is Navy slang for on-the-job training.
22. Balochistan is one of four provinces of Pakistan.

My driver was Nashti Gaffar, a Pathan from the Pamirs, the Afghanistan frontier. He could have been a character out of Kipling from his attitude and appearance.[23] He was a slender, medium-height man, straight as an arrow. He was simple and direct with no effort at subterfuge. He said, "Chauffeuring is not a man's work." He didn't like it, adding, "I'm a soldier. See, I got this in Kashmir." And he pulled up his robe to show a great slash across his leg.

John T. Mason Jr.: Somebody had tried to cut his leg off.

Admiral Eller: He said, "I drive a car well, but I shoot a rifle better." That's where his heart was, back up in the mountains, shooting and fighting.

Captain Paul Jackson was the naval attaché. He met me at the ship and took me to his home for a few minutes before making a call on the ambassador. I could see why some people aspired to be attachés. His home was about 100 feet long, a large, sprawling building in a walled compound with beautiful grounds around it. He had nine servants to take care of him. He was in Rassieur's class, 1923.

He took me to call on Ambassador Avra M. Warren, whom I liked.[24] He seemed a very capable man. He was energetic and dynamic, very frank and courageous. He and Loy Henderson and Grady, whom I met later in Tehran, were all out of the same pattern. We had picked good people to send to the area at this crucial time.

The Pakistani are the same way. They are frank and courageous and sincere. They don't like anything that appears to be subterfuge, anything that appears to be hiding the truth. Any that I talked to and all that I met seemed to be the same.

We had excellent relations with Pakistan then, partly because of the ambassador and partly because they trusted us and believed that we would support them and help them build up. These good relations have been unhappily dissipated in the years since by our faulty foreign policy and poor thinking of our leaders in Washington.

---

23. Joseph Rudyard Kipling (1865–1936) was a British author and poet. He was born in British India and set many of his stories on the subcontinent. In 1907 he received the Nobel Prize in Literature—the first English-language writer to achieve that honor.
24. Warren was U.S. Ambassador to Pakistan, 1950–52.

I called on and dined with the Governor General, His Excellency Khawaja Nazimuddin.[25] He was from Eastern Pakistan, a short, chubby man who didn't impress me at all. He may have been a better man than I thought, but I saw him several times, and he seemed weak. The East Pakistani that provided many of his staff are not the same people as in West Pakistan. They are more like the Burmese, I suppose, and the Eastern Indians around Calcutta.

John T. Mason Jr.: They are separated by 1,000 miles too.

Admiral Eller: Yes, they were before the East seceded to form Bangladesh. Next I called on the governor of Sindh, H. W. Din Mohammed, a knowledgeable man much interested in the ancient history of the area. He mentioned places I'd never heard of, such as one I may not spell right, Mohenjo-daro. It was an archaeological site they were excavating then on the Indus River. The earliest civilization in India, they believed, was on the Indus River. This would be logical, because, as in Egypt with the Nile, the Indus is a tremendous river bringing life to the land.

Another man I called on was Admiral J. W. Jefford.[26] The British Navy still headed the Royal Pakistani Navy, as they did that of India. He was one of the typical salty admirals of the British Navy, a short, compact seadog. He had more confidence in the Pakistani building themselves into a nation than I found in Admiral Barnard in India. I liked him and I dined with him in the frigate *Sind*, flagship of the Pakistani Navy.

I inspected the schools and training centers. The principal naval training center for all of India had been in Karachi, so Pakistan fell heir to a good naval training center. They were building up as fast as they could. Their main trouble was language. They were teaching everybody English so as to have a common language. They seemed to be efficient. The ships were clean, and the men seemed eager to learn their jobs. I think they had developed a good navy.

The man who impressed me most on the sub-continent was Liaquat Ali Khan, Prime

---

25. Nazimuddin was later Prime Minister of Pakistan, 1951–53.
26. Rear Admiral James W. Jefford, RN, in 1947 became the first Commander in Chief Royal Pakistan Navy.

Minister of Pakistan, who directed the country's course most capably.[27]

John T. Mason Jr.: He's the father of Pakistan.

Admiral Eller: He was the second father; Jinnah was the father.[28] Liaquat Ali Khan was an Oxford graduate, a brilliant lawyer and statesman before he came into office, and a leader in the Muslim League. He was very astute, frank, and sincere. He was a little older than I, maybe six years older. In my several visits to Karachi, I became attached to him and thought very highly of him.

Now, contrary to Indians, he was thinking of the situation in Korea, which he considered very serious. It was strong in his mind and concerns. He was also concerned about the Soviets, because he said only Afghanistan stood between his country and the U.S.S.R. He was afraid that Afghanistan would fall to the Soviets as she has since fallen to Communism, instigated and supported by Moscow. Pakistan sent out troops to Korea, one of the handful of nations that did. He strongly supported our stand there and was eager to see us overwhelm the Communists.

He also, of course, was concerned about Pakistan's situation in the Free World. They are very independent people. They thought of themselves as a key part of the Free World, but far isolated from any strength that could support them. At the time, of course, Liaquat Ali Khan was much concerned about their dependence on the sea in tying together Eastern and Western Pakistan, which was a strange situation for a country. It's one of the reasons they were trying to build up the Navy as fast as they could.

One of his primary concerns, about which he talked a great deal, was Kashmir. Kashmir is largely settled by Muslims and should have, by rights, gone primarily to Pakistan, with a small part to India. But the leader of Kashmir had been bought by India, I think. He arranged for it to go to India, not by vote but by edict.

---

27. Khan served as Prime Minister from 15 August 1947 until his assassination on 16 October 1951.
28. After the partition of India in 1947, Muhammad Ali Jinnah became the first Governor General of Pakistan.

John T. Mason Jr.: The plebiscite to decide this issue had passed by, had it?

Admiral Eller: Talk of a plebiscite was still going on, because Admiral Nimitz was called in about 1948, and he stayed on with the assumption that it might. It was hoped that it might become a fact for more than two years, wasn't it?

John T. Mason Jr.: Yes, about 1950, I think, he bowed out, because it was a hopeless situation.

Admiral Eller: It was hopeless. It so happened that our visit coincided with Liaquat Ali Khan's return from a conference with Nehru.[29] And he was quite unhappy with Nehru. They had met several times to confer on Kashmir, and they had had their foreign ministers meet, but to no avail. He said, "Conferring with Nehru is like hitting into a feather pillow. You can't reach anything solid. He talks forever around an issue but will not come to grips with it. He will never give you a 'yes' or a 'no' or offer a compromise solution."

This apparently was Nehru. He was noted as an orator, but he was also noted for his intransigence over Kashmir and his refusal to take one side or the other—although he really took the Communists' side, I think, in issues between the Free World and Communism. Liaquat Ali Khan disdained Nehru's view on Communism. He said, "You can't be a Third World. You're going to be affirmative on one side or the other. Neutralism in Indian was really favoring Communism." I'm sure it did then and has since.

At the time we were shipping large quantities of grain to India. The publicity on the arrival of grain was practically nil in India. The Soviets shipped small quantities, and there was great publicity. I saw other examples of this hypocritical bias during the period I was there.

Here is another quotation from Liaquat Ali Khan that I like very much: "We do not like Communism. How could any people believing in God accept it? We're good Muslims.

---

29. Jawaharlal Nehru was India's first Prime Minister. He served from 15 August 1947 until his death on 27 May 1964.

We love God. We love our families; Communism denies both." This is something I can't understand of ministers in our country being deluded to the point that they can accept Communism and that it is a way of life for people. You can't be a Christian and be a Communist, too, if you're sincere.

John T. Mason Jr.: They fall victim to social action and that sort of thing. It becomes overriding.

Admiral Eller: Their mind just blots out the truth. Recently I went to a board meeting of the Church League of America. The director said that Billy Graham had come around to saying that he believed that you could get along with the Communists, that Communism was all right for the people that embraced it.[30] This shocked me.

Liaquat Ali Khan was one of the world's great statesmen. If he had lived, I'm sure Pakistan would have had a far brighter future.

On a later visit, I witnessed an omen perhaps of his fate. In 1951 I arranged change of flagships there during an important Pakistani national anniversary. It may have been the anniversary of Jinnah's death or birth; I don't remember. As part of my official duties, I laid a wreath on Jinnah's tomb as a tribute from the military side of our government.

Jinnah was the George Washington of Pakistan. He was the father of the country. A lawyer educated in England, he had been head of the Muslim League for years. He was, I guess, 20 years older than Liaquat Ali Khan and was the principal figure in the formation of Pakistan.[31] He held out for a division of the Indian subcontinent. He was the first Governor General when Pakistan was given dominion status in 1947. He died the next year, in 1948. Then was that Liaquat Ali Khan became the leading figure in Pakistan.

I took off my shoes preparing to enter the shrine, which was a simple one, very much like the Temple of Heaven in Peking in simplicity, open to heaven. My interpreter

---

30. William Franklin "Billy" Graham Jr. is a Christian evangelist who came to national prominence in 1949 and had associations with a number of U.S. Presidents.
31. Khan was born 1 October 1895; Jinnah was born 25 December 1876.

said this was the mystery man of Islam, Amin al-Husseini.[32] He was the ex-Grand Mufti of Jerusalem. The British had appointed him during their administration of the area after World War I. He was very strongly opposed to the Jewish state in Palestine. From a friend of the British, he turned into a violent opponent when they formed the state and became an agitator, a fomenter, and an instigator of assassinations. Many of the assassinations in the Middle East, legend had it, were maneuvered by him.

John T. Mason Jr.: He was the forerunner of the present Palestinians, wasn't he?

Admiral Eller: Yes. They probably revere him as being their principal leader. He was pro-Axis. He was supposed to be a cousin of the Arab Kings and supposed to be a descendent of Mohammed, which all of them claim to be.

Liaquat Ali Khan was assassinated with the next two years. The world lost a great man when he went.

Busy days in Karachi prevented my getting far inland. I wanted to get up to Kashmir and into the interior of the country to learn something about it. First of all, to see what the problems would be of defense if we should bring carriers in to provide air support for Pakistani troops, but I didn't have time. I did get over to the Persian border and flew over Balochistan. You go out of Karachi to the northwest on a good little road, a narrow road but a good one. We passed a caravan of camel coming in as we went out. You go a few miles to the Hab River, which is sometimes a river and sometimes dry. When you cross the Hab River, you run out of road and come into a camel caravan trail. Beyond is Balochistan, which is divided between Persia and Pakistan. There are Belochi in both countries. They want independence from both states.

Later the attaché plane flew me over Balochistan and on to the frontier. Balochistan is wild and rugged country. It looks as if the sea and the wind and earth just met together in a wild uprush. The land is uptorn, keep knife-like gorges, highlands. All that I saw was completely barren. I don't know how the nomads lived, and I don't know why they want a separate country. They must have some area along the rivers that are arable.

---

32. Amin al-Husseini (1897–1974) was a Palestinian Arab nationalist.

Alexander the Great found out the problems of Balochistan. When he came back from conquering Northern India, including what is now Pakistan, he tried to take his army across this coastal route, across Balochistan. He came in through Afghanistan, I believe, and he lost a good part of his troops through thirst and hardship.

I also got time to go out briefly by road to the Indus and then farther by air. That's when I saw that it is the food bowl of Western Pakistan, as it is of the Punjab of Pakistan and India farther inland. In fact, some of the nation's differences have been over the water of the Indus River.

After several days in Pakistan, we got under way for Ras Tanura in the Persian Gulf.[33] Here was the oil refinery with a little port ARAMCO had built for the then-modest oil export.

On the trip up, I prepared a brief report to Admiral Sherman of what I had experienced on the first two weeks on the job. I might read part of this into the record.

John T. Mason Jr.: Yes, and would you tell me what your actual mission was in this command?

Admiral Eller: The mission of the command was to show the flag, to make people of the countries aware that the United States was interested in them. And to be a small evidence of the United States strength that would show them the Free World's interest in maintaining freedom around the world. In addition, it was to keep the oil flowing. I had a deputy ashore in Bahrain whose job was to clear up any hitches in the movement of tankers from Bahrain and Ras Tanura to the Pacific Fleet.

A major portion of the fuel and gasoline for our ships and planes off Korea was flowing from the gulf at the time. In fact, we activated every old rust bucket we could to haul petroleum. It was so greatly needed that it makes me shiver today to think if anything stopped the flow from there now, what would happen both to our fighting forces and to our country industrially.

It's an area that few understood and few realized its importance. At the time it had become critical to our destiny and has become increasingly so. That still hasn't been driven

---

33. Ras Tanura is a Saudi Arabian port city on the Persian Gulf.

home enough to our government. I think the Navy has always appreciated it, because we had to have the fuel. And we have, generally, a global viewpoint.

John T. Mason Jr.: Yes.

Admiral Eller: Also, our presence was an encouragement to Americans in the area to realize that they were not forgotten. And at the time, one of my missions was to supervise evacuation of Americans there, if it became necessary.

"Our greetings [this is to Sherman] in both countries have been sincere and warm. In Bombay and Karachi we have to of the best men in our diplomatic service: Timberlake, consul general in Bombay, and Ambassador Warren in Pakistan.[34] They are both levelheaded and aggressive, go-getters with political acumen and commonsense. We are particularly fortunate to have Warren in Pakistan, where his influence is steadily growing at a time when a strong and balanced man may be badly needed. The appreciation of our American colony for our visit is almost pathetic."

Actually, we had quite a bit to do with our Americans in both Bombay and Karachi, as much as we had time for. We had softball games between the crew and American civilians. I gave press conferences in both places and also gave speeches to groups at luncheons.

"First of all, they are proud to have part of their Navy in port. Second, they gain a sense of security and reassurance that they are not really forgotten halfway around the world. They know what power means in the world, particularly in the East, and grasp at the slightest show of it by our forces. When the size of the Navy permits, it would be worthwhile to consider operating a small squadron in these waters in the same manner as in the Mediterranean." (We then had a very small Mediterranean squadron.)[35]

"For a number of reasons, this squadron might include at least a CVL.[36] Prime Minister Liaquat Ali Khan, the governor of Sindh, Pakistan's most important subdivision,

---

34. Clare H. Timberlake, a Foreign Service officer, was counselor of the embassy and chief public affairs officer in New Delhi, India, 1950–52.
35. In 1995 the U.S. Fifth Fleet was activated, an upgrade of the former U.S. Middle East Force. It is responsible for U.S. naval forces in the Persian Gulf, Red Sea, Arabian Sea, and part of the Indian Ocean. The fleet commander is based on the island of Bahrain in the Persian Gulf.
36. CVL was the designation for a small, fast aircraft carrier built on a cruiser hull.

and the ambassador all spoke to me of the need for air protection of Karachi. They feel that Pakistan's ground forces, given equipment, could handle any possible threat from overland unless, of course, Indian forces should be employed against Pakistan, which is a possibility. As did happen, of course, subsequently.[37]

John T. Mason Jr.: We did give them a carrier, didn't we, the Pakistanis?

Admiral Eller: I don't remember. The British did, but I don't remember if we did or not. I don't think they had one then.[38] I don't remember seeing it.

"In these distant waters, the submarine threat dwindles." I wouldn't say that now, but it was true then. "Hence, should Pakistan be attacked, the most likely means would be bombing, and the most likely target would be Karachi, the only port on this coast, the center of government, the terminus of the single road and rail line, supplying the forces and airfields on the upper frontier. It is the principal storage center, especially for petroleum.

"Their thinking is in terms of aid in antiaircraft and land-based fighters, which are both now inadequate. Should they see and periodically visit the carrier, the sea-air concept would begin to become obvious to them. The Pakistani leaders are smart, practical men. Karachi lies on almost exactly the same parallel as Bahrain and within easy striking distance. It would become obvious to everyone here that carriers would economically perform multiple functions, offensive against appropriate targets, defensive in the Persian passages, and protection for Saudi Arabian oil and Karachi."

Then I spoke again of Nehru and the recent conference with Liaquat Ali Khan: "Liaquat Ali Khan, who has a reputation of tolerance and friendly cooperation, is dissatisfied with Nehru. He stated that in the recent Kashmir negotiations, Nehru did almost all the talking, confused issues with words, and dealt in cobweb thinking, which is what others

---

37. Since the partition of India in 1947, that nation and Pakistan have been involved in four wars against each other and a number of other skirmishes. The largest was in 1971.
38. Britain sold HMS *Hercules*, not yet complete, to India in 1957. She was completed in 1971 and commissioned as INS *Vikrant*. She served until decommissioned in 1997. Pakistan did not have any aircraft carriers.

told me, and is apparently Sir Owen Dixon's thinking.[39] Both the Indian and Pakistani top officials, and down to coolies, have been friendly in the extreme. If Nehru will come around—and a number of important citizens of Bombay are against his foreign policy maneuvers—I believe we can keep India on our side, and she can be a worthwhile ally. Our real allies at present, and with adequate equipment, stout fighters, are the Pakistanis."

Sherman sent this part of it over to Joe Collins, who was then head of the Army.[40] On our trip to the gulf I got rid of a lot of paperwork with long days of cruising, and I sent in several official reports. I can't cite from those, because they had been shipped out of Washington to bulk storage. Dean Allard got me the letters to Sherman, since he happened to have Sherman's papers in the classified archives.[41] I wrote also to Admiral Conolly, but his files are also stored out of Washington.

Our trip was a rough one until we got well into the Persian Gulf. High seas battered the ship. We traveled as close as we could to the Balochistan coast and then the Persian coast, photographing and making notes. There is no possible port there of any importance except Karachi in Pakistan. Of course, this is the route that has been followed for thousands of years as the Arabian boats, principally of Kuwait and Muscat, came through the Straits of Hormuz down to India and some around India to her east coast or even beyond.

One afternoon we arrived in the Straits of Hormuz. The seas were still rough. It was getting toward dusk, and the atmosphere became completely different. I'd seen a similar effect from the Gobi Desert over the Yellow Sea. The air became a misty red. The sun was low. As it set, it became a fiery red. The mountains of Persia, to the right, which had been like gray-white marble, turned rose red. Pretty soon the wind was blowing strong out of the sands of Arabia, picking up fine red sand, which filled the air. It got into your eyes and nose and clothes. I could see why the Arabs had scarves that they wrap around their faces. It made it very difficult to stand on deck.

---

39. In May 1950, the United Nations asked Sir Owen Dixon, an Australian, to act as a mediator on its behalf in the dispute over Kashmir between India and Pakistan. His role ended in frustration in October 1950.
40. General J. Lawton Collins, USA, was Army Chief of Staff from 16 August 1949 to 15 August 1953.
41. Dr. Dean C. Allard, later Director of Naval History, was at the time of the interview head of the operational archives section of the Naval Historical Center.

I wrote a description of that, just a paragraph, that I'll read: "Sunset this day transformed one of the old dhows—"

John T. Mason Jr.: It's a fishing boat, isn't it?

Admiral Eller: It's a general term used for all Arabian craft of different sizes. They are sailing craft, though some have motors now to kick them along. But they are sailing craft with a lateen rig, usually one-masted, of various sizes. They can be used for fishing or freighting. These trading vessels, these dhows, are relatively small, though some might be 80 or 100 feet long. They carried the commerce of the Persian Gulf in the early traffic between the Indus civilization and the Mesopotamian civilizations.

"Sunset this day transformed one of these rickety dhows en route from the Pirate Coast, perhaps to Bandar Abbas, a small Persian port. It became a crimson fairy craft belying certain smells of goats and fish long departed. A red mist lay in the air and a red burgundy tint on the water, undulating in opulent shades, where incoming tankers had pumped their ballast. Flying fish in rows and lines splashed blood in the water. A sea snake looked uglier than ever in his bloody coat. Dolphins arched gracefully in the blood-red sea. A shamal was blowing." (Schmall, or shamal, is the term given to these sudden—)

John T. Mason Jr.: It's a storm with sand, isn't it?

Admiral Eller: A sudden storm that erupts over the gulf and desert. I'm sure it's caused by an upsurge of current from the heat. The sands get burning hot in the sun and cold at night.

"A shamal was blowing, one of those sudden wild northerlies which are dreaded on desert and sea. It lifted the red sands of the Dahanas and filled the sky with shades of red and the bitter sting of sand. The evening watch was gasping with heat and coughing the fine sand. Some of us on the bridge watched a blood-red moon rise. 'It looks like the Iron Curtain has moved south,' said the navigator, half joking and half in earnest."

The war wasn't going too well in Korea then, so anything red looked ominous to us. Of course, this was now getting close to the first of September. Harvesting had finished in Russia by then and also in Persia, and historically in Europe, the world wars have started in or at the end of the harvest season. So we weren't too sure but what we would have a start of a war then, especially since conditions were touch and go in Southern Korea. It was a while yet before the landing at Inchon.[42]

During that trip through the straits and up to Bahrain, we passed a number of tankers and some cargo ships. At that time, happily, some of these flew American flags. I think we saw a half dozen or so flags then, with a good sprinkling of the "Star-Spangled Banner." Now we are practically down to none.

Most of the oil then was going to the Pacific, largely to supply our war needs. Some was going to Europe and some to the United States. Today Europe and Japan both depend heavily upon this oil, and so do we to a lesser extent. The Arabian peninsula, as Admiral Conolly had pointed out, has three of the world's strategic bottlenecks: the Straits of Hormuz, which we had just passed; Bab-el-Mandeb at the southern end of the Red Sea; and the Suez Canal. We were all worried about these and still should be.

We stopped briefly at the sheikhdom of Bahrain. The principal island is 20 miles long, not very wide, and generally low lying. We stopped to pick up mail and take on supplies from our supply ship. Our provisions, except for a modest amount of fresh ones we could buy locally, came from the United States in a supply ship that made periodic runs.

Then we went to Ras Tanura, a small port with a little pier sticking out into the gulf. ARAMCO had built a modest refinery there not far from the port. I went ashore, and Consul General Hart came up. Ras Tanura is a few miles from Dhahran, which is the oil town ARAMCO's headquarters in Saudi Arabia and a few miles from Dammam, a major port being built on the gulf below Ras Tanura.

The ruler of the eastern province of Hasa was Saud Ibn Jiluwi. Saud means that he is of the ruling family of Saud. Ibn is the son of Jiluwi. I believe his father had saved

---

42. On 15 September 1950, U.S. troops under the command of General of the Army Douglas MacArthur, USA, commanded an amphibious landing at Inchon, the port for Seoul, South Korea. The surprise landing, 150 miles behind enemy lines, temporarily turned the tide of war in favor of United Nations forces.

King Ibn Saud's life in one of the many battles early in the century when Ibn Saud was consolidating the various tribes into Saudi Arabia. Since then, the Jiluwi family had been the rulers of Hasa. Saud Ibn Jiluwi had two homes, a diplomatic and commercial one at Dammam and his real home in Hofuf, an oasis some distance in the desert—a big, rich oasis, the biggest one I saw.

Hart took me to call on Ibn Jiluwi, a fierce and warlike man. His principal interest in us, after listening to our own plans, was to see cowboy movies and war movies on the flagship. He loved those. The Arabs were really childlike in a way, very simple and direct in their—

John T. Mason Jr.: Well, they are not very sophisticated, or they weren't.

Admiral Eller: They weren't. The only ones that were sophisticated were some of the princes and their cousins who had gotten into the Western world. These few had become sophisticated, but old Ibn Saud must not have realized it. After he had consolidated the country, because he thought the Arabs had broken away from the strict religion of Islam, he required the strict Wahhabi sect discipline: no smoking, no alcohol, nothing that would take away from strict following of Mohammed's teachings.

I made numerous calls on sheikhs—major ones like Sheikh Sir Salman bin Hamad al-Khalifa, ruler of Bahrain—and ones with subordinate duties.[43] A description of one is more of less typical, although they all might vary some. Each sheikh, if he is a good man—and most that I saw seemed to be—feels that he is a ruler, a father of his people. He has responsibility for them as much as they have duties to him. Each one has a reception room. Saud Ibn Jiluwi's in Damman was a large room, where he would meet with the tribesmen who had any complaints or statements or pleas they wanted to make.

Some sheikhs would get up early, make their first prayers toward Mecca, and spend the whole morning dealing with these issues as a judge and father. In this same room they formally received callers. Ibn Jiluwi's large room had a number of fine Persian rugs on the deck. When you came in, you sat on the rugs. There were no chairs. The first ceremony, after greetings, was to bring in coffee. A villainous-looking man came in bearing a huge

---

43. Sheikh Sir Salman bin Hamad al-Khalifa was Hakim of Bahrain from 1942 to 1961.

pot with a long curved spout. He would take a little cup, like a sake cup, hold it some distance from the pot, and with a flick of the wrist pour a thimbleful of coffee scented with cardamom seed without spilling a drop. He would hand this to the honored guest and then would proceed around the circle.

John T. Mason Jr.: That was a symbolic greeting, wasn't it?

Admiral Eller: It was a symbolic greeting. Properly, you could take up to three, but it was discourteous to take any more. You were supposed to drink all of it. I didn't know that, and I left some in one time, and this fellow reached down and grabbed the cup out of my hand. He started to fill it and saw some coffee still in, so he threw this on the rug and then filled it. After the third cup, maybe the sheikh would wiggle his cup to show that it was time for the next course. Servants brought in little glass cups, about three inches tall and an inch and a half in diameter, filled with syrup-sweet tea. You had one cup of that; happily that was all.

    This routine was going on as you conversed through an interpreter. Then followed a third ceremony of another series of coffee. This time whenever the sheikh wiggled his cup, it was time to go. I'd like to adopt that system in some of our conferences here.

John T. Mason Jr.: The conference was over?

Admiral Eller: The conference was over, and you should leave.
    Ibn Jiluwi came to call on me in the ship several times. Hart told me that he loved war movies and that he loved to see guns firing. So we always had war movies, and at times arranged to have target practice. We brought him on board for lunch with Consul General Hart, of course. He stomped on board with his retinue—six or eight bodyguards, heavily armed. Each one had a rifle, a saber, a dagger—maybe two daggers—a pistol, and bandoleers of cartridges draped around his shoulders. They never let Ibn Saud get out of their sight. If you got in the way, you were rudely pushed aside. About half of them were black, and others were pretty dark. I have a feeling that they were slaves, because the word

going around was that the Saudi Arabians were still bringing slaves over from Africa.

We went below to have lunch, and the guards stomped down there too. They stood around the bulkhead watching me and seeing that no one bothered their sheikh. Ibn Jiluwi wouldn't eat any of the food, such as rice or chicken or lamb, but he devoured the ice cream and kept asking for more until he was filled up.

Then we put on a war movie, and I went to my cabin to get out some important reports. I told Briner when the movie finished to take him up on deck, and I'd come up for target practice arranged for that day. I was in the middle of dictating a letter when suddenly, Boom, our 5-inch gun fired. I jumped up and ran topside. There was Ibn Jiluwi standing on the bridge, very happy, with Briner by him. I asked Rip what had happened. He said, "Well, when we came up after the movie was finished, the sheikh saw all of these men gathered around the gun. He said, through the interpreter, 'Shoot' so I thought I ought to shoot." We completed the target practice, and this pleased him greatly. He loved the sounds of guns.

John T. Mason Jr.: Tell me, Judge, how many ships did you have in your command?

Admiral Eller: Only *Greenwich Bay* was of value as a fighting ship, and she wasn't very much of a fighting ship, but valuable for scouting with seaplanes. Most of the time I also had USS *Maury*, an oceanographic ship engaged in surveying the waters of the gulf.[44] Of course, we were responsible for the tankers, which were not warships but vital for the fleet off Korea. Occasionally we had a supply ship.

John T. Mason Jr.: Were you responsible for arranging their schedule?

Admiral Eller: Not necessarily, just seeing that it was carried out. The schedule was arranged between the oil company, my representative ashore, and the people in the Pacific who supplied the tankers. They all came from the Pacific.

---

44. Originally commissioned as the attack cargo ship *Renate* (AKA-36) in 1945, she was converted to a survey ship and renamed USS *Maury* (AGS-16) on 12 July 1946.

Occasionally a destroyer came through and would be part of the force for a short time. Essentially we didn't have any real fighting strength out there. Other than showing the flag and diplomatic missions, it was a planning job. I was working on war plans all the time, especially at sea.

Because I wanted to learn the area fast, we only stayed two days at Ras Tanura. We refueled and sailed up to the gulf to Ras al Mishab, a port that a consortium headed by Bechtel Engineering had built. Much like an Arab encampment, the buildings were portable. They were erected to be there as long as needed to bring in equipment for building the Trans-Arabian Pipeline. The Americans lived in portable buildings. The administration building was portable. The Arabs who did a great deal of the work on the Tapline were in tents. Everything could be picked up and moved. In fact, I saw that happen later on at an island working center.

I was then anxious to get on up to Persia to see the route across the Caucasus Mountains, and then over to the Elburz Mountains and the Zagros Mountains from the Caspian on down to the gulf, to determine how to develop our war plans more effectively.

The first day at Ras al Mishab I called on various people, including Ibn Khuwaiter, sheikh of the area. He received me on the roof of his home-administration building with the tents of his retainers clustered on the sand below. We sat on a raised platform under an awning. Fresh air came through, so we were fairly cool above the desert. Most of Eastern Arabia, Hasa Province, is desert-like sand, rocky barrens, and mudflats.

The ruler was a subordinate of Ibn Jiluwi, as sheikh for the northern area and for the Tapline construction. I brought the Tapline supervisor on board, including George Colley, a splendid leader in charge of construction in the Middle East for Bechtel and the consortium. George had been in Manila at the outbreak of World War II, building naval facilities there with Bechtel. He had escaped when Manila fell, in a small boat with some friends and his new wife, got down to Indonesia and was on his way to Australia when they were captured and put in a Java prison camp. Many died there, and his wife almost died. He found a way to get out of the camp without setting off electrical alarms, by crawling out through the latrine. At a native village he found a doctor who gave him medicine.

Repeated trips over the years saved his wife and others. Normally he weighed about 170 pounds, but went down to 90 pounds in the prison camp. After the war he had gone back with Bechtel and was now building Tapline.

I told him I'd like to see something of the Tapline. The next morning we got into a car at dawn, because I had plans to leave that afternoon. We drove about 200 miles into the desert along one of the finest highways I've seen. The engineers had gone into the desert and found the proper components: sand and marl and something else. This was a packed-down-hard six-lane highway. We had a wild Arab driver who drove 70 miles an hour, with great trucks rushing along carrying construction equipment.

We got to Quaisuma, the number-three pumping station from the Dhahran oilfields, about 300 miles, I think. This was a temporary camp like the one in the port. We inspected the equipment, and I talked to several of the men, including a skilled mechanic who was in charge of one of the pumps. I asked him why he was there. He had had trouble at home, so he decided to get a job out of the country. His pay was good and expenses nearly nil. He could save $20,000 a year on the job, he said. I was making then about $8,000.

For lunch that day, they had steak, flown in from the United States; fish, brought in by refrigerator vans from the gulf; and vegetables and chickens, most of them brought in from Eritrea and Cyprus. They had ice cream, free beer, coffee, tea, cake, fresh bread. They had nearly everything possible that a man could want and three times as much as you could eat. They gave the men free soft drinks any time they wanted or beer at certain hours. They had movies. They gave them short vacations down to Baghdad or down to Asmara. If they stayed a year, the company would send them back home on fully paid leave.

John T. Mason Jr.: They did the same thing with the people on the pipeline?

Admiral Eller: Yes. It was to induce the men to stay. Colley told me that if they could keep a man a year, he would practically stay on. If he got unhappy and left—they could leave any time they wanted to—he would get transportation out. Then the company had to start all over again recruiting and training.

They were building the pipeline from both ends at once, in length about the distance from Seattle to San Diego. It ran northwest across Saudi Arabia, paralleled the Iraqi border, then the Syrian border, went through a bit of Jordan, and then across Lebanon to the sea at the ancient port of Sidon. There the tankers filled from fuel buoys offshore since there isn't much of a harbor at Sidon.

We flew back in a company plane. On that whole trip the only life I saw in the desert was two or three flocks of camels and goats, and troops in a dry wadi at a curiously shaped fort. It was squarish with round corner towers. You could see the soldiers in it; the camel cavalry were outside. The Arab tribes were camped in their black goathair tents outside the wadi.

I have felt the closeness of the divine most at sea and in the mountains, but you feel it also there in the desert. It's a hard land, a cruel land. It breathes the Old Testament. Many of the people, nomads especially, were still living as they had in the time of Abraham.

Returning to the ship, I took a plane down to Dhahran to go to Tehran. Admiral Conolly had asked me to deliver the shell case as soon as I could. I felt it more important to get up to Tehran and the Caspian; hence, I had sent a dispatch saying I was coming to Arthur Richards, counselor at the embassy in Tehran. He had been in the National War College with me, in our class. Brigadier General R. J. O'Keefe, U.S. Air Force, at the Dhahran airfield had a plane going to Tehran the next morning.

I got no sleep in the barracks that night, because planes were flying in and out all night on missions. At 4:00 o'clock, passengers boarded the Tehran plane and flew up the gulf. By sunrise we were at the head of the gulf, over the great refinery of Abadan, then the world's largest. We flew over lower Mesopotamia, which is a sea of palms. All the dates in the world could come from there, I think. Then we turned east to cross the three-mile-high Zagros Mountains. It's one of the most spectacular and, in a way, pitiful sights that I've seen. You stare down into clefts, just V's, almost straight down, thousands of feet, to what may be a stream or a dry streambed. The mountains are completely deforested, except for little niches hiding in the shadows where sunlight can hardly reach, it's so deep down. It is a denuded land.

The plane had a little trouble getting over the range. We had to fly through a pass 10,000 feet high, and you could look down into these deep gorges. Think of how mistreatment of the land had brought this about, plus the change in climate, I guess.

We reached Tehran's airfield late in the morning. I stepped out of the plane to an impressive sight. Tehran lies at the base of the Elburz Mountains, which run between the Caspian and the high plateau that constitutes most of Iran. Mount Damavand towers nearly 19,000 feet back of the city. The wind was blowing, sweeping down from the high mountains, and it was cold, although it got hot later.

I was surprised that no one from the embassy was there to meet me. In the plane were some Marines coming to relieve the guard in the embassy and a number of Army soldiers. An Army officer was there to meet them. I spoke to him and said I'd expected to hear from the embassy. He said that he was meeting the soldiers for Colonel Jim Pierce's organization but would take me first to the embassy.[45] That perked my ears up, because I'd known Pierce when he served in Army Public Information under General Collins. So I said, "I'll go with you."

Fortunately, as we passed Colonel Pierce's compound, I asked to stop to greet him. We were both very happy to see each other. The car was waiting to go on to the embassy when he asked, "What are you up here for?"

I said, "I want to go to the Caspian and see the roads over the mountains that the Soviets might use headed for the gulf."

He said, "Well, I can arrange that."

There were two separate U.S. Army missions in Persia. One was a mission to train the Iranian Army, the other to train the gendarmes.[46] General Evans headed the one for the Army and Colonel Pierce that for the gendarmes.[47] He only had a small number of men compared to General Evans. He said, "I can arrange that without going through the slow diplomatic process. When do you want to leave?"

"Well," I said, "in the morning."

---

45. Colonel James R. Pierce, USA.
46. During the interview Admiral Eller frequently referred to the nation as "Persia," sometimes as "Iran." He used them essentially interchangeably.
47. Major General Vernon Evans, USA, Chief of the U.S. Military Mission with the Iranian Army, September 1948 to June 1951.

He said, "That's a little sudden, but we'll try to do it."

Then it turned out that I had to have photographs, so I couldn't leave in the morning. I had to make it a fast trip, because a conference in Rome was coming up on evacuation of Americans. It was a worldwide conference called because of fear that the Korean War would expand.

So we got the photographs and then went through the paperwork. I had a chance, therefore, to talk to Richards and to call on Ambassador H. F. Grady, whom I'd known about and greatly admired.[48] He had been in Greece and had been a strong factor in inducing our country to back up the Greek government throughout the so-called revolution there, which was really Communist-led, inspired, and supported by Moscow. Luckily, my dispatch to Richards had gone astray, since it would have taken weeks to arrange my trip through diplomatic channels.

The next morning we did take off, under the guise of a gendarme inspection trip. In the car with me were Major Robert Carver, one of Colonel Pierce's officers, and an interpreter. The interpreter was a Baha'i. I'd never heard of the Baha'is before.

John T. Mason Jr.: Oh, there are plenty of them around.

Admiral Eller: I know there are now, but I'd never heard of them. He was one of these talkative individuals and very much impressed with his pseudo religion. So he brought me into the world of Baha'iism quite swiftly.

Both with Grady and Pierce, and with Carver, I discussed the problems of Iran. Longstanding ones were the lack of water, the deforestation and denuding of the mountains by goats and the dry climate. But the government was taking care of these in a measure. Another problem was money, but this was coming from their oil. A serious problem was selfish landowners.

The Shah wasn't there, so I didn't see him, but I did meet him later on in Washington and read about him constantly.[49] I think he was highly motivated to improve the welfare of

---

48. Henry F. Grady was U.S. Ambassador to Iran, 1950–51.
49. Mohammad Reza Pahlavi (1919–1980) became Shah of Iran in 1941 and held office until his regime was ousted in 1979 by the Ayatollah Khomeini.

Iran. He gave away large portions of his land, which had come to him through his father, and was appropriating other land, with compensation to give to the peasants. Most of the country was dominated by a handful of rich families and religious leaders who used, unhappily, the power of their office, just as some Popes and subordinates did in the Middle Ages to aggrandize their own selves and their families.

But Iran had, as Grady said, almost limitless possibilities compared with Greece, where he had been. She had minerals, petroleum, and possibilities of food production 100 times those of Greece. And she had a sturdy population. The Iranians are sturdy people; given the leadership and the means, they could be a very effective force for the Free World.

The route to the Caspian was interesting. We drove almost west from Tehran, a little northwest, because the mountains run close to the city. We turned northward at Qazvin. The good road ran out, becoming rough and potholed. There were some trucks in it and some buses, almost no cars. The buses were overloaded, dingy, and old. The trucks were old and top-heavy, tired trucks that you would think would break a spring any minute, and many of them did. We saw them often along the road trying to install a new spring. Later on, we would break a spring ourselves.

It was very arid on the plateau from Tehran to Qazvin, almost a desert. But there were rich green fields of grain and vegetables near Qazvin, and there were beautiful melons, which our interpreter, whom we called Mac, said were the best in the world. We tried one, and it was good, but not quite up to the Georgia melons.

John T. Mason Jr.: What about the Eastern Shore?

Admiral Eller: The Eastern Shore melon is pretty good too.

Here the farmers lived very much as they had for, I guess, time immemorial. They were threshing grain. Oxen were plodding around in small circles, held by a line, pulling a cart with large rollers with wooden teeth. There was enough wind to blow the chaff away; I'm sure this is the way they had always done it.

On the way to Qazvin, I wondered how it was that they were able to have such good agriculture in so arid a land. As we passed along, I saw that I'd seen from the air, a great number of what appeared to be giant prairie dog holes coming up out of the ground. We stopped by one of these. Two men were cranking a windlass. It turned out that this was an entrance pit down to an underground water channel coming from the mountains. This and many other qanats had been dug by the Persians hundreds and hundreds of years ago. Every few hundred yards there would be another pit where you could go down. And periodically men would have to go down and clean out the dirt that had settled in the water course. Two men were down below filling goatskin buckets, and two men were topside cranking the windlass, hauling them up and dumping the mud. These qanats were largely owned by wealthy men, landholders, who would sell the water to people along the way, charging so much for water rights. The water then, in turn, was drawn up and put into irrigations ditches for the fields. I talked to the men through the interpreter. He sort of pitied them. He said it was poor work, but they were proud of it.

They said, "This is a man's work. You're doing God's work. You're providing food and water for the people of the land. We get good pay. [They got 80 cents a day] And we're proud of it."

This made me realize, as I've often realized, if you dedicate yourself to anything that is difficult and do it well, you're happier with it than with something that is easy.

After we left Quazvin, we turned northward and wound through the mountains. Now we had no road. It was a trail, rough and rocky and rutted. Part of the time it was a dry riverbed. We condemned it, but then I thought back to my youth in North Carolina in the mountains, and it wasn't very much different than many of the roads there in the rainy season. The U.S. had very few paved roads in the early part of this century.

There were long, tortuous passes through the mountains. One of the reasons I wanted to see the roads was that I thought they could possibly be easily blocked—for a time, anyhow—by demolitions and with trained people in the hills, well dug in against motorized attack. And if we had aircraft carriers from which we could fly planes to support the defenders, perhaps we could make a real barrier of the mountains. All we could have hoped for, even if we had gotten planes there, would have been delaying defensive tactics. But it might have been enough to have gained time to bring more strength in.

In the mountains where were plain pueblo-like villages of mud, straw, and stone, half shaped out of the mountainside. Each district, except this, unfolded its special claim to fame, according to Mac. When we left the gorges behind, we wound through silver olive groves that produced, Mac assured us, the finest olives in the world. Later we would see by the Caspian the finest tea and the finest silk, the finest oranges, the finest lemons.

John T. Mason Jr.: National pride.

Admiral Eller: Yes, sir. He was proud of his country, and yet, at the same time, he was very critical of the government and the landowners.

As we descended to the sea, the mountain became heavily forested except for some precipices over 1,000 feet high. We passed many charcoal oven caves. These have helped the goat denude the Middle East.

One worker stands out in my memory. Black with smoke, he was stalwart, tough, free of stance, and free of speech. He spoke with emotion, "We do not like the Russians, and we don't like the landlords either. We want to be free to earn and to get ahead. Look at these black rags! I cannot buy more. I work from 6:00 to 6:00 and don't get enough to feed my wife and boy."

They, too, were proud of their work but unhappy because they weren't getting enough pay. The qanat laborers were getting 80 cents a day. I don't know what these poor people were getting.

Between the Elburz Mountains and the Caspian is a narrow plain sometimes scarcely a mile wide. At other places it spreads out considerably. We hit it right after we got through the passes and then came down toward Rasht and Bandar-e Pahlavi, which are on the Caspian itself.

Unlike the plateau we'd left, here were trees—all sorts of fruit trees, grain, and every type of fruit you could think of. Beautiful flowers and tropical or semi-tropical plants and flowers and vegetables. Even the dunes were carpeted with grass where cattle grazed. I saw few cattle during my tour, except in the Indian subcontinent, and the many cattle here, fat and healthy, good meat.

The beach is wide and shallow, giving easy access to anybody who wants to land. Of course, the Iranians have no strength afloat there. I think they had one little coast guard-type ship on the Caspian. The Russians have enough warships to come in with no trouble at all and could easily make a large landing.

We wanted to get up to the border. There was a border zone that you could not get into except for very important business. This was under Army control, and although Carver was with the gendarmes and was on an inspection trip, his area ended at this border zone. When we got to the zone, he said to the guard, through the interpreter, "We're going on to turn around."

So we went on and then speeded up; he was driving at the time. We got about to the border when we were overtaken by a car that came roaring after us and forced us to turn back. But we got where we wanted to go, anyhow, and saw the whole coast up to the border. It was all the same, wide and shelving, giving easy access. Also it was not a bad road in that area.

We turned back then and drove far into the night in order to reach Ramsar. This beautiful development was built by the old Shah, the father of the present Shah. He built a place there and then a gorgeous hotel in a gorgeous setting. The hotel sits about a mile, I guess, from the sea. An elevated roadway runs from the hotel to the beach. Orange groves, flowers, and trees flourish on each side. It's very much like the palace of Kubla Khan in Coleridge's poem.

It was a luxury hotel. I don't think there was anyone in it at the time except us and a whole staff of servants. The accommodations were a little different than in a comparable hotel in the United States. The bed was a thin mattress on a hard, raised platform, very much like I'd seen in China, where they slept over a stove. The commode was a hole in a marble floor. The bed was good for me, because I had a bad back, and it was aching then, of course, after a rough day. The food was good and the grounds beautiful. It was a superb place, where I would have liked to stay on vacation. I wonder what has happened to it.

From there we drove east along the southern Caspian to Babolsar, another fine hotel, a resort if people could get there and had the money to stay. The old Shah had also built this hotel. There were a few guests in Babolsar and entertainment that night, including movies. But the principal one was strongmen, first wrestling, and then one lifted heavy weights. They claimed he got up to 1,000 pounds. He was huge. He must have weighed 300 pounds. As he lifted the weights, he would cry, "Allah, Allah."

The next morning I awoke, and there was giant Mount Damavand looking into my window. The day before it had a cloud cover over it all day. Now there was a glistening white cap on top. It had begun snowing. Soon we saw what the snow had precipitated. Returning to Tehran we took the eastern road over the mountains, now practically to the Soviet border on that side.

As we started up the mountains, we began to meet tribes coming down with their flocks. They had horses mostly and sheep, with some goats. Everything they owned was packed on their horses, great bundles of clothing and tents, equipment, and maybe some chickens cooped up on top or a baby with blankets around it. Most of the people walked, except the leader of the tribe and maybe his newest wife, well bedecked and beautifully dressed. A few of those walking might be carrying some things but not much, except for weapons. Frequently we saw a boy carrying a newborn lamb draped over his shoulders. Well up the mountain a chieftain had camped with part of his tribe. We stopped to talk to him. He was fiercely independent. These tribesmen felt themselves completely independent of the government in Tehran.

John T. Mason Jr.: They still do.

Admiral Eller: They had common land on the Caspian coast, where they grazed their flocks, and they had common land up in the mountains, where they grazed. This was all their land, not any one man's land. They traveled 10 to 20 miles a day till they came to a good, grassy spot. Then they would unbundle all this gear from their horses, set up camp, and spend two or three days or more. They were moving leisurely because this was early September.

John T. Mason Jr.: It was seasonal, wasn't it?

Admiral Eller: It was seasonal. They moved north to the warmth of Caspian in the winter and south up the mountains in the summer. I don't think these tribes ever crossed the mountains down to the central plateau. Their migrations were back and forth in the mountains and to the sea. They would winter on the Caspian.

There is a very fine book I read as a young officer, by Fitzhugh Green called *Grass*. A movie was also made of it.[50] He graduated from the Naval Academy in the class of 1909 and resigned after World War I to start a second career. He followed and lived with the tribes, then wrote this book.

John T. Mason Jr.: I think Justice Douglas wrote one also.[51]

Admiral Eller: He did? I didn't know that.

John T. Mason Jr.: He went over to that area.

Admiral Eller: Yes, he was a great mountain climber. A great drinker, too, as I witnessed.

One of the tribesmen we stopped to talk to said, "The Old Man Damavand has grown whiskers, so it's time to be on the move."

I might read a little out of my notes at the time, and then maybe we'll stop.

"I shall never forget this day—steep mountains, rugged mountains, forested ones, and rock-bare ones. We ceaselessly climbed and dropped between sky and earth, now in deep ravines where rain torrents sweep away such roads as there are; now along the great shoulder of mountains with the land spread far below like an uptorn sea. From the citrus fruit, cotton, and rice farmers of the semitropical Caspian, where red hair and blond traces are common, we passed through to wild, dark mountain men like hawks in their aeries. Actually, many of the tribal children are redheaded and change to dark hair as they age.

---

50. The 1925 film was titled *Grass: A Nation's Battle for Life*. Commander Fitzhugh Green, USNR (Ret.).
51. William O. Douglas was an Associate Justice of the Supreme Court from 1939 to 1975.

"Swinging around a sharp curve in a pass two miles high with the cliff dropping into depths, we came upon what looked to be the largest flock of sheep in the world. Thousands covered the mountain, dividing into a living tide to flow by us.

"The tribesmen, in their black goatskins and felt hats, scurried along the flanks as nimble as goats. Their guiding cry settled into a singsong and a chorus of 'Shhhhhhhh, shhhhhhhh, shhhhhhhh,' and the sheep followed it.

"Later, descending thousands of feet into a gorge in advance of another large flock, we came upon a group of tents belonging to this particular tribe. They had camped there to graze and refresh their horses. The chieftain talked of the great trek to his land rights beyond the mountains. He hospitably pressed sweet tea and coffee on us before we rushed on through the flow of migrant life."

That lasted more than 50 miles. There would be intervals between groups, but the route was alive with flocks and people with their horses.

"Only one group near Firuzkuh [that's some distance from Tehran, but we were getting down toward the high plateau now] cradled in the heart of the mountains, appeared unhurried. A dozen tents clustered together on a hillside. The tents, woven of black wool, were some 20 feet wide and of varying lengths, up to 40 feet. They stood over semi-permanent foundations of mortar."

That's the only place I saw such foundations.

"The shipshape interior of the chieftain's tent was divided into one large room 20 feet square with a smaller room set off by cloth partitions. Part of the large room consisted of a raised platform, white and very clean. Bright tribal rugs lay on it. A young mother, dark and falcon-like, alternated between weaving and tending her youngest of five, a fair baby with hazel eyes and red hair, suspended in a homespun hammock cradle."

Women are more in evidence among the tribes than in Arabia. They are kept out of sight entirely in Arabia.

John T. Mason Jr.: Yes, yes. Did you see much rug making?

Admiral Eller: Not much. I saw them weaving some in their camp, but I was on the move so much I really didn't have much time to stay long anywhere.

The next day, that evening, late, we came down from the mountain to the plateau and got to Tehran. Meanwhile, the embassy had set up a meeting for me with the Prime Minister, General Ali Razmara.[52]

---

52. Haji Ali Razmara was Iran's Prime Minister from 26 June 1950 until his assassination on 7 March 1951.

Interview Number 16 with Rear Admiral Ernest M. Eller, U.S. Navy (Retired)
Place: Annapolis, Maryland
Date: Monday, 10 September 1979

John T. Mason Jr.: We stopped last time, Judge, almost in the midst of a sentence, and you were about to talk about Prime Minister Razmara of Iran.

Admiral Eller: He had been the general who helped push the Russians out of Azerbaijan. At the end of World War II, the British and Americans agreed with the Russians that we would leave the respective spheres into which Iran had been divided. The old Shah of Iran had been pro-Axis. So the British and the Russians had gone in and had divided the country into spheres of control. Then we had used that route to send part of the great flow of supplies to the Soviets that enabled them to stop the Germans.

After the war, we had agreed on a certain time to leave Iran. The British and Americans left on schedule, and the Soviets theoretically left, but they set up a puppet republic in Azerbaijan with their minions in charge and left forces to help them. Under great pressure from us and from the United Nations, to a degree, but largely through the skill of the Persians, the Russians retreated from this area, and the republic did not last. Iran was unified again.

Razmara had been the Persian general whose firmness had helped push out the Soviets and subdue the insurrection. When I got back into Tehran, after conferences with Ambassador Grady and Richards, I had a long talk with General Razmara. I think he was one of the world's outstanding leaders at the time. He impressed me. He was a short, steel-eyed, resolute, small man. He knew what was going on, and he was determined to carry out his mission of helping shape a strong, unified, modernized nation.

John T. Mason Jr.: He spoke English?

Admiral Eller: He spoke English well. He had a very difficult job, because the young Shah was trying to modernize Persia, as he continued to do throughout his rule. One of the first things the Shah was trying to do was to give the land back to the peasants. He first gave vast tracts of his own possession, the imperial lands. Then he was putting pressure on the large landholders—by hearsay, some 400 owned most of the land. He tried to persuade them to give the land, or let the state buy it to transfer to the peasants. He was having difficulty over this, and ultimately it would cause considerable trouble. The Prime Minister knew the world situation very well, and knew the problems with Russia. He was patriotic, levelheaded, and strongly pro-American. Had he lived, conditions in Iran would have been far different.

John T. Mason Jr.: When did he die?

Admiral Eller: He was assassinated within the year, like Liaquat Ali Khan.

John T. Mason Jr.: By?

Admiral Eller: By a fanatic, someone who opposed him. It might have been a Khomeini type.[1] I can't remember the circumstances of the assassination. There were three great leaders assassinated in that same year. He, and Liaquat Ali Khan, and King Abdullah of Jordan.[2]

Here is one of the statements Razmara made that I jotted down. He said, "Iran has given much to the world in the past. She has much to give in the future, and I intend to try to help her do this." The Shah was away, though I would meet him later in Washington. As I mentioned, he was dedicated to bringing Iran into the modern age without turmoil if he could. When I was there, Tehran was a mixture of modern and ancient, but mostly ancient in sanitation. The gutters running down the street were open sewers. You would see people even dipping water out to use in their homes.

After a very short time in Tehran, I had to leave because of the conference coming up in Rome. To understand the problems of the route, I went by road to Iraq. The Iranian army gave me escort, and one of the officers in the mission went with us to Hamadan.

---

1. When the Shah left Iran in January 1979, the Ayatollah Ruhollah Khomeini seized power and declared the nation to be an Islamic republic.
2. King Abdullah I was Jordan's head of state from 25 May 1946 until his assassination on 20 July 1951.

Hamadan is on the ancient road of conquerors going down into Mesopotamia. It runs west from Tehran. It wasn't a very good road; we broke a spring on the way. At Hamadan, while the spring was being repaired, the Iranian escort, Colonel Rezavit, took me to see what is reputed to be Esther's tomb, and that of Aviana, the great Arabian philosopher and scientist of about 1,000 A.D., I believe.

Then he took me to his paternal home. The streets of Hamadan, like most of the eastern cities then, were narrow and unpaved. The house looked very unpretentious on the outside. It sat back in a courtyard, whose street walls were dingy—the walls of the court. The door looked like it was in a very sad state. But when we opened the door and stepped inside, we were in a little paradise. I think they kept the street side that way deliberately in order not to flaunt their wealth. His father claimed it was the oldest inhabited city in the world. In ancient times, it was the capital of the Medes, and Ecbatana under the Greeks. His father was a priest, and this gives me some insight into—

John T. Mason Jr.: A mullah?

Admiral Eller: A mullah. He was a very gentle and interesting man, but I think very avaricious. From the beautiful courtyard with flowers, we went into the house. He gave us tea and sweet meats, and so on. After half an hour or so, I figured we ought to be going, because I was trying to reach the next town on the way before dark. But he refused. He said, "You must wait until my younger son comes in." The younger son finally came. He was a schoolteacher, and he had just been out purchasing a village. Most of the villages and land in Persia were owned by a relatively few landholders, and the priestly clans were using their power to become large landholders. So I'm sure they are not as favorably received by the people—they weren't then—as we get the impression in the news from Khomeini.

John T. Mason Jr.: Perhaps you have a clue to their opposition to the Shah as well.

Admiral Eller: Yes. Although the Shah was trying to correct this.

John T. Mason Jr.: Well, but they didn't want him to.

Admiral Eller: Oh, you mean the priestly opposition. That's correct. They wanted to hold onto the land and villages. At this point, the priest insisted that we go into another room and opened a tremendous room filled with all sorts of food on the table, sweet meats and all types of foods in which the Persians are artistic.

We finally broke away and drove over the Zagros Mountains to Kermanshah. My escorts had to turn back here, because it would take days to get diplomatic permission to go through the border. So at Kermanshah, I stayed at a decrepit hotel, and the next morning tried to hire a car. That was very difficult; I heard there was a bus going. It was pretty well broken down and loaded with produce, chickens, geese, sheep on top, and all types of people. But we made it over the mountain into Mesopotamia. After a long stop at the border for customs, I got to Baghdad the next day.

The counselor put me up in the embassy; the ambassador was away. I made calls on the Prime Minister and the Minister of Defense to discuss politico-military matters, and I saw Baghdad at night before I left the next day. It was like the Arabian nights. Just as in Peking, the individual artisans had their own street or section. Many of these—the silversmiths, the goldsmiths, the ironsmiths, and the bakers—worked at night.

Bread baking was one of the most interesting activities. It was typical of Persia and adjoining lands. The bakers had a beehive oven and would get it very hot. Then they would take the dough, roll it out thin, put it on a long paddle, and slap it against the inside of the oven. It would cook almost instantly. They would bring it out as the crisp thin Middle East bread that you see everywhere.

At this point, I might read a little from a letter I wrote to Admiral Sherman after this part of the trip. This is talking of the routes through Persia to the Persian Gulf, where the Soviets would come for the oil. Remember, this is September 5, 1950, and we were very much troubled that World War III would break out, and the Soviets would move in and take the oil in the gulf.

"Each route is different. In general, however, there are long sections of every road that are torturous and rough, but negotiable by tanks and large trucks. In fact, petroleum trucks and buses run on all the roads I covered. These cannot be blocked for long by demolitions, though the railroads could be. On the other hand, even small ground forces well positioned and aided by air could enforce considerable delay. With good air support and with any sort of buildup, we could gain weeks, and perhaps months of time in the Iranian mountains. Carrier air would be especially useful in support and in forcing delay in the mountain roads of southwest Iran leading to Baghdad and Abadan. The most difficult sections of these routes are in the western and southern portions. Hence, air routes to them are shorter and emergency landing fields are nearby in Iraq. Conversely, an opponent would be far removed from his usual bases."

From Baghdad, I flew to Dhahran, thence to the worldwide conference on evacuation in Rome. I went representing the only naval forces we had in the Middle East, and those very minor.

John T. Mason Jr.: This was sponsored by whom?

Admiral Eller: By the State Department.

John T. Mason Jr.: It was purely a U.S. conference?

Admiral Eller: Yes. I don't know why it was held in Rome, except, perhaps, it was about as central as it could be, because representatives came from Europe, all Middle East nations, South Asia, the Philippines, and from various points of the globe.

John T. Mason Jr.: And you say evacuation.

Admiral Eller: Evacuation of Americans.

John T. Mason Jr.: Oh, evacuation of Americans in case of a confrontation.

Admiral Eller: Yes. Men came from the different embassies and from the principal military forces that would be involved: the Army, Navy, and the Air Force. This conference, like other State Department conferences I attended, lasted a week. It was a tedious eight- or ten-hour-day of just sitting and conferring and working up papers; then further paperwork in the evenings. Of course, our problem in the Middle East was that we didn't have very much in the way of transport. We had a large number of people in Arabia and lesser numbers scattered through the embassies and on business in the area.

To break the routine, we had a couple of hours off for lunch. In those two hours I managed, first, to call on Admiral Ferreri, head of the Italian Navy, whom I'd met when over with the Joint Chiefs to set up the military side of NATO.[3] I, of course, went to the Vatican City and St. Peter's, the Sistine Chapel, which I'd never seen, and found fascinating. There were organized groups of pilgrims at the time pouring through St. Peter's and other churches in Rome, very much like the Moslems going to Mecca, which I saw later.

I was impressed with the ambassador's residence, an Italian palace he had rented. It had beautiful silken drapes on the walls, marble furniture, acres and acres of landscaped ground around the house. He had us for dinner one evening. Happily, my friend, Pete Hart, consul general in Dhahran, came.

Among the others was a young man from Manila, who had been in the U.S. Navy in World War II as a reservist, and had served in Rome during the occupation after the war. Our last day there, a Saturday, we took the afternoon off when we finished, and he drove us through the countryside visiting two of the most impressive sights I've seen anywhere. One was a village, Polombara, on top of one of the Sabine Hills, inland from Rome. It was a fortified medieval village that hadn't changed, I don't think, in hundreds and hundreds of years. From there we drove up to Tivoli. Here there are the most fountains in a single place in the world, I believe, on the grounds of the palace of Trevi built by a cardinal.

John T. Mason Jr.: Yes.

Admiral Eller: You've probably seen it.

John T. Mason Jr.: No, I haven't seen it, but I know about it.

---

3. Admiral Emilio Ferreri, Italy's Chief of Naval Staff.

Admiral Eller: It's a world's wonder to me. Water flowing out of fountains in all directions and everywhere.

That evening I flew via Athens to Cairo, preparing to join my ship, which was coming into Massawa, Eritrea. I had two days in Cairo and visited with the British Middle East Command on the Suez Canal at Fayid. It so happened that the chief of staff was another National War College classmate of mine, Brigadier Jim Woodford, one of several I ran into during my time in the Middle East.

John T. Mason Jr.: One of the values of the course.

Admiral Eller: Yes, very much so.

I saw pretty much of the length of the canal while I was there. Then early one morning in the midwatch. Commander Phelps, the assistant naval attaché with whom I'd stayed, and I drove to the airport, whence he flew me down to Massawa. We went up the Nile to Luxor. Except for the Nile itself and irrigation out from it, this is nothing but a barren eroded land of sand and mountains. Then we turned toward the Red Sea and landed at Port Sudan to refuel. This scorched spot is like part of Hades, and the Red Sea coast on south is no better.

I got to Massawa, and *Greenwich Bay* had arrived. It was like entering a cauldron to board her. Massawa is one of the last places in the world you want to be stationed. It's on the Red Sea, under the mountains going up to the capital of Eritrea. Both the humidity and the heat are high. So it is an abominable place.

John T. Mason Jr.: The Russians seem to want it though, badly.

Admiral Eller: They want it because of its useful location, of course. We were to change flagships there. *Greenwich Bay*'s tour was ending and USS *Valcour*, Captain Robert Stroh, was relieving her.[4] In the highlands at the capital of Eritrea, Asmara, we had a large Army communication unit and a small Navy unit of about 30 people who supported our worldwide

---

4. Captain Robert J. Stroh, USN, commanded the *Valcour* (AVP-55) from 25 July 1950 to 5 April 1951.

communications. It was a marvelous place. The loss of Eritrea has been serious.

John T. Mason Jr.: This was a very significant base, was it not?

Admiral Eller: It was, though we had few people there; it was very important for our worldwide fleet communications.

John T. Mason Jr.: As I understand it, the Russians have it now.

Admiral Eller: I'm sure they do.

The road up from Massawa to Asmara is one of the most winding roads, one of the most beautifully engineered roads that I've seen. It covers a tremendous rise in a very short distance. I think Asmara is 4,000 or 5,000 feet above sea level.

John T. Mason Jr.: Who had built it, the Italians?

Admiral Eller: The Italians when they occupied Ethiopia and Somalia and the coast through there. Eritrea was still under British administration. When they captured it from the Italians during the war, they kept it separate from Ethiopia. Ethiopia wanted it, but it isn't populated by Ethiopians. They are a separate people who didn't want to be part of Ethiopia.

Brigadier F. G. Drew was the governor general. He was a very capable man, austere and typically British, reserved and haughty in air, but when you got underneath, he was a very warm and interesting man. He invited us up for dinner. Captain Briner and me, the next night after I had called on him. He then insisted that we stay the night. After the dinner was over with a number of local officials, he sat down and talked until midnight about the importance of Eritrea to the West and the importance of keeping it out of Ethiopia. He said there would be insurrection and difficulties, and stressed its value to the Navy, both of England and the United States. His wisdom shows today, but he was not heeded, and it was turned over to Ethiopia later on, to our sorrow.

Mrs. Drew was an interesting lady. She was a slight lady, short and slender and cultured, but she had gone throughout Ethiopia and Eritrea exploring the caves and underground settlements of the early Christians. She was an artist and had copied the inscriptions and drawings she had found on the walls of the caves and underground dwellings. She was preparing to publish a book on them. I thought at the time that when Philip was sent into the desert to the Eunuch and baptized him, that he must have found a very powerful convert.

John T. Mason Jr.: This is the beginning of the Coptic Christians.

Admiral Eller: The Coptic Christians, who had gone underground during periods of persecution.

Valcour arrived. We transferred the flag files and the staff, codes, classified publications and so on. *Greenwich Bay* sailed happily for home, and *Valcour* soon left for Bahrain. I had to fly to Jeddah to present Admiral Conolly's gift to Prince Mansour at the first opportunity, because Admiral Conolly was being detached that autumn. I had tried for weeks to get a date with Prince Mansour, but our embassy said that the foreign office of Saudi Arabia, which is in Jeddah, the diplomatic capital, had said they couldn't locate him and didn't know when they could. Weeks had passed since I'd sent the first dispatch from the flagship in the Persian Gulf. I kept inquiring and nothing was happening. So as *Valcour* prepared to sail for the gulf, I sent a dispatch advising I was flying to Jeddah and couldn't stay beyond a certain date, and that Admiral Conolly was being detached, so I hoped to make the presentation.

Valcour sailed, and I went up to Asmara to catch a MATS plane that was coming through.[5] Its engine broke down, so I had to spend a couple of days in Asmara with the governor general who put me up again. During that time I took the opportunity to drive far inland into Eritrea and down to Ethiopia. It's an accordion-like land. Eritrea is a plateau, presumably, but it is filled with deep ravines. If you're going anywhere, you have to go

---

5. In World War II the Army Air Forces operated MATS, the Military Air Transport Service. It became an Air Force command with the separation of the services in 1947.

down and up and down and up constantly. And as you get to the Ethiopian border, the mountains rise higher and higher like great waves on the sea.

We finally flew to Jeddah. Our ambassador was away, but Hayward Hill, the counselor, was very helpful. He met me and held a reception so I could meet a great number of people. Among them was one of the most helpful men I met in the Middle East, Gary Owen, ARAMCO's vice president for government relations, naturally stationed in Jeddah. He did everything he could to help me, then and later.

I was put up in the ambassador's residence outside where the old city walls had been; these had been torn down fairly recently. I arrived at the residence in my whites, because I had gone to the reception and made calls. When we got there, it was the siesta hour, and the driver couldn't wake any servants. The huge, uninviting house sat in a barren courtyard, surrounded by a high wall. Unable to raise anybody, I found a ladder, climbed over the wall in my whites, got into a room, and finally roused Abbas, "father," a most impressive Muslim. Six feet tall with a large frame, he could do anything with the greatest of ease. Nothing fazed him; nothing bothered him. "If Allah wills, I can do it."

I still had to wait for Prince Mansour. No word from him yet. So I took the opportunity to drive toward Mecca. You can drive some 15 or 20 miles toward the holy city. Then you come to a large sign printed in various languages saying, "Forbidden to those who are not Moslems to pass any further." I had an Arab driver, but I'd taken the wheel, which I often did, and went on beyond the sign to turn around. He nearly fainted. He was sure he was going to have his head cut off.

Jeddah itself then was quite interesting. There were a few modern buildings of our architecture, but most were still the old buildings. And being the port of entry to Mecca for the pilgrims, it was a rather prosperous city. The main buildings were four or five stories high, built of coral or limestone. They had balconies with ornamented tops, decorations in stone or adobe, very attractive, at least from a distance. These were called harem balconies, because it was said the harem would lean over and look down into the narrow streets to see what was going on. All the streets were narrow and winding, except in the new part of the city, with modern buildings. These included a Coca-Cola plant run entirely by machinery. Nothing was touched by hand after it went into the boiling water.

That's the way Coca-Cola sets up its plants all over the world. I drank only Coca-Cola there for a cooling beverage.

John T. Mason Jr.: Knowing it was sanitary?

Admiral Eller: Afraid of the water.

Finally I got a date for meeting the Prince, but I still had a little time, and a Pakistani destroyer came for the hajj, the pilgrimage. There were thousands of people coming through. It was a special month for pilgrims, apparently. Now they went up by bus, largely, rather than by caravan or by camel, or by foot as they used to do. I went to the destroyer to call on the captain. There was nobody on deck. So I walked up the gangway, and a sleepy sailor showed himself. I said, "I'd like to see the captain."

He didn't understand me, I suppose, but he went below and up came a neat lieutenant. I said, "I came to call on the captain."

"Well," he said, "he's not here, and there is nobody else here but me. They have all gone to Mecca."

I asked, "Are you going?"

He replied, "No, I'm a Christian. That's why I've been left behind to take care of the ship."

I asked, "How did you happen to be in the Pakistani Navy?"

It turned out he was born in Bombay and had been in the Indian Navy before the partition. I asked, "Why did you leave that?"

"Well," he said, "I couldn't stand their strange gods. The Moslems have a single god. They think straight. If they give you their word, you can rely on it, But the Indians, they have all of these strange gods. They can use one of them to deceive you. I wasn't happy with that type of life." This, in a way, describes the two nations and my experience with them. Not everybody, of course, but my general reaction to them.

Prince Mansour received me in the royal reception room. He was by rumor the King's favorite son. Old Ibn Saud had unified the country in part by war, and in part by visiting the different tribes and by marrying the daughter of the chieftain, and then leaving her with the tribe and going on to marry another wife. He may or may not have had more than one wife in Riyadh, where he stayed, because he seemed to be very fond of his home. But he had these scores of others that had been temporary wives. They said nobody knew how many sons he had.

Mansour was the son of his favorite wife, probably the one in Riyadh.[6] He was very much like the old man in build, tall, and fine-looking, excellent presence, nice personality. We spoke through an interpreter, but I think he knew English, as many of the princes did. At that time, as since, Saudi Arabia was much disturbed by our Israeli policy and was doubly so then, because we weren't sending much in the way of assistance to Saudi Arabia, though it was apparent that the oilfields were becoming more and more vital to us, and, of course, to the Saudi Arabians.

But the prince said that he hoped that the United States would stay strong, "We in Saudi Arabia understand what it means to be protected by the sea," he said. "I have visited a number of your ships and have been impressed by the efficiency and cleanliness. The carrier *Valley Forge* particularly, impressed me; 1,800 men worked as a single man. Their organization, discipline, and skill were unbelievable. You have reached a power there for peace or war unequalled in history, controlling the sky and the sea with an unbelievable force. We hope you will keep your Navy strong, not only to protect America, but the rest of the world. Ships like USS *Valley Forge* show that the United States has reached a peak in material achievement never before approached by any nation. It is a good thing for the world that the one to do this is the United States, because she devotes these achievements to the welfare of the world, to help all nations and not just herself. I am glad that it is not another nation, for you alone will use your strength at sea for peace and not for imperialism."
That viewpoint seemed to be a general one of the Saudi Arabians I met. Old King Ibn Saud also strongly believed in sea power.

Immediately after the conference, I flew across Arabia in an ARAMCO plane. That was quite an experience. There was a mélange of passengers. They were bringing in workers from all over the Middle East and Indian Ocean area. There were Indians, Goanese, who didn't consider themselves Indians; Africans from Somalia and the Sudan; Pakistanis;

---

6. The King was known in the West as Ibn Saud and in Saudi Arabia as Abdulaziz. Prince Mansour was the first Defense Minister of Saudi Arabia, serving in that capacity from 10 November 1943 until his death on 2 May 1951. His mother Shahida was Armenian; she died in 1938.

Indonesians; Arabs; East Africans; Italians; and one wild Yemeni, a mountaineer. Although it was hot as blazes, he was wearing a shirt, a jacket, a sweater, and a coat. I suppose these were most of his possessions, and he wasn't taking any chances of somebody stealing them. Their baggage was every sort of strange contrivance you can think of.

It was a very rough flight, and my discs were bothering me. So I ended up by lying down on the deck and periodically getting up to see what was going on. We passed first over the coastal plain of sand and salt flats, then barren hills with a very rare oasis. Then we crossed a lava waste with thousands of small volcanic craters and floods of lava congealed in the sands. I thought of Sodom and Gomorrah. It must have been the same period when this volcanic action took place. Then we came to the central plateau. The land is rising all the time in this lava waste mountain, which is sand, gravel, rock, and sand, gravel, rock. It's the most barren land you can think of.

We stopped at Kharg and refueled. This is an oasis below Riyadh, where ARAMCO was developing a large experimental farm. The experts were growing wonderful vegetables there and were greatly appreciated by the Saudi Arabians for their contributions. From there we passed over the Dhanas. These are golden red sand dunes that are crescent shapes and interlocked. They rise 60 or 100 feet or more in height. They form a great beautiful pattern on the desert. I would camp among them later on.

That night I stayed in ARAMCO's guest house at Dhahran. I was always happy to stop there, because it was beautifully run by Goanese, who were perfect servants and gentlemen with it. They were much concerned at the time, because Nehru was taking over the little enclaves in India the French and Portuguese had at the time. The Goanese were hoping the rule would stay under the Europeans, but it didn't, of course.

I had a brief time in Bahrain, where *Valcour* had arrived, and called on the political resident, Sir Rupert Hay, of whom I became quite fond. He was a short, jolly, John Bull-type veteran of the Indian Service. In essence, he was Britain's ambassador to the gulf states. He had political agents in each of the gulf sheikhdoms.

Another important man there, and one of the most important in the area, was Charles Belgrave, later knighted. He was the economic and financial adviser for the sheikh of Bahrain. He apparently was a younger son of a titled family—you know,

Belgrave Square in London. After service in World War I, he was looking for a job and saw an advertisement in *The London Times* for someone interested in going to the Persian Gulf. He applied and ended up in Bahrain as a young man, an adviser to the sheikh. He had now become, I believe, the most powerful man in that area, because he practically controlled the finances and economy of Bahrain.

I also had a quick look at our tanker operations. I had an officer and a couple of men ashore in charge of getting our petroleum out to Korea from the gulf. Nearly a tanker a day sailed, showing how important the gulf was during the Korean War.

This was one of the few times we had a chance to have regular Sunday services on board. There was an American Dutch Reformed mission there that had developed a good reputation, because of a hospital and service to the people. A young missionary came on board to hold service for us that Sunday. Actually, none of the oil companies observed our Sunday, but observed the Moslem Sunday of Friday.

We then sailed for Bushire, a small Iranian port near the head of the gulf. I was trying to get permission to travel the road from Bushire toward Shiraz and Persepolis and Isfahan in order to see that approach to the gulf. Answering my dispatches, Ambassador Grady advised that he was having difficulty getting permission, but by emphasizing the desire to see Persepolis, he thought he would get it. When we got to Bushire, permission had come through. The government had sent Captain Mohammed Ardalan, Iranian Navy, to escort me. He might have been taken out of ancient history. He was a Mede in ancestry and looked just like the ones I've seen in the sculpture of the period. In fact, I saw him on one of the sculptures in Persepolis on that trip.

I wanted to make the trip fast. By pushing, we could have done it in one day up to Shiraz. But the Persians overwhelm with courtesy entertainment. On the way, we had to stop at all of the headquarters, the army general and the governor general of each province. We went through two provinces. We also visited other dignitaries on the way, and each had to serve food and usually a great number of sweets with it. We had a high-wheeled vehicle that could negotiate atrocious roads. It took us two days to go 250 miles to Shiraz. That is a city of roses and poetry. One of their great poets was born there. It's a lovely city when the roses are blooming.

John T. Mason Jr.: The rug makers too.

Admiral Eller: And one of the unique rooms in Iran. Everyone told me to see it, if possible, to get entry, the "Mirror Room." Every bit of the bulkhead, with the ceiling, is covered with mirrors of different sizes—tiny ones, mostly. When the lights turn on, flashes of radiance shoot in every direction—shiny sparkling room. The home in which it is located was owned by the cousin of the general in charge of that tribal area. He arranged for us to see it.

The tribes were on the move in the Zagros Mountains just as they had been earlier in the Elburz Mountains. Most of the tribes of southern Iran are located in Pars Province, of which Shiraz is the capital. That is one of the places where they are now having trouble.

The governor was rather optimistic about the conditions. I might read a little of the letter I wrote to Admiral Sherman concerning this. I was talking about Arabia, and I said, "Whatever we do there, our great hope for real development of strength, and where it is most needed, is Iran. While writing these comments, I received some clippings from Washington on Iran. They point out our difficulties there, the declining U.S. prestige, the inadequacy of our aid, and the instability resulting from the Tudeh Party causing trouble and unrest. These statements are true; they deal with the past more than the present. In a 250-mile trip northward from Bushire through much tribal country, I was in contact with a number of the army and gained several favorable impressions. They are snappy, neat, and well disciplined. The officers appear to be intelligent and zealous. They have just finished maneuvers defending the Bushire-Shiraz passes and claim success with improvised defenses. The day I was in Shiraz, the chief of staff left for Tehran to confer on developing permanent defenses.

"The army has constant contact with the tribes, keeping an officer with a radio with each major group. I spent an evening with the general in charge of tribal duties in Pars. He is in constant touch with his field officers and handles most tribal problems direct. He says he has no serious ones.

"Tribal youth, as other Iranians, serve two years and make superior soldiers. With the army control net throughout the country and the additional gendarme and frontier guards, communism will be kept down unless the government weakens, or Russian marches in."

I think, just as an aside, that the government did weaken. I think we put pressure on them to try to be more lenient in handling political activist radicals. And I believe the Shah could have held on in Iran if we had not begun to withdraw our support. Of course, he made a serious mistake in trying to push modernism too fast, especially with the women. That, probably, was his wife's influence on him.

We went on the Persepolis, a fascinating place. It's not too distant from Shiraz. It has the ruins of the great palaces of King Darius and Cyrus (though I think Cyrus's main palace was at Susa) and Xerxes and several others. These are elevated on terraces with tremendous columns 60 feet or so high. There are ruins of the treasury and the archives. There are also huge marble or fine stone carvings showing processions of people bringing their tribute to the shahs. One of them, as I mentioned, could have been Captain Ardalan, a Mede in ancestry.

On the mountain beyond Persepolis on the face of a cliff, the tombs were carved out of Xerxes and other ancients. I don't think it was very accessible, or that many people went there, but it was a sight worth going to see. As soon as I got back to Bushire, we sailed to Ras Tanura. The company took me into the desert to see two oilfields they were developing. Arabs were doing much of the work. When the drillers had completed a well, they would take away the derrick, and you would see just a little pumping area. The Arabs were operating these with skill.

John T. Mason Jr.: What seemed to be the attitude of the Arabians toward ARAMCO?

Admiral Eller: I didn't find anyone who seemed hostile. ARAMCO paid them well, fed them well, trained them in a technical school, and brought more and more Arabs into the work force. The company had a hospital for them and seemed to do everything possible for the men. It was a very forward-looking policy. I don't think there was ever any hostility between the government and ARAMCO, even when Saudi Arabia later took over the oilfield, because the rulers realized ARAMCO was there to make money, but trying to do it in the best way possible for the country, as well as themselves. I didn't meet any hostility nor see any then in those early days. The whole operation was well organized. The drilling derrick had just finished drilling a well at our field. They merely hoisted it up on its wheels and rolled it across the sand on its huge balloon tires to wherever they were going to drill the next well. It might be a mile or two away. There was no delay in taking it down and setting it up again.

We then sailed to Kuwait at the upper end of the gulf. This is one of the ancient sheikhdoms of the area that is noted for its boatbuilding, of which a great deal was still going on then. It was also noted for its trading and smuggling in the far areas where they sailed—to Ceylon and beyond—and pearl diving. It was a center of the pearl-diving activity in the gulf, a grueling, killing vocation. Divers would go down, they claimed, 100 feet or so using stone weights, and stay down for two or three minutes before coming up for air. They would keep repeating dives.

John T. Mason Jr.: Short-lived careers, I would guess.

Admiral Eller: It was. One of the sheikhs I talked to had been a pearl diver as a youngster, or maybe just tried it out. He said, "The perils of land are nothing to the perils of the sea—the octopus, the barracuda, the spiny creatures that you meet down there. Then, of course, this inability to stay more than two or three minutes before your lungs burst."

In 1950 Kuwait still was a walled city with dirt streets and the usual adobe-coral buildings. In the market I was looking for some rugs late one day. The merchant took them out of little cubbyholes and threw them down in the dirt street to let me look at them. There was better care of them afterwards in their homes, of course, because you would take off your shoes to walk on them.

Kuwait was still very much as it always had been. The sheikhdom wasn't much larger than the District of Columbia, but had more oil than Texas. It's the richest per capita country in the world, I'm sure. The sheikh was Abdullah Al-Salim Al-Subah, then in his 50s.[7] I called on him. He had a kindly face, much gold in his teeth, and apparently was very philanthropic, though. He was spending quite a bit of money on improving his palace

---

7. He was the Emir of Kuwait from 1950 to 1965.

and building a royal yacht, 100-foot yacht, which he took us to see after the call. It was built in the old manner of roughhewn boards, but it was going to be lavishly furnished.

He was, however, using most of the oil money wisely as a steward for his people, building schools and hospitals and housing and roads. A desalinization plant was being considered and later built. For water then, they would sail up the Shatt al-Arab, the confluence of the Tigris and Euphrates, and fill up tubs, buckets, and barrels. Mr. L. T. Jordan was general manager of the Kuwait Oil Company. He was quite knowledgeable about the area and was very hospitable to us and our crews.

The crews couldn't ordinarily go ashore freely on liberty in the Arab cities because of the restriction on alcohol, and, of course, the segregation of women, and the fear that they would get in trouble. So we could only send them, when in the gulf, or in most Moslem ports for that matter, on sightseeing parties or shopping parties. There was never any evening liberty. The Kuwait Oil Company employed a number of Americans and other non-Moslems, and they made it a point to take care of the crews whenever we were there. They were very kind to us.

One of the noted men in all Arabia was Colonel H. R. P. Dixon. And his wife was almost as noted. His father had been in the diplomatic service in the Middle East. When he was born, his mother couldn't nurse him, so an Arab woman had. That automatically made him a member of the tribe to which she belonged. As he grew up, he took advantage of that and became a true Arab from every standpoint whenever he was with them. He lived with them, dressed like them, and spoke their language perfectly. He understood their thinking, their philosophy, and their reaction in any sort of situation better than any European in the area, and was highly regarded by the Arabs. King Ibn Saud spoke of him with admiration, and even the workmen in distant parts of Arabia spoke of Colonel Dixon as one greatly honored and revered.

The Kuwait Oil Company had wisely employed him as a consultant and used him very much. He and his wife had sort of a ramshackle house, but a very comfortable one—cool and airy, sitting over the harbor. I got to be good friends with him, liked him, and on every visit learned a lot from him. Every time I reached Kuwait, I would go up and sit on their balcony and talk to them or have them on board. A large, angular woman, Mrs. Dixon was the expert on the flora and fauna of Arabia. She ultimately wrote a book on them.

John T. Mason Jr.: An English woman?

Admiral Eller: Yes. They were both English.

At that time, too, we saw and later visited the head of AMINOL, American Independent Oil Company. Between Kuwait and Saudi Arabia are two neutral zones. The tribes know no boundaries as they move back and forth for grass. So when Arabia was split up into various countries, there was difficulty between Kuwait and Saudi Arabia, because they both claimed this same land for their tribes. Finally it was settled by providing neutral zones, which neither country owns. Each has a half interest, and the tribes come and go without interference.

One of these neutral zones extends to the Persian Gulf. Oil rights in it for Kuwait had been purchased by the AMINOL. J. MacPherson was director in charge. At this time he was a little dispirited, because they had drilled several dry holes. Later on I went out into the desert with him when they were hoping to complete a real well, and it turned out to be a dry hole too. But, subsequently, they found considerable oil.

From Kuwait we sailed down the gulf to Qatar. This is a large godforsaken peninsula that juts out from—

John T. Mason Jr.: Very strategic, however.

Admiral Eller: Yes. It juts out from the coast of Arabia below Bahrain for some distance. It's very strategic. It could have been part of Saudi Arabia. We anchored at Umm Said, which was the oil port then. The British had found oil there. They named the operating company Petroleum Development Qatar, PDQ for short. Percival Lilly, manager of operations, unlike some of the British oilmen in the Trucial coast sheikhdoms, was very friendly and had no hesitation in showing me around. When we arrived, Lilly came out to the ship and insisted that we go ashore with him. The next day he took us to the oilfields, which were across Qatar to the north, a rough, barren drive.

I said that Saudi Arabia was barren, but Qatar was a land God forgot completely. I didn't see palm trees anywhere except, perhaps, a few in the little capital of Doha, some 70 or 100 miles up the coast. Here the sheikh had his headquarters and fort, Sheikh Ali Ibn Abdullah. We seldom stayed anywhere more than three or four days. That was our routine to try to get around to show the flag and learn the area. That was more than ample time for Qatar. We next sailed to Bahrain for a brief stop. The flagship captains especially liked to go there, because the British had a little base called Juffair. It had an enlisted men's club and the crew had an opportunity to shop in the town. They would play baseball and other games on the base. It was a pleasant place for all hands.

While there, whenever I could, I tried to do something with the crew. I took them across the island to a deserted beach on the other side where we could operate independently. We had a picnic with beer, a baseball game, and fishing. The ride was quite interesting, because you passed through some ancient tombs in a burial area that completely covers a good portion of the north part of the island. There was much wonder then about why they were there and who built the tombs. There were large stone slabs of a sarcophagus on some of them with inscriptions.

The next time I saw Charles Belgrave, I said these were hieroglyphics. He said, "What? Are you sure?" He was very much of an archaeologist at heart. They had not deciphered the writing and didn't know the date of the tombs.

John T. Mason Jr.: The origin of them?

Admiral Eller: Later, there was considerable excavation, and it turns out that they date back to 2,500 to 3,000 B.C. I don't know that they have ever deciphered the inscriptions. But they believe this was a trading port mentioned in the Assyrian and Babylonian records. It must have been something more than that, perhaps a holy island where important people were brought to be buried. I considered bringing back one of the large slabs to present to the Smithsonian, but was never in Bahrain long enough. I suppose I could have done it. Nobody seemed much interested in them other than Belgrade.

I hadn't yet called on Sheikh Sir Salman bin Hamad al Khalifa.[8]

---

8. Salman bin Hamad Al Khalifa was the ruler of Bahrain from 1941 until his death in 1961.

John T. Mason Jr.: Is he Bahrainian?

Admiral Eller: Yes, the ruler. I had not called on him because I hadn't been in Bahrain long enough. So I called with Charles Belgrave. Usually you would call with the political agent of a sheikhdom, but Charles Belgrave was so close to the sheikh and so knowledgeable that he took me this time.

I think Sheikh Khalifa was the most progressive and enlightened and philosophic of the sheikhs that I met. He had a good face and a good heart. He tried to live up to his responsibilities. He said that, in a sense, it was like being in biblical times when the priest was the father of the people, and he felt he was. The ceremonies when you made a call on him were very much like the 23 Psalm. "He anointed my head with oil, my cup runneth over." This is done. After the anointment, which is an incense, comes the coffee, tea, coffee ceremony using small rice cups. One of the servants—usually a slave in some of the sheikdoms—hauls a large coffee pot off about a yard away, then just flicks it, and hits the coffee cup every time. He'll fill it up to a quarter of an inch of the brim with a single flick and not spill a drop. When you drink it, if you don't want any more, you wiggle your hand. He will keep refilling until you can't take any more. If the sheikh is ready for you to go, he wiggles his cup and you go.

I discussed world conditions with Sheikh Khalifa. On calls, I always tried to find out what the sheik's interests were. His interests were his people most of all. Then world conditions. He said he had never been out of Bahrain. "However, a man can travel all over the world by reading." He said, "I've been everywhere in the wonderful world of books."

John T. Mason Jr.: Was he educated in Britain?

Admiral Eller: I don't think he'd been educated abroad. These were Moslem books. He was speaking through an interpreter, sometimes Belgrade. "My duty is at home with my family, the people of Bahrain. A ruler is the father of his people. He has duties to them, and they have duties of obedience and respect to him." I think he had respect. He was the type of ruler that you look for anywhere. He, like others of the sheikhs, always had audiences for the people after the first break of day prayer. Anyone that had a problem could come in to see him. Audiences might last all morning. Then he would go hunting or do something else.

In early November Hydrographic Unit Number One arrived in the gulf on surveying duty. I think it was also partly to be sure we had some facilities there in case of real trouble.

John T. Mason Jr.: Tell me about that unit.

Admiral Eller: It was USS *Maury* (AGS-16), also two fleet tugs, *Allegheny* and *Stallion*. She had, I believe, two long-range patrol planes. Both by boat and by plane we were surveying the Persian Gulf and the Arabian coast.

John T. Mason Jr.: Now, was this for the Navy?

Admiral Eller: Yes, for the U.S. Navy Hydrographic Office. The group was a great comfort to me, because it increased the capability we had for evacuation and for early warning. It also added to the available air transport. I requested a flag plane soon after I took command of the area, and it arrived sometime in December. It has been there ever since for the Commander Middle East Force. *Maury* also had a helicopter that I used a great deal to join a ship at sea or to go or come from ashore. Landing on *Maury* was easy since she had a landing platform. But the process of getting on board the small flagship was a different matter. They hitched a horse collar under your arms and had a winch in the plane. You stepped out the window, and the winch lowered you down. The stern of an AVP seaplane tender was covered with all sorts of apparatus. There wasn't much clear space. The pilot was a master. He would hover right over the ship, lower you gently, and a couple of the crew would catch you. Boarding the helicopter was a reverse process.

John T. Mason Jr.: It was the same sort of equipment they used for rescue purposes?

Admiral Eller: Yes. In fact, I used the helicopter about the time *Maury* arrived to go to Dhahran, because I wanted to travel into the desert to see how it would be possible to get up to Riyadh by road if the Soviets came in. ARAMCO was sending a geological party to survey deep into the desert of Saudi Arabia below Riyadh and down toward Muscat.

John T. Mason Jr.: Was that for the purpose of finding oil?

Admiral Eller: Yes. ARAMCO had a concession covering a large part of Saudi Arabia. They were seeking to expand production all the time, to expand their fields. During my time there, they were really just getting under way in all the Persian Gulf area on important production. In Iraq and Iran, they had been producing for some time, but had stopped or slowed down during the wear. I'm not sure that ARAMCO had produced any oil when war broke out. They had drilled wells, and, I believe, had found oil. But when the war broke out, everything closed down.

John T. Mason Jr.: From your description, I get the impression that the oil was found largely along the water's edge.

Admiral Eller: Much of the initial oil, yes. The first oilfields in Saudi Arabia were found not too far from the coast, and the Saudi Arabians built a port, Dammam, now a major shipping point for the oil. Saud Ibn Jiluwi, sheik of Hasa province, has his coastal headquarters in Dammam. From the original field in Saudi Arabia, slanting inland for a long distance, ARAMCO began to find oil in different fields, apparently one immense oil stratum running south and west.

Of course, Kuwait is on the coast, and all the sheikdoms are on the coast. So the oil that has been found in them is near the coast. In Iran the oil, the first fields, are not too far from the coast, maybe 50 or 100 miles. But now they have found fields well inland, up on the high plateau of Iran. In Iraq, where oil was first produced in quantity in the Middle East, the fields are far inland.

We must have gone at least 400, maybe 500 miles into the desert. As soon as we got into the desert, there were no roads. Once we got beyond where the oil company had developed their fields, there were no roads. So the vehicles we had had large balloon tires. We had a van, which I believe was air-conditioned for the geological equipment, a half truck, and another vehicle. The first night we camped, then the second night we stopped at Kharg and had some fresh vegetables, and then went on into the Dhana dunes. Two of our party were Bert Beverly, a chief geologist for ARAMCO, and Alexander Chapman, a geologist and a long-time oilman from Texas. But he was also serving as a CIA agent to develop plans to deny the oilfields to the Soviets. He was very helpful to me in plans of various types. This was something that no one wanted to do, of course, but if the Soviets came in, the plans were to try to blow up the wells.

You saw practically no life in the desert. Occasionally there would be a fox or a gazelle. These are beautiful little creatures like the ones I'd seen in Eritrea in the police chief's office. He had a pair as pets. They stood two or three feet high. Their horns were thin, pencil-like. Their legs were little more than pipe stems, and their hooves were like walnuts. They had the biggest, most soulful eyes. Lovely things. I don't see how anyone could shoot them. The male in his office, if you weren't looking, would come around and butt you in the stern. Then he would come up and rub against you to show you it was all in fun. Well, we occasionally saw a gazelle and a bustard, which I'd never heard of before—it's turkey-like in size— and occasionally a dove or a partridge, maybe, but very rarely did we see anything. We did pass one camel caravan lonely in the desert. I saw those periodically in the sheikhdoms. Camels were used considerably then as in the past, and may still be.

But then, when we got deep into the Dhanas, it was like camping with God. We were alone under the stars. The sands were hot and blazing by day, and as quick as night fell they turned freezing. We had a cooking stove with bottled gas, and we scraped up some dry vegetation wherever we could find any and would save it for a fire at night.

You could see why the Arabians became such able astronomers. They were, I suppose, among the earliest and greatest. In the sand dunes one of the geologists got out a magnifying glass and had me look at the grains of sand. They looked like reddish-gold gems. They sparkled. They had been polished by the wind for ages. One night when we were camped amidst the dunes, in the distance we saw the lights of a vehicle. Somebody said, "That's a taxi." A taxi here in the desert? But that's what they called it. This was a car with balloon tires, on government business going to Riyadh from the coast. There were no roads. They just steered by the stars.

John T. Mason Jr.: A trackless waste.

Admiral Eller: Yes. After several days, I left them, because I had to get back to the ship. Chapman and I returned in the half truck with a driver. In late afternoon we came to Hofuf, the largest oasis in Saudi Arabia and home headquarters of Saud Ibn Jiluwi. I thought it would be appropriate to call on him. I didn't realize how seedy we looked, having been out in the desert for days with dust all over us. The city itself is walled, though some of the gardens are outside. We came to a gate, and the sentry stopped us. Our driver and interpreter told them what we were doing, and that I wanted to call on the sheikh. We waited, and we waited, and we waited, and nothing happened. Finally, I got word to the sentry that we had to go on, that the flagship was sailing the next morning and we had to get back to Dhahran and Ras Tanura. So he sent us on with a guide through the city to the palace. The city has large walls around it, and has many irrigation ditches. A great number of vegetables were growing under the palm trees.

We were taken in to the palace and put in a barren reception room, as most of the sheiks were. We sat down and nothing happened. Another half hour or more passed. I finally said, "Well, we've got to go." And at just that time a little man came in—a small Arab. I had no idea who he was, but he proved to be Abdul Aziz Ibn Saud, Ibn Jiluwi's son, named after King Ibn Saud.

I got across to him that we came to call and had to go on our way. So we had the coffee, tea, coffee ceremony. Then I said, "It's late; we have to go."

About that time he received a message. Apparently there had been a lot of telephoning back and forth, trying to reach his father in Dammam. Suddenly he became very cordial. He said, "No, you can't go. You have to stay for something to eat."

I said, "We can't. We've got to go; the ship has to sail."

He insisted, so there was nothing to do but stay. A couple of hours passed, and finally after dark, when I'd hoped to be back, he took us up on the roof and here was a great spread of several whole sheep on rice with vegetables in dishes around it. This was characteristic of their feasts. So we had to sit down. He had several of the officials with him, and we had a banquet that lasted an hour or so. I was getting more and more itchy, and said we had to leave. Meanwhile, we had been talking about his interests. A special one was hunting. He spoke of how he loved to hunt, and then, finally, he got to the gazelles.

I said, "They are a beautiful creature. Don't you find it difficult to hunt them?" He got the word beautiful, and I'd made a mistake, because now I had indicated I wanted one.

He said, "I have some in the compound. You must take them."

I said, "No, we haven't got any way to carry them, and the ship is sailing. I haven't got any place to keep them."

"No," he said, "you have to take them." We went down to the truck, finally. They had crated a couple of them and stuck them in the half truck. So we had two gazelles.

As we drove through the streets towards the north gate, we saw a whole troop of people carrying food on their heads, coming out of the palace. The young sheikh had given food to the people of the city for their feast afterwards. They always welcome anybody, any visitor, because that means they get most of the food. We couldn't have eaten a hundredth of what was on the long table. Happily, ARAMCO had a compound where they kept gazelles. So I put the two there and named them Hasa and Hofuf. They probably have many descendants by now.

We now sailed for Muscat, a fascinating place. En route, I completed a revision of our war plans with my staff. These were essentially delay and early warning, evacuation, and denial of the oil. We worked into the plans not only our few naval vessels and patrol planes, but all the planes and vessels we could put our hands on in the gulf. We couldn't consider any real defenses, because we had nothing to defend with.

John T. Mason Jr.: What were the implications of a possible Russian move at that time? Was it related to Korea and the Russian interests in that war?

Admiral Eller: Yes, to Korea and our support of it and by the entry of China. When China entered, of course, it then began to look like the war would keep expanding. The Soviets had been building up their forces, kept them built up after World War II, and continued to build up. So it was natural for everyone to think that since they had sent the North Koreans into South Korea and brought China in the war, that the next step would be for the Soviets to enter directly.

John T. Mason Jr.: Admiral Sherman himself was terribly much concerned, wasn't he?

Admiral Eller: Yes.

John T. Mason Jr.: And had contemplated setting up a new fleet?

Admiral Eller: Oh, yes, these were the plans. In fact, I think *Maury* was sent ahead of schedule, and there were destroyers tabbed to come out. He had wanted a carrier to be in the area. But unless the fleet could have been there when the Soviets struck, only the delay worked into the plans we prepared could be followed.

Muscat is a most interesting place. It's an ancient seafaring country. It once had possessions as far south as Zanzibar and the coast of Africa, and north to Kuwait, as well as islands or toehold possessions elsewhere. They still have a little enclave in Pakistan called Gwadar.

John T. Mason Jr.: Is Muscat part of the Trucial States?

Admiral Eller: No. You go out of the gulf and come around the cape, and then it faces on the Arabian Sea. It's called Muscat and Oman.

John T. Mason Jr.: Yes, I know.

Admiral Eller: The harbor itself had a narrow entrance not over 1,000 yards, if that much. It's quite picturesque. There is a little island that closes off the starboard side of the entry as you sail in, and cliffs running up hundreds of feet. The palace was right on the water. It was a large building, but not impressive. The town itself was of modest size. Oil had not been found there then. It was a poor country. They lived largely on fishing, trading, and some farming—quite a bit of farming in some areas—but it was a poor country.

John T. Mason Jr.: Has oil been found there?

Admiral Eller: Yes, since then.

John T. Mason Jr.: Not in any great quantity?

Admiral Eller: Not enormous quantities. I think liberal quantities, though. Stribling Snodgrass, a graduate of the Naval Academy, was adviser to the sheikh. I had seen him in Jeddah when I was there. He had gotten out of the Navy not long after graduation, and then had gone in the oil business. He invited me over to see the sultan of Muscat four or five years ago, but I couldn't go.

When the ship visited Muscat, the sultan was away, down toward Aden in that part of his domain. His uncle, a very shrewd, shylock-looking man, was ruler in his absence. His brother Tarik, who had been educated in Europe and spoke Turkish, English, and German fluently, was very helpful to me. We exchanged calls. Of course, the sultan's uncle came on board.

John T. Mason Jr.: Well, was this a customary thing for each commander out there to make this general tour?

Admiral Eller: They kept the ship moving, yes.

John T. Mason Jr.: So it wasn't a novelty to these people that—

Admiral Eller: No, they would expect the ship to come in occasionally. However, the conferences that I went to and my trips inland, I don't think anyone had done them before, nor several of the port visits. In fact, my predecessors had operated more in the Persian Gulf than I did.

I don't think any of our warships had been to Muscat for a good while. On the cliffs, several hundred feet up, there were painted the names of a few ships in large white paint. There was a Dutch Reformed mission in Muscat. The head of it asked me if we would repaint the names on the cliffs, particularly that of *Isla de Luzon*. The *Isla de Luzon*, a gunboat, had been captured at the battle of Manila Bay and commissioned in the U.S. Navy. After operating in the Philippines for a couple of years, she had come to the States westward and had stopped in at Muscat. When they were there in 1902, the sailors had climbed the cliff and painted their ship's name, starting a custom followed by the rare U.S. warship that visited the small harbor.

John T. Mason Jr.: Graffiti even at that point.

Admiral Eller: Yes. We had a very old treaty with Muscat, the first east of Suez. It goes back to the 1830s, a commercial and maritime treaty. I went up the cliff with a group of volunteers, and we painted the *Isla de Luzon*, *Valcour*, and others.

As I said, Tarik was very helpful to me, and his cousin or nephew Thuwainy bin Shinab took me in tow as adviser and guide. He was likable, modest, and spoke English well. He had been educated, I think, in India. He drove me into the country, up the coast and inland. It was rocky and arid with very few oases or verdant spots over underground water where the dry wadis reached the sea. There were no roads, only tracks. We saw no other motor vehicle on our all day trip. The tribesmen we met, particularly those from the mountains, carried rifles and daggers. They were ready to shoot at any time and to go to war. They lived as they had always lived as far as I could see.

On Thanksgiving Day, we sailed from Muscat. I held services on board. At noon I had as many of the crew as I could on the forecastle to dine with me. We ate a big Thanksgiving dinner then, and they ate a second big Thanksgiving dinner that evening. You couldn't stop them.

From Muscat, after stopping in at a deserted bay around the cape to let the crew swim and fish, we sailed to the sheikdom of Sharjah on the Trucial coast. The approach to Sharjah is pretty well sanded up, so we had to anchor several miles offshore. From afar, the city looked beautiful—white buildings rising out of the sea and palm trees. It looked like a jewel. It wouldn't be exactly like that when we got ashore with the flies and the dirt and the dust. But it was impressive from the sea.

To make the usual formal call, I took the barge and ran in as far as we could go. There is a wide sand island lying off the coast. A quarter of a mile from it we ran out of water. Nearby were fishermen with their dirty little fishing boats. Captain Stroh and I were in starched whites, but there was nothing to do except to hail one of these and hire it to take us to the sand island. The boat had inches of water in it with dead and dying fish floating around. It smelled as if the fish had been there for a hundred years. So we sat on the ports and held our feet up on the gunwales. The rower would splash us with his oars and laugh. The boat grounded near the sand island, and we still couldn't get ashore dry shod. So a couple of them hoisted us in their arms and carried us to the beach. Then we walked across the sand to the other side, maybe a quarter of a mile. There were cleaner boats. One of them took us on to the mainland. By then it was dark. A radiant moon was shining, and that was one of the most beautiful, peaceful rides. They poled the boat soundlessly. We were gliding in the moonlight on this mirror-like lagoon. So I thought Sharjah was a heavenly place.

The young political agent, H. O. Michel, was an Oxford graduate, a new breed in the area. He was kind and intelligent. With him we called on the sheikh, and the sheikh called on us. Then Michel took me to see some of the other sheikhdoms. The next one going toward the cape and the exit of the gulf is Ajman, which is a pretty little city. Then you come to Umm Al Qaiwain. It's dreary and sand-blown and flea-bitten.

John T. Mason Jr.: What are these? Just little towns?

Admiral Eller: They are little port towns, the capitals of sandy sheikhdoms, some of considerable area. Ajman, I think, has only a few square miles. The town is an oasis, with ample water welling up from underground. It is a lovely little oasis. The last one nearest the cape, which we didn't drive to the, but I visited later, is Ras Al Khaimah, a large sheikhdom. Another day we drove to Dubai, which is toward Bahrain. It's the principal town on the Trucial coast.

John T. Mason Jr.: And they have oil, don't they?

Admiral Eller: They hadn't struck oil then, but have since.

John T. Mason Jr.: Does this complete the list of Trucial states or are there more?

Admiral Eller: There is one more, Abu Dhabi, the largest, which I visited later, as I'll mention.

Dubai is quite an impressive place and picturesque. The buildings are built of coral stone, dull to gleaming white. They are two or three stories high, have ornamented balconies with stone carvings, and squarish Persian towers for "air conditioning." They go up some distance and have a scooped interior. Any wind blowing from any direction comes through openings at the top, hits the scoop, and comes down to cool the house. They also sprinkle water at the top as the air flows down, and it's very comfortable. Souks, markets, lined each side of a lagoon that ran through the center of town.

John T. Mason Jr.: What's the Arab word?

Admiral Eller: S-O-U-K is the way we anglicize it. The souks on the Trucial coast, as they were in Kuwait and much of Tehran, for that matter, are usually covered with a mat, or just a piece of cheesecloth to cut out the sun, and keep the flies in. I called it the Venice of the East, because there are many little inlets running into the town. And a number of the houses are built so that the stone comes right up out of the water as in Venice. The city was transformed that evening by the moonlight mirrored on the little lagoons and waterways. The darkness hit the flies and the dirt so that it was very picturesque. Sharjah and Dubai were my favorites on the gulf coasts next to Kuwait.

From Sharjah we sailed to a presumably deserted mountainous island, Abu Musa. I wanted to give the crew a day or so there for recreation. Most of the red ochre of the world comes from here. But as we approached, it was an island of many colors: mold green like the green on a copper-roofed building, rust reds, pastels, mauves, pinks, heliotrope, and orchid. The low mountains are cut by erosion and the different colors are from minerals that have colored the earth.

Mining was not under way at the time, so I thought there would be nobody on the island. As we were crossing it, I heard a radio, and here was a shack built out of driftwood with a radio bellowing out news in English. I went in and found a Pakistani. He had gone to Mecca. He had saved all his life to make the pilgrimage, had spent all of his money, and was working his way back. His last job was on Abu Musa. When they stopped mining and left, he didn't have enough money to go on, so he had stayed behind. I suppose he lived on fish. He actually was listening to events in Moscow, New York, Korea, and talked about them intelligently. It made me realize what radio has done throughout the world.

John T. Mason Jr.: Even more so, television.

Admiral Eller: Yes, though it hasn't spread to quite the extent of radio.

We went back to Bahrain, and from there I made it a point to fly to Abu Dhabi, the biggest of the Trucial sheikhdoms, and the first going down the Gulf from Qatar. It was rumored that they had an oil strike, but the oilmen were quite secretive. I asked to go where they were drilling, but no, it was inconvenient; the roads weren't good. They kept delaying and I could only stay two days. So I didn't get to see what they were doing. This is now the major producing sheikhdom on the Trucial coast.

John T. Mason Jr.: Were the British in charge?

Admiral Eller: The British. All of these sheikhdoms were under semi-protection with political residents, very strong factors in the foreign affairs and other decisions of the sheikhs.

John T. Mason Jr.: At the time you were there Oman was not threatened, was it?

Admiral Eller: No.

John T. Mason Jr.: By Aden?

Admiral Eller: Aden hadn't been given up by England yet. It was a mistake to do so.

After a few days in Bahrain, we sailed to the oil port of Kuwait—the first time we had gone into Kuwait itself, the harbor of Kuwait. Down the coast a few miles is Mina al Ahmadi, the Kuwait Oil Company loading point. They had the biggest oil pier in the world when I was there. It was a T, and we used the two ends of the T for navigational points, they were so far apart. Instead of riding up in the ship, I wanted to see the condition of the coast and whether or not there were any roads. ARAMCO gave me a car and drove me to the neutral zone, then to Mina al Ahmadi.

After three or four days there with the usual calls and visits into the desert, we sailed to Basra. Then on to the gulf and the Shatt-al-Arab, which I believe means the River of the Arabs. We got to the entrance of the Shatt-al-Arab at dawn near low tide and had to wait briefly off the sand bar there. A dozen or so other ships, mostly large tankers, were waiting to cross when the tide raised the level of the water enough. We, being of less draft, didn't have to wait long, and soon started up the Shatt-al-Arab, about a 70-mile run. One saw practically nothing on the way up except date palms, stretching out of sight inland and up ahead. The two important breaks were on the starboard hand, Abadan, the great Persian oil refinery, and a few miles above it Khorramshahr, Iran's naval base on the gulf.

I took a certain distance and counted the trees, and then ran the estimate inland for a mile. I calculated there were 40 million palm trees, at least, en route to Basra. It's just an endless sea of them. You can see why dates are one of their principal exports and food. Basra is a very busy and important port. In the times of Sinbad the Sailor, it was on the sea. All of the 70 miles following the river is really silted in land and very rich. We promptly started the many official calls, far more than usual, because there are various embassies in the port. However, our embassy was in Baghdad, with a consul general at Basra.

In the midst of these calls, the death of the Queen Mother was announced. All official calls were canceled, agreeably to me. Instead, the governor of the province held a reception in the mosque for visits of sympathy. So I went, took off my shoes, and sat down cross-legged. We drank coffee, as always, while the mullahs chanted their sorrow over her death. The next day I got word from the consul general that Senator Green was arriving.[9] He was around 90, I think.

John T. Mason Jr.: And slightly dote.

Admiral Eller: Yes and bent over. I met him at the airport in the consul general's car and brought him to the ship. He wanted to see the sailors from Rhode Island to get publicity. He came on board and had lunch with us. We got all the sailors from Rhode Island together and photographed him with them. I had a good photographic shop on board, which developed the film right away. He took prints with him and sent some to the papers in Rhode Island.

That afternoon—I don't think he had stopped long anywhere—he got on a plane and went on. It would have killed me today, even at my age, to try to do this.

John T. Mason Jr.: He was one of the early joggers.

Admiral Eller: He was jogging around the world.

The next day I took a car to observe the road toward Baghdad. We drove up as far as Ur of Chaldees, where Abraham started—about 125 miles. It's just a pyramidal ruin now, but still there. You can imagine Abraham starting out along the Fertile Crescent on a journey that was to affect the future of all men.

Late Christmas Eve, I took the attaché's plane and flew up to Baghdad. On the way we passed over a great number of tels, ruins, that are just mounds rising up out of the bones of cities. Mesopotamia is literally a relief map of ancient history. Everywhere you go you find ruins. We passed over Babylon on the way up. It is extensive. It runs for miles. Just about the time we were passing over a place called Nippur—an important city under the Babylonians, I believe—a storm struck. As we jostled around in lightning and fury, dark came, and it was a difficult trip for a time. Then all of a sudden the clouds

---

9. Theodore F. Green, a Democrat from Rhode Island, served in the Senate from 1937 to 1961. He was born in October 1867 and was 93 years old when he retired.

broke and there was Baghdad shining below us in the night with its lights ablaze. It was sparkling like the jewels of the Arabian Nights, a spectacular entry. I was put up again at the ambassador's residence. He was there this time—Edward S. Crocker II. The next day after noon dinner with the assistant military attaché, I broke away at coffee time and left for a drive to see the British Air Force base, about 70 miles to the west. Baghdad is on the Tigris River, and the base was close to the Euphrates.

John T. Mason Jr.: Let me interrupt and ask how you arranged this itinerary and with what facility?

Admiral Eller: You had to arrange a port visit for an important country well in advance. We could go to a sheikhdom making arrangement at Bahrain fairly rapidly. But to go to Basra, for example, I would have to make my schedule three months in advance. So the actual port visits were made up each quarter, going through the Navy and State Department to get diplomatic clearance. The request went to the embassy of the particular country in Washington. The embassy would send a message to its foreign office. They would let it lie around for a week or two, and finally give permission.

These trips inland I arranged simply with the attaché or the ambassador. If I was in Saudi Arabia, the oil company took care of everything. Once you got inside a country, there was less difficulty about your movement in it. Until you got there, you had all of the red tape official requirements and clearances to combat. En route to the British air base, we passed, so it was claimed, the traditional location of the Garden of Eden, some 30 or 40 miles west of Baghdad.

After inspecting the base, they wanted me to spend the night, but I returned in the evening. The next morning early, the air attaché gave me a flight up over the northern part of Iraq to the Kurdistan area and the Iranian border, and up to the Turkish border, and also to the Syrian border. I wanted to see, first of all, the passes through the Zagros Mountains there that came down into the plains of Mesopotamia and then the oilfields.

John T. Mason Jr.: Was Kirkuk in operation then?

Admiral Eller: Yes.

John T. Mason Jr.: Did you go there?

Admiral Eller: I flew over it. After we'd flown to the northeast border, we came back over the oilfields and Kirkuk. Like several other places, it rises up on a pyramidal mound. It's truncated, cut across the top, and the present city must lie on scores of previous cities that have risen on the same site and been destroyed by war or time or disease. On the ruins of each of its predecessors, each one has risen above the plain higher and higher.

From Kirkuk, we flew to the northwest and west to Mosul, which is also in the oil fields. It's across the river from the ruins of Nineveh, which spread out in an easily visible map. There were ruins everywhere like this—Samarra covered miles. It seemed nearly as big as Babylon.

Another place I want to mention is Qadisiyah. From a distance it looked like the Pentagon, but was a perfect octagon. You could see the courtyards and foundations of the houses, and the gardens. Everything was laid out just as if it were a relief map of the city. It dated back, I understand, 1,500 years or so.

John T. Mason Jr.: But not occupied now?

Admiral Eller: Not occupied. Just ruins like Babylon. I got back that evening. And the next day I still had a little time, so I took the road south from Baghdad toward Basra to see the upper end of the route. We went on past Babylon for some distance and then came back and stopped there for a little while.

Babylon was just the way Isaiah prophesied. It was an immense tumble of ruins in all directions. The river had run by Babylon at one time, but now it was several miles away.

John T. Mason Jr.: The waters of Babylon.

Admiral Eller: You could see fragments of houses and palaces and a fragment of the hanging gardens, one of the wonders of the ancient world. These were a series of arches with a terrace on top of them where they planted the lower gardens, then stepped back rose other arches from a higher terrace. And then, as I understand it, a third level stepped back some more. I suppose the plants trailed down over the sides.

Babylon was uninhibited, except for one guide named Hamed. He was quite knowledgeable, a semi-geologist, I think, and keeper of the place. He said practically no one ever came there. As we walked around, I saw ducks fly up out of the pools that had been formed deep in the pits beside the ruins and a jackal slinking through them, just as described in the prophecy. Hamed was something of a philosopher too. I took this quotation down. He said, "Russia will make all the world desolate like this. The communists are like the rulers of Babylon; they turn men into slaves. That kills opportunity to go forward. It kills initiative. It kills God and home, and man must have these to live as a man."

I think most Arabs are not deceived by Communism. Those who do accept it are like the criminals of any country.

From Baghdad I flew back to the ship, and we dropped on down the river, maybe 25 or 30 miles to Khorramshahr, the Persian naval base on the gulf and the terminus of the railroad to Tehran, built during the wear to transport supplies to the Soviets. The commander of the naval base and commander of Iran's Persian Gulf activities was Captain Shahin.[10] Some years later he became head of the Iranian Navy and visited Washington. Arleigh Burke, then CNO, had me, among others, to dinner with him at the admiral's house.[11] He was unusual for a Persian, heavyset and fairly tall. He didn't have the eagle-like tribal look so many of them have, or the dapper look of the Shah. He could have been a Russian in his build.

Khorramshahr also required many calls and receptions. There was a constant boom of our saluting battery for dignitaries coming and going. One visitor was the governor at Abadan. A short, stocky Pickwick-like man with a deep horseshoe-shaped scar that

---

10. In 1958, as Chief of Staff of the Imperial Iranian Navy, Vice Admiral Havibollah Shahin visited the United States.
11. Admiral Arleigh A. Burke, USN, served as Chief of Naval Operations from 17 August 1955 to 1 August 1961. His oral history is in the Naval Institute collection.

covered almost all of his forehead. He had been governor of Azerbaijan when the Soviet-inspired revolution took place. He had been wounded, but had stayed on and was given credit as being partly instrumental in getting them out diplomatically by promises that were never kept. Not by him necessarily, but by the legislative body of Iran.

Eric Drake, head of the Iranian Oil Company, a subsidiary of British Petroleum, was very helpful and kind and thoughtful in arranging matters for me. He arranged for a tour of the Abadan refinery, then the largest in the world. They were bringing more and more Iranians into the company. I don't think it was as high a percentage as ARAMCO, but they were following the same wise course. Drake was in his early 40s, I think, and forward looking. Years later he became head of British Petroleum. We saw him just a few years ago in England.

John T. Mason Jr.: Was there evidence then of the workers' unrest—the Arabs—in contrast to the Iranians?

Admiral Eller: I didn't see any.

John T. Mason Jr.: That's a problem today, isn't it?

Admiral Eller: I know it is. Of course, Iran has problems with these different ethnic groups. The tribal groups consider themselves independent still. They just suffer the government. Some Kurds clamor for independence. Arabs predominate in the coastal province that includes Abadan. Then in Fars Province, just inland, are tribes again. So few of them consider themselves as part of the Persian family, really.

I wanted to see the roads up toward the oilfields. They go on up over the mountains like the railroad to Tehran. My excuse this time was the ruins of Susa, built by Cyrus, that became the winter capital of ancient Persia. Cyrus's palace was being excavated at the time. It was a long drive of about 250 miles inland. People said that I needed three days: one to go, one for Susa, and another day to come back. But I persuaded them to try to do it in a day, because I had to sail. So we left early, before dawn with my very pleasant liaison officer, Captain Afkhami, a true Persian, the same type as the Shah and looking something like him, in fact—a short, slender, capable young man.

A German archaeologist, Ghershman, was working on the ruins with his wife, also an archaeologist. They opened their mouths, and archaeology and history poured out like a fountain. Hence the visit, though short, was interesting. I might read a little of my report to Sherman after this trip:

"The more I learn of this area, the more clear it becomes that Russia's first objective will be the Abadan refinery. This plant turns out over 600,000 barrels a day of refined products. A large, new catalytic cracking unit for high-test aviation gas will soon be ready. No fixed defenses protect this prize. There is little evidence of denial preparation, even if time permits. As a result, the Soviets have waiting for them here all the aviation gas, motor gas, and submarine diesel required for major operations in the Near East, including an attack on Turkey from the back door, easier submarine attack in the Indian Ocean, and movement onto Suez.

"Many British talk of Abadan's being bypassed. On the contrary, the Russians would be mad not to grab this plum on the first day with a battalion or two of airborne troops.

"Supporting ground forces moving with light equipment via Pahlavi and Abadan, could join them within two days unless we do something to strengthen Persian resistance.

"Russia bulges here to the south like flood waters against a weakened levee. She has acquired a barrier of other nations, or of seas on every part of her frontier except from Turkey to Pakistan. Strong Turkey on the west, tough Pakistan on the east.

"In our buildup along this vital crescent, we and England have concentrated on the two nations offering most promise: Turkey and Pakistan. We will benefit from this, and it would be unwise not to continue supporting them. It is not impossible that all this aid will be neutralized, since the Soviets quite logically disregard the strong ends and plow through the weak center. The center can be strong. Most people will tell you we can do nothing about Iran; the leaders are weak and corrupt, the people have no spirit, the nation has no promise. Ambassador Grady won't tell you this. He knows, as you do, that the first essential is a leader with resolution and purpose and strength. The Persians are good people. They have brains; they have an ancient culture. They have pride, with an inferiority complex. What they need is for somebody to say, 'Be strong!' and to take firm steps to make them so. Razmara may be the man, even though a dozen forces try to tear him down. He will not be the man, however, unless we in the United States back him. By backing, I don't mean hesitant, begrudging, slow in assistance.

"India consistently supports Communism against us, and we offer a $200 million wheat grant. Persian usually opposes the Soviets, and we give them only a small loan.

"We should make the same powerful and determined effort we made in Greece, where we took the bit in our teeth with a spirit of whatever the obstacles or problems, we would do what we set out to do. This is the spirit we have lacked here so far. Until we adopt it, the kind of backing we got from the Muslim states on branding the Chinese Communists as aggressors is the kind we have deserved."

I think, unhappily, this forecast what we failed to do.

John T. Mason Jr.: Yes.

Admiral Eller: Now we hurried back to Bahrain via Ras Tanura, because Admiral Carney was coming down for a visit.

John T. Mason Jr.: He was what?

Admiral Eller: He was CinCNELM.[12] He had relieved Conolly some months earlier.

We stopped at Ras Tanura to refuel. While there, we were blasted by a shamal, a wild gale that sweeps over the desert and is a sandstorm over the sea. I had left the flagship at Khorramshahr and flew to Dhahran, because I wanted to go back to Tehran. I had some business with Ambassador Grady. But the plane had engine trouble one night.

The next night we got all the way up to the head of the gulf over Basra, and then swung east only to find the mountains covered with clouds, and storms blocking the two-mile-high passes. And another time we were aborted. So I gave up Tehran in order to

---

12. Admiral Robert B. Carney, USN, served as Commander in Chief U.S. Naval Forces Eastern Atlantic and Mediterranean (CinCNELM) from December 1950 to June 1952.

get ready for Admiral Carney. After talking to the oil people and to Hart, the consul general, I made a last call on Emir Turki, the sub-sheikh for that area. I liked him. We seemed to get on very well. I was not going to be back since my ship wasn't to return to Ras Tanura while I was on board. So I called on him. Afterwards, as the shamal raged, I couldn't get to the ship with my barge, because it couldn't run in the heavy seas. So one of the oil company's tugs took me out to the ship.

As I came on board, there came a truck at the landing. Emir Turki had sent a feast for the crew. It was a half truck loaded with about a dozen bleating sheep, bags of onions, potatoes, and rice for the feast. Well, I was in a dilemma. I got in touch with Hart by radio. He suggested a natural solution. I couldn't turn the gift down, because this is bad taste. So I regretted to Emir Turki very much that because of the conditions of the sea, we couldn't get the provisions on board for some time and we were sailing right away. Therefore, would he, as a favor to me, give a feast for the poor people? Well, of course, this worked.

Admiral Carney arrived about the middle of January on a whirlwind tour of his command, principally the Mediterranean. He inspected the crew and then had a series of conferences and calls with the oilmen and the sheikh and Sir Rupert Hay. We had the usual receptions and dinners all in one day. Then early the next morning, a little after the midwatch, we drove to the British Air Force base north of Bahrain on the little island, Muharraq. It is connected to Bahrain by a causeway.

Admiral Carney's plane had landed there. We took off and flew to northern Saudi Arabia, to Qaisumah, the pumping station 150 miles or so inland from the coast. Despite the busy day, Carney brought his fishing and hunting gear. At Qaisumah, we drove out the pipeline a way and saw the marvelous work they had done laying the pipe. Then he got in one of the oil company's cars and drove into the desert and shot some doves. Joe Bolger, who was also along, took another car, and I went with him and Charlie Buchanan.[13] We drove in the desert, and they ran down a fox, for whom I felt sorry.

John T. Mason Jr.: Well, Carney was always adamant to shoot doves.

---

13. Rear Admiral Joseph F. Bolger, USN; Captain Charles A. Buchanan, USN.

Admiral Eller: Yes, he loves to shoot and loves to fish.

We were to be received by King Ibn Saud that afternoon, late. So we soon flew from Qaisumah down to Riyadh in the desert. We were met and taken to the guest palace. The king's palace itself, the guest palace, and other buildings were grouped inside a walled compound. They were two-story buildings, white and sand brown with crenulated, serrated fringes and flat open roof. Charlie Buchanan and I shared one of the rooms in the guest palace. It had large, cold, and hard ancient European style beds that had seen their day. They were desert-worn. The bathroom was just a barren cement floor with a hole in it. No windows. The door opened on the sandy inner courtyard, where the guards were always banging their guns as they marched around.

John T. Mason Jr.: It had been a former harem, had it not?

Admiral Eller: I don't know.

John T. Mason Jr.: That's what I was told.

Admiral Eller: It could have been. They didn't have very good quarters.

John T. Mason Jr.: No, they didn't.

Admiral Eller: After our call on the King, there would be the sunset prayers. In Moslem time, or in Arabia, anyhow— and I guess it's true in most Moslem countries—12:00 is sunset wherever you are. The day started when the sun rises. At 1700 our time, 10:35 Arab, we called on the King. Her was six feet or more tall, very muscular, and he radiated power. He was quite feeble, in a way, yet seemed powerful. He had a richly furnished majlis, the reception room. We walked the length of the room to greet him and shake his hand, which had a bent finger as a result of one of his battles. The conversation gravitated to the Navy at this reception and later at dinner.

I like the Navy," Ibn Saud said. "I rode in one of your ships once to Great Bitter

Lake to see President Roosevelt. He was a great man and a good friend of Saudi Arabia."[14] Then he showed us a wheelchair and was very proud that Roosevelt had presented it to him. I think he had to use it quite a bit himself then.

He also said, "The Navy is valuable for many reasons. It keeps the enemy far away. It destroys him before he can come to capture your cities. It is satisfied to fight to protect the country, and not to try to take over the government." He was very touchy on this. "The Navy stayed at sea where it belongs. It doesn't try to run the country or fight wars for wars' sake. It is more moderate than the other services. It loves freedom more. It is the Bedouin of the sea."

He himself brought up the Soviets. He didn't trust them. He had refused to build a road to Riyadh since it could facilitate invasion. He did allow a railroad to be built since, he said, a railroad could be broken more easily than a road. From this reception just before the evening prayers, we went out to Crown Prince Saud's summer palace some miles from the city, built with oil money.

Thousands of people thronged the road. I believe a good part of the populace of Riyadh had come out. Prince Saud threw out coins as we passed along. His palace had a swimming pool and flowers with date palms all around, a millionaire's place. He was a tall, big man like his father. When he joined us, he brought his little three-year-old son with him, of whom he was very proud. The Arabs love their children, their boys especially.

When the call came for evening prayers, rugs were carried from the palace out into the desert, and Prince Saud and his brothers and retinue held their prayers on the sand. Afterwards we dined with the King and a number of his sons and officials. It was the longest table I saw in the Middle East, set up to honor Admiral Carney. Along it were at least a dozen whole roasted sheep on mountains of rice with many platters of other food spread over the table: chicken, meatballs, salads, saffron rice, tomatoes, beans, okra, whole chickens, cooked tomatoes, and other trimmings. There were tower-like cakes rising up like a ziggurat. I liked the chicken and the sheep, but not the rancid ghee, the fat

---

14. In February 1945, shortly after the Yalta conference in the Crimea, President Franklin D. Roosevelt met with Saudi Arabia's King Ibn Saud. The meeting was on board the heavy cruiser *Quincy* (CA-71) in the Suez Canal's Great Bitter Lake.

they love. But the King didn't eat much of it. He ate largely bread dipped in broth. He was having stomach trouble.

We first talked about the problems he had uniting the country. He told us of some of his campaigns of which he was most proud. Then he passed from settling the tribes and controlling them, to religion. War, religion, and the welfare of his people animated his mind as they would, naturally, anyone tracing back to Ishmael.

"It is necessary," he said, "that the people of a village worship as well as work together for the common good. You know that, for Christ and Mohammed are similar. We Muslims believe in all the books and prophets of the Bible, though some of them have been changed. Abraham, Moses, and Christ—these are prophets. Mohammed was the last. Some of the books of the Bible have been lost; some have been deliberately changed. Much of it is not exactly as written, but the Koran is unchanged since the day it was written, more than 1,000 years ago. Its language is pure and unchanged from the moment that God gave it to Mohammed as inspiration of His purposes. It is the last and final word of God, the pure word of God, and I intend to keep it so."

As we dined, the king gave some directions, and the servants brought in sour goat milk. He watched our reactions as we tasted it. It was abominable. He questioned us on it. He said, "Doctors claim this is good for your health, especially the belly. This is not true. God alone gives health and ordains man's life."

One of us said, "Well, maybe He gives goat's milk to give man his health."

When this was interpreted to him, he smiled a little bit, which he seldom did. Others at the feast laughed. "No," he said, "it is ordained. At six months before a child is born, an angel comes from the Lord and touches the back of his neck. This determines his life, the length of his days, the quality of his achievements or crimes. Nothing he can do thereafter can change anything. All comes as God wills. This is the truth, and all men must know it." Quite a philosophy, wasn't it?

We went to the majlis after dinner and had the coffee, tea, coffee ceremony, and the incense, and rose water on our hands. He said, "This gives you pleasant dreams." He was in good spirits and in a good humor. Then he brought in one of his younger sons with a grandson, Faisal, age one and a half. The king kissed him and fondled him, and delighted in making the baby do tricks. He was pleased beyond measure when the handsome little fellow held out his hand to Admiral Carney and stayed with him for a moment. Then the King asked an interesting question. He asked, "Do you let your staff and others in the Navy go home to their families occasionally?"

"Yes," Admiral Carney said, "many of them have their families with them, even in foreign lands, like Admiral Bolger and Captain Buchanan."

The King said, "That's good. If it were possible, I would not be away from my family even one day. God made the family to be together. Without a family, man is bankrupt. Nothing else that a man has matters. If he has a family, he needs nothing else."

Ordinarily you were supposed to stay two or three days with the King in order to receive proper hospitality and to show your appreciation. But Carney was on the move and had to go, so the King gave us dispensation.

We turned in early and got up before 6:00. We were supposed to have breakfast in the same room where we had dined. We got to the doors and they were locked. Charlie and I banged on the doors, and finally a sleepy-eyed servant stuck his head out. They had had no idea of fixing breakfast.

Ibn Saud was very firm against alcohol, tobacco, and any other violations of the Koran. Nobody was supposed to smoke or drink. Yet in this large room over against the bulkhead were piles of cigarette butts. After we had banqueted and gone, the servants had held their own feast and somehow had gotten cigarettes. If the King had seen this, which they knew he wouldn't, their heads would have been off.

The night before, we had all received a gift. The most precious one was for Mrs. Carney.

John T. Mason Jr.: According to the rank.

Admiral Eller: According to the rank. Mrs. Carney wasn't with us but was in Bahrain. She had flown there with him. So the King sent her a beautiful matched pearl necklace that must be worth $20,000 or $30,000. They were beautiful. He gave a sword, I believe, to Admiral Carney and to Bolger. And he gave the rest of us one of their gold-sheathed daggers with the sheath turned like a J. Everybody received an outfit of Arab clothes, outer garments and inner garment and the headpiece with the golden cords, which only the royal family is supposed to wear.

John T. Mason Jr.: Yes.

Admiral Eller: We got back to Dhahran early that morning and spent the day there in conferences with the oil people and a trip to the oil field. It was almost midnight when Carney took off for Malta. I then took a plane across to Bahrain, reached the ship toward dawn, and we sailed for Bombay.

The highlight of that visit was similar to previous ones. It was the celebration of India's first anniversary as a republic. This was about 26 January, I believe. It was very picturesque and colorful. After the parade of the troops and the games, the governor general had a reception at his rich palace. It was equally striking and outstanding.

We sailed from Bombay to Karachi, arriving on the first of February. *Duxbury Bay*, relief flagship, came in on the third. Three seaplane tenders rotated as flagship. I think I was the first to have all three, because I stayed longer than my predecessors. The highlight of my trip there, besides the labor of shifting to the new flagship, was a flight up the Indus River and up to the Persian border again.

We now sailed to Bahrain to prepare *Duxbury Bay* for a long journey south. Soon after we got to Bahrain, I flew to Constantinople to join Admiral Carney, where he was holding a conference with the Turkish general staff on the defenses of the Mediterranean and the Middle East. Turkey is the entry to the Middle East. The Turks, like others, wanted more backing from the United States. They felt neglected, though they were furnishing the most useful contingent in Korea. In fact, they spoke about that at one of the conferences.

John T. Mason Jr.: Was CENTO in being at that time?[15]

---

15. CENTO – Central Treaty Organization. Originally known as the Middle East Treaty Organization (METO), it was established in 1955 by the Baghdad Pact as an alliance of Iran, Iraq, Pakistan, Turkey, and the United Kingdom. The United States joined CENTO's military committee in 1958. CENTO was dissolved in 1979, the year Iran seized U.S. embassy personnel as hostages.

Admiral Eller: No, I don't think it was. I think this was part of the arrangement setting it up. This was still in early 1951.

John T. Mason Jr.: Yes.

Admiral Eller: I liked the Turks. They are resolute and tough and determined, and, I believe, reliable. They made it very clear they would resist any aggression, whatever help they got from us. I'm not so sure how they think today, but that was the feeling then.

Carney's flagship *Columbus* came in while we were there. There was a little time outside the conferences, but not much, to make quick trips to the naval and military installations, including the Turkish Naval Academy, and to the Black Sea. In doing this, I saw something of Constantinople's highlights. The Blue Mosque and the sultan's palace, and the city wall remnants were of interest to me in particular. Constantinople—Istanbul—has probably the greatest souk in the world. It spreads out tremendously.

The night the conference ended, I got up in the midwatch once more, this time to catch a plane for Beirut. Meanwhile, *Duxbury Bay* sailed from the Persian Gulf on the long voyage to Ceylon, where I had another conference coming up.

At Beirut I was to join George Colley, who was building the Tapline and in charge of all other construction by the Middle East consortium. He planned to show me the terminus of Tapline coming down to the sea at Tyre and Sidon, and also the pipeline coming in from Iraq for which, I believe, they were increasing the number of lines, or else bringing it to a new terminus.

John T. Mason Jr.: That's the one that went through Kirkuk.

Admiral Eller: That left Kirkuk.

John T. Mason Jr.: Yes.

Admiral Eller: He hadn't arrived when I got to Beirut. We were to meet that evening. Richard Sanger from the legation in Beirut was at the airport and helped me through customs.

While we were going through, some legation people from Damascus were returning to their posts. I told Sanger I wanted to see the roads going out of Beirut inland toward Saudi Arabia and Syria.

He said, "Why don't you go with these people as part of the diplomatic party? That will save days of delay for clearance." Well, I jumped at that, of course. So I rode with them over the snow-capped Lebanese mountains—a beautiful sight—into Damascus.

Damascus is part modern and part ancient. I was shown what was alleged to be the street called Straight, which was still covered over. And still you pass compounds where the camels of a caravan were kept with little alcoves around the compounds, where the people slept. These were the hostels, I suppose.

I returned to Beirut, met Colley, and we stayed at the George Hotel, a superb place. It pains me to see what has happened to Beirut, because it was a little Paris then. The George Hotel sat right on the seacoast, jutting out on the rocks. Our rooms looked over the sea. The moon gleamed on the dark water, and the waves lulled you to sleep. It was a delightful place to stay, although we weren't there much. We drove down to Tyre and Sidon, which were miserable remnants of past glory. The Trans-Arabian Pipeline (Tapline) ended at Sidon.

The next day we drove up to the road of the conquerors through Byblos. You could see the ancient inscriptions on the cliffs as you crossed Dog River. Conquerors going from Egypt north, and from the north towards Egypt, had carved their names and inscriptions on these high cliffs. Byblos is an ancient port with records of commerce with Egypt thousands of years ago. It is claimed that the Bible derived its name from the city, because they made paper out of papyrus at Byblos. I saw papyrus rowing there in a little pool amidst ruins.

We then crossed over the Homs Gap into Syria, past the massive crusaders' castles. We drove to Tripoli where the Iraq pipeline reaches the sea, and also at Banus above Tripoli. Then we drove over the gap into the desert. Crews were working on the pipeline then. They would weld hundreds of feet of pipeline together. A giant machine scraped rust from the pipe, primed it, wrapped it with glass wool, tarred it, and wrapped it with heavy paper. Then it walked behind a huge ditch digger that was digging a ditch, dropped in the pipe, filled the ditch, and started on the next section—a continuous operation astonishing to watch.

John T. Mason Jr.: Who was in charge of this? The French?

Admiral Eller: No, it was a consortium of construction companies, which may have included French ones, but I think they were mostly American. Colley of the Bechtel Corporation was in overall charge. We saw a little bit of Palmyra, an ancient desert empire for a time. Then he said, "There is one thing that you have to see. It is the most impressive ruin I know, and that's Baalbek." So on our way back to Beirut we drove south through the desert and dry hills of Syria into Jordan to Baalbek. This most impressive ruin goes back to the time of the Romans and earlier. I believe the Romans built it to its principal magnificence. It must have existed in early Old Testament times.

John T. Mason Jr.: Yes, because of Baal.

Admiral Eller: But the Romans had made it a shrine to Jupiter. We got there at dark. While we were standing in the temple to Jupiter surrounded by 60-foot-high columns with tremendous carved stones on top, we looked up and there was Jupiter shining through the columns. Hidar, our guide, could have been a Phoenician mariner. He had the same profile and shrewd face that shows on Phoenician coins.

From Beirut I flew down to Colombo. That is a good stopping place this time.

Interview Number 17 with Rear Admiral Ernest M. Eller, U.S. Navy (Retired)
Place: Annapolis, Maryland
Date: Tuesday, 18 December 1979
Interviewer: Dr. John T. Mason, Jr.

John T. Mason Jr.: We broke off as you were preparing to depart from the Eastern Mediterranean to Ceylon.

Admiral Eller: The flagship had sailed south for Ceylon during the Constantinople conference, a long voyage of about two weeks at economical cruising speed.[1] So I flew to Colombo to attend the South Asia and Southeast Asia Conference on military-political affairs.

John T. Mason Jr.: Was this a SEATO thing?

Admiral Eller: I'm not sure that SEATO had been organized.[2] It may have been preliminary to it.

I got to Colombo, which is a very attractive city with broad streets and flowers. It's as hot as Hades and humid in February. I stayed with the naval attaché for a couple of nights until the flagship arrived. She was to furnish the security guards for the conference, which was held in the high mountains of Ceylon, at Nuwara Eliya. I went on board the flagship, collected my papers, and got under way for the conference. It's on a mile-high plateau in the mountains, very beautiful and interesting country en route. There were many cattle and caribou and elephants, and many strange trees such as the Jack tree. The fruit sprouts out of the trunk like warts.

On the way, I stopped a little while to go through the Temple of the Tooth and the botanical gardens, one of the most famous in the world, near Kandy, one of the old capitals of Ceylon. There I saw for the first time, with fascination, cinnamon, nutmeg,

---

1. The Middle East Force flagship was then the small seaplane tender *Duxbury Bay* (AVP-38).
2. The Southeast Asia Treaty Organization (SEATO) was an international organization for the defense of Southeast Asia, formalized by the Manila Pact, signed in September 1954 at Manila in the Philippines.

and other bushes and trees that make our spices and made that such a rich part of the world.

The mountain road was like some of the most breathtaking ones we have in the Blue Ridge or in the Alps. We contested the route all the way up with elephants. You would see them bathing in the streams. They work half a day, then the caretakers give them a halfday off and bathe them. And that's what they love.

John T. Mason Jr.: They must belong to a union.

Admiral Eller: No doubt, the elephant union.

As you get higher up—about 3,000 or 4,000 feet—you pass through tea plantations with heavy-hanging mists and clouds over the mountain peaks. It looks very much like Scotland. And the sea glistens far below. It's a spectacular island as you get up into the mountains that rise abruptly. It's a large island, but in a straight line it's still not too far from the seacoast to the mountain peaks. Nuwara Eliya was something of a summer capital, a mountain paradise. We stayed at the Grand Hotel, a large rambling, old building, very comfortable.

The attendees were ambassadors, or their first or second in missions, from most of the countries of the area—from Indochina around to Iran. I guess there were about 20 countries represented. Some also sent their naval and military attachés. I was the sole Defense Department representative. The head of the conference was Loy Henderson, ambassador to India, who was one of the handful of most distinguished and able men I've seen in our country. We became friends and kept in touch for many years.

Ambassador Joe Satterthwaite was there from Ceylon, a very nice gentleman, and Ambassador Avra Warren from Pakistan.[3] There were two members I'd known at the National War College, and ran into all over the Middle East, it seems. One was Art Richards from Tehran, and the other, Ed Gullion from Saigon.[4] It was an outstanding conference with sound thinking and hardheaded men leading it.

---

3. Joseph C. Satterthwaite was U.S. Ambassador to Ceylon from November 1949 to July 1953. Avra M. Warren was U.S. Ambassador to Pakistan from February 1950 to November 1952.
4. Arthur Richards was deputy chief of mission in Tehran, Iran. Edmund A. Gullion held senior positions in the U.S. embassy in Saigon from 1949 to 1952.

John T. Mason Jr.: What was the theme?

Admiral Eller: The theme was what to do about South Asia in peace or war—our interest in, and the political military importance of South Asia and Southeast Asia.

I was conference leader for what, I think, was in many ways, the most important subject taken up, because it dealt with something very practical and hard: what we were going to do about the United States strategic interests in South Asia? I gave two talks and headed this conference and made a report on it. Here is a little from one of my talks:

"The United States, on the whole, has tended to leave this quarter of the world blank in its thinking. That we have retained some military interest is due, in part, to certain military air bases, to the availability of ground forces in Pakistan, and to the fact that the seas of the world dominate the area. Ships can travel freely and operate so satisfactorily from remote bases that the U.S. Navy has been able to maintain our small force here from bases in the United States.

"The trend of growing interest in South Asia during this past year has been encouraging. This has occurred in several fields, including military thinking, where there is an increasing realization that this is the last great area of the world open to us to take a positive stand." [Unhappily, we haven't in the generation since then.]

"It is there where the balance of world power may be overthrown. It is an area, however small or great its importance now, that will certainly be a powerful factor in the future.

"The current emergency has demonstrated that we may need at least a portion of the oil of the Middle East in case of war, as we need it now for current buildup. We are beginning to think about developing plans for, at least, a part of the Middle East area. Perhaps the most important step in our actions has been the beginning of the shift in our thinking concerning this area as the sole responsibility of the British. We begin to understand the importance of its raw materials, of its strategic position in providing operating bases, especially air and naval, including protection of oil from the Persian Gulf, of its large population, which provides today some military forces, and a large reservoir of other manpower, its control of communications between the Far East and Europe.

"However far removed this region appears to be from the front lines today, in this generation if the Soviets can affect it—and certainly in the next—South Asia will certainly play a major role in our destiny. I'm encouraged that conferences like this may ensure that it is a favorable role." I'm not so sure now, nearly 30 years later. I might read a couple of the many recommendations in my report:

"The most effective military defense of this area will be provided by strong flanks, which on the west would include Pakistan. Therefore, our principal effort should be to strengthen these flanks, both militarily and with emphasis in the east on Indochina and in the west on Pakistan, Iran, and Turkey.

"Pakistan can provide important ground forces now, either directly in South Asia or to the Middle Eastern flank, provided the Kashmir question is settled. It would be useful to the United States and the United Kingdom to bring about an early buildup of Pakistani ground forces in which we would assist by providing military equipment. This policy would require a settlement of the Kashmir question.

"Unless her foreign policy changes, India will not give the Free World military assistance. In the event of war, she will initially probably attempt to posture neutrality. If her policies should change prior to the war, it would be useful to provide military aid to India. She has a great deal to offer to the world: her military potential, her raw materials, her industrial output, manpower, and communications can be developed for us.

"Ceylon and Pakistan contain a number of bases, particularly air and naval, which can make an important contribution to allied military operations at the outset of war. It is recommended that we take every feasible military and political step to build up the strength of the east and west flanks of South Asia, which for the short term, can be best effected by increasing military strength in Indochina and Iran, Pakistan and Turkey."

We did that for a while, and now we're just going against our very best interests.

John T. Mason Jr.: We've lost practically every one of those.

Admiral Eller: We've lost practically every one, and that's all happened in the last few years, unhappily.

John T. Mason Jr.: Those papers eventually will be in the Naval Historical Center, will they not?

Admiral Eller: Yes. If they can handle them. I've got so many.

From Nuwara Eliya, coming down the mountain, one little scene I saw on the way shows the benefit of discipline. There was a group of elephants having an education class, I guess. They were handling trees. One little youngster about a year old was malingering. He wasn't doing much. So a big bull elephant came along and whacked him on the stern with his trunk, and immediately the young fellow got to work.

I joined the ship in Colombo in mid–afternoon, and we sailed within a few minutes. We rounded Ceylon during the night on a two-day trip up to Madras. I had sought permission to go to the French enclave of Pondicherry, but India objected.

John T. Mason Jr.: Was Trincomalee a base at that point?

Admiral Eller: Yes, the British were still using it. We came back by there, as I'll mention.

We went to Madras, an ancient city. As you know, by legend, and perhaps by fact, St. Thomas went there and was martyred there in A.D. 68. They have the St. Thomas Mount, and St. Thomas Cathedral to commemorate him. It's a Catholic church.

John T. Mason Jr.: Well, it's not Roman Catholic. It's Middle Eastern—branch of Christianity under a Metropolitan. Or at least it used to be under the Metropolitan of Jerusalem.

Admiral Eller: Oh, it fell under the Metropolitan of Jerusalem?

John T. Mason Jr.: Yes.

Admiral Eller: I saw it, but didn't learn much about it, obviously.

John T. Mason Jr.: There were at least a million Christians out there on the coast.

Admiral Eller: Yes. The country was suffering at that time badly from drought. They had had four years of low rainfall, and it was almost semi-desert. Madras was an interesting city. The old part of it had beautiful architecture, trees, and flowers. But once you got out into the country, it was tragic.

Madras has the tomb of Elihu Yale, who was born in Boston. While he was governor of St. George in Madras, he made contributions and supported the beginning of Yale that was named after him.

I went into the country to Conjeevaram, the "Golden City of a Thousand Temples," where Clive won one of his famous battles. He had gone out as a youngster in the East India Company. Immediately troubles had developed, and he had shown his military genius and became the most famed man in the area.

The British had planted trees along all the roads. Now most were dead or dying, because the poor people had ringed them to get firewood. The people themselves looked like they were also dying. The arms of the women and children, I don't believe, were more than an inch or an inch-and-a-half in diameter. There was no flesh on them at all, only skin and bones. They still maintained their temples, though, their heathen temples--some over 1,000 years old. In several of them were gigantic juggernauts, which must be bigger than our biggest trucks—huge, two-wheeled vehicles under tall straw cones. Strange looking superstructure of straw.

In the Temple of Shiva there was a huge elephant waving his trunk as people came in and out to worship their gods.

John T. Mason Jr.: These were Hindus?

Admiral Eller: Yes, and the crash of gongs and the beat of drums. It was just as if they had gone back to ancient heathenism.

Then on the way back we came by one of the wonders of the world, a place called the Seven Pagodas. It spreads over acres along the coast, and part of it is submerged in the sea. There is a tremendous amount of carving, people and animals and gods carved out of the rock. There were also many poor, emaciated people, scarcely alive—a sad and sickening sight. They crowded around us with their claw-like hands and gaunt faces begging madly. It's an almost impossible situation for India to handle this tremendous mass of people unless they can control the population growth.

The governor of the state had been an independent prince and also in the navy. He was Commodore Sir Krishna Kumarsinhji Bhavsinhji.[5] He had ruled one of the northern principalities. They had moved him down to be governor of Madras state, which is two or three times as big as North Carolina, for example, or Virginia, and had a population of 50 million people—over a third of the population of the United States at the time.

His house was every contrast to the people in the streets. It was palatial, filled with stairways, carvings, rich ornaments, carvings on the stairway. It could have been a museum in itself. I suppose it had been the home of the British governor of Madras. As usual during a port visit, I had a press conference. That was one of the places it was reported in the Soviet press. A clipping from there reported my saying, "This area is of interest to both the United States and the Soviet Union. It is a very important area of the world. And the Soviet Union has a weak navy, and, therefore, cannot trouble them much at the time." I wouldn't say that now, but it was true at the time. That's nearly 30 years ago; today Soviet ships roam the area.

One of the nice things we were always able to do for the crew was to arrange softball games and other athletic activities with the local Americans, and British. So it was an especially interesting place for the crew. In fact, it was the first time any ship of the Middle East force had visited Madras. I think I was the first one to round the coast.

We next called at Trincomalee, which is on the northeast coast of Ceylon—Sri Lanka now.[6] It's one of the finest natural harbors in the world, a huge one. It could take most of the fleets of the world at the same time. It could be the most important naval base in all of South Asia, because it's right on the vital oil route between the Pacific and the Persian Gulf.

Ambassador Joseph E. Satterthwaite came over from Colombo to be there during my visit. Vice Admiral Geoffrey Oliver, commander of the British East India Force, was based at Trincomalee. He took me around the base that had been developed extensively during World War II and was then in partial upkeep. I think he had eight ships, a cruiser

---

5. Krishna Kumarsinhji Bhavsinhji was the first Indian Governor of Madras from 1948 to 1952. He was an honorary commodore in the Indian Navy.
6. Under British rule the island of Ceylon had dominion status; it 1972 the country ceased being a dominion and became a republic known as Sri Lanka.

and several destroyers and corvettes. Then he had the Persian Gulf force that stayed in the gulf.

We were there three or four days. One night he had us for dinner. It was the first and only time I saw an Indian magician. He did a number of tricks, such as charming a deadly, hooded cobra, which I wouldn't think would be a very long-lived profession. Then he made a mango tree grow out of the dust. I still have some of the leaves, and how he did it, I can never tell. He also had a rope climb up in the air by itself.

Satterthwaite took me one day into the island to talk privately and to see some of the spectacular ruins. Ceylon, like South India and Southeast Asia, must have had a very great culture thousands of years ago and immense energy was expended in building temples and monuments. One of the largest carved statues I've seen was of Buddha at Polonnaruwa. I'll let you look at this. I kept it just to show you the carving. I think he's 40 feet high. And he was much better than their later carvings, which became very grotesque. The site had a number of temples, palaces, structures of every sort, and immense carvings. It became the capital of Ceylon in the 8th century. There are three statues like that at Polonnaruwa of Buddha sitting, reclining, and standing.

Another place that interested me was a most difficult and exciting climb. This was Sigiriya. A prince killed his brother, hoping to be king, and fled to the top of this almost unscalable mountain. It is just bare rock. We had to go on a narrow ledge around the bend of it to get part way up, passing the hazards of swarms of wild bees. At one point on the narrow ledge, a niche had been carved in the rock for a cage so that if they attacked and you didn't fall down the cliff, you could get in the cage until they departed. From there we climbed up just bare toeholds and handholds to the top of the mountain. The murderer fled there with his followers, built a palace refuge, and held it for a year before he finally died.

From Trincomalee we sailed around Ceylon up to Cochin on the southeast Malabar Coast of India. That's where the Indians had established their naval base and naval college, which had been at Karachi before the partition. It's a very ancient port. It was there in the Old Testament period and was one of the communicating links between the Persian Gulf or Red Sea on the other side of Arabia and China.

The first explorers from Europe, the Portuguese, came to the Malabar Coast in the late 1400s. Vasco de Gama has a memorial slab there, where he was first buried. The body was removed and taken to Lisbon. There was a St. Francis church, San Francisco, built by the Portuguese in the 1500s. I inspected the naval base and the schools, and then the Paradise Synagogue, which the naval commander of Cochin insisted I see. It's antecedents trace back more than 2,000 years. By legend, the first Jewish people came to this coast after being freed from Babylon. This was by Cyrus, wasn't it?

John T. Mason Jr.: Yes, Cyrus the Great.

Admiral Eller: The synagogue had a copper plate dated 379 A.D., of which the rabbis were very proud. It was a deed to land one of the local princes had given them. I have a tracing of it. The sector around the old synagogue is filled with people that look like Spaniards: long, hooked noses, red hair, tall. They must have come down during the Spanish Inquisition. Their Old Testament scrolls interested me very much. Written as they were originally, they are huge scrolls kept in gold-encrusted cases and in a safe along with the copper plate.

I took one day to go up into the tea country. We had an Indian driver. I wouldn't drive there under any circumstances, because the streets were packed with people. It's like Annapolis at the waterfront on a weekend. They filled the streets, a living tide. The driver drove madly, blowing his horn, and they would scatter just at the last minute as he hurtled through them. The mountains that are close inland to Cochin show a dreadful devastation. They had been heavily forested. When the heavy monsoon rains come, there is plenty of moisture, and the trees hold it in the ground. In the short time since the British had left, the Indians had cut them away completely. It will take no time, unless they remedy it, to become just barren, eroded mountains, like those in Iran. When the monsoon rains hit, they come with great force.

At about the 4,000-foot level, we came to the tea plantation country. It looks much like Scotland, a broad hilly plateau with higher peaks above it. Women were picking the tealeaves. It's all done by hand. They have to be experienced so as to know which leaves are to be put in which bag to get the quality that certain of the leaves give.

John T. Mason Jr.: It's interesting that the selectivity is right there.

Admiral Eller: Yes. The plateau, where the Scotch manager lived, was just a beautiful, green, rolling country, completely unlike what I'd seen on the opposite side at Madras.

From Cochin we headed for the Persian Gulf. On the long voyage, I had time to redo all my war plans and finish my reports. It was a very relaxing period for the first time in months.

Admiral Freddy Boone was to visit us almost as quick as we got there. He had just become Carney's new chief of staff, relieving Joe Bolger.[7] He arrived for indoctrination on Great Sabbath. We interrupted calls and visits to the oil fields of Saudi Arabia and Bahrain for two Easter services. We held the first one in HMS *Wild Goose*, flagship of Captain A. H. Wallis of the British Persian Gulf Force; then an hour later, one in my flagship. On Easter Monday, Boone departed, and we sailed for Kuwait.

About this time one of the tragic things for the world happened when General Razmara, the Prime Minister of Iran, of whom I thought so much, was assassinated. That's when Mosaddegh came in as Prime Minister.[8] And exactly the same situation occurred in Iran then as when our present Ayatollah Khomeini took over. Mosaddegh was a wild fanatic. He was a lawyer, I believe, one of the wealthy landholders who were very unhappy about the Shah's taking their land for the peasant, although they were remunerated. He soon took over the British oil fields and other property of the Anglo-Iranian Oil Company.

For months thereafter, there was tension between Britain and Iran, a diplomatic struggle, the threat of British forces coming in to try to take back Abadan, the big refinery, and the oilfields. I don't think the issue was finally settled until Mosaddegh was ousted some months later by the military of Iran. And, hopefully, the same thing can happen to the present fanatic.

We got to Kuwait just a day before Rear Admiral Don Felt flew in to relieve me.[9] We had several busy days there introducing him to the top people: the ruler; the British political agent, Cal Dixon; the oil executives; reviewing war plans and many

---

7. Rear Admiral Walter F. Boone, USN.
8. Mohammed Mosaddegh was the elected Prime Minister of Iran from 1951 to 1953. The U.S. Central Intelligence Agency was involved in a coup that overthrew his government. At that time the Shah became the head of the Iranian Government.
9. Rear Admiral H. D. Felt, USN, served as Commander Middle East Force from May to October 1951. The oral history of Felt, who retired as a four-star admiral, is in the Naval Institute collection.

other matters. We held the change of command ceremony on 2 May. To conclude on the Middle East, I'll read a short extract from a letter I wrote that day:

"The world situation is little different today in the spring of 1951 than in the spring of 1950, just before Korea. Then, however, it was impossible to get our government interested in, or disturbed about, the U.S.S.R.'s growing military strength. Even though the Soviets had most clearly stated what they intended to do, we progressively cut back military strength. Anyone trying to get it increased was a warmonger trying to ruin the country economically. Today we are far better off than a year ago. We're much nearer to readiness to meet Soviet aggression in mind, in material preparation, and in organization. If our leaders will not swing back to the other extreme when this crisis wanes, if they will maintain our strength, we shall probably avert major war."

The more things change, the more they stay the same. Witness our decline in recent years.

I flew back by London and stayed several days there being debriefed. Admiral Carney took me out to their house in Virginia Water. He and Mrs. Carney lived in London during the week in their apartment. It was the first time I had been with the two of them alone for an extended period. During the drive, and in the evening when he played his banjo, his spontaneous remarks kept not only me laughing, but kept her laughing also—true spontaneous wit.

From London I flew to the Burtonwood-Lancashire Air Base, and thence to Iceland. On the way I asked the pilot to fly low over Barra, where the McNeils came from.

John T. Mason Jr.: Came from where?

Admiral Eller: The island of Barra, the outermost island in the Western Hebrides, a low, bleak island, storm-beaten by the Atlantic. There is nothing between it and the continent of North America. It's cold and drizzly. You can see why my ancestors left. Why they stayed initially, I don't know. We landed in Iceland for refueling. And it's another bleak and barren land, with the smoke of geysers and steam escaping from the underground heat. We arrived at Newfoundland at midnight, landing in high winds, blustery and cold, a somber and unappealing place to stay. We left early the next morning and got to Washington in the afternoon.

I had several days of debriefing and a few happy days at home. During this time, at the editor's request, I wrote an *Americana Encyclopedia* article on "The History of Guns, Land, and Naval." And made preparation to take command of the fine cruiser *Albany*, which Admiral Sherman had arranged.

One of the amusements, as my short leave ended, was the Gridiron Club. The club had, I think, canceled the usual annual, clever show spoofing the government the first year of the Korean War, and this year too—1951. Instead, they presented excerpts from their previous entertainments. This happened to be the Sunday afternoon before I joined *Albany* at Norfolk. Agnes and I attended with Jim Wright of the *Buffalo Evening News*. As usual, it was delightful. Of course, they cleverly panned Truman, as they always do the President at a Gridiron dinner, where he is the principal guest.

Happily, we still had the little seaplane base at the experimental station, the naval station across from the academy, site of our Navy's first air station. An amphibian flew to Norfolk every Monday morning on a regular schedule. I was able to get passage, the easiest way I've ever had of getting to Norfolk.

Captain John H. Sides, a classmate, commanded *Albany*.[10] We held the change of command ceremony the next day. In my talk to the crew at the ceremony, as in all talks to them, I tried to build pride in themselves and understanding of the importance of their service to the country in the finest ship in the Navy.

John T. Mason Jr.: She was a heavy cruiser?

Admiral Eller: Yes.

John T. Mason Jr.: With 8-inch guns?

Admiral Eller: With 8-inch guns then. Years later guided missiles replaced them, which made her look like an ugly duckling. But she was a beautiful ship then, number CA-123.[11]

John T. Mason Jr.: And the date was the 14th of May?

Admiral Eller: The 15th that I actually relieved, less than two weeks since leaving the Middle East. I told them I was proud to be in this fine ship. She had had a distinguished career as a flagship for years and was then Holloway's flagship, though he rode a battleship on our first cruise.[12] I told them it was a good ship because of them, because of their industry and their initiative, their devotion to duty, and their good conduct, and I hoped they would keep it that way. I believe they did. I also emphasized the grave world situation then in the middle of the Korean War. The fleet was essential to the country, and their service to the fleet made them particularly important.

We had a short time to get ready for the midshipmen's cruise. At my request, Admiral Holloway assigned the squadron's radio-controlled drone detachment to *Albany* on board. The drones were radio-controlled planes about 12 feet long and almost the same wingspan, with a speed of 180 knots, making them good antiaircraft targets. We had the control party on board and were able to use the drones all during the cruise, not only for ourselves, but for the other ships, of course. As a consequence, we stood one in AA all my time in *Albany*.[13] The drones could be recovered. They had a parachute that lowered them to the water. As long as you could see the drone, you could direct it, maneuver it against antiaircraft fire. Even if damaged, it was easy to repair—just canvas and a little wire. We had several of them in case of losses.

John T. Mason Jr.: You say this ship was used for a midshipmen's cruise that summer?

---

10. Captain John H. Sides, USN, commanded the *Albany* (CA-123) from June 1950 to May 1951.
11. USS *Albany* was commissioned as a heavy cruiser (CA-123) on 15 June 1946. She had a standard displacement of 13,700 tons, was 673 feet long, 71 feet in the beam, and had a draft of 21 feet. Her top speed was 33 knots. She was armed with nine 8-inch main battery guns and twelve 5-inch dual-purpose guns. The ship was subsequently decommissioned in June 1958 for conversion to a guided missile cruiser.
12. Rear Admiral James L. Holloway Jr., USN, served as Commander Battleship-Cruiser Force Atlantic Fleet, 1950–53.
13. AA – antiaircraft.

Admiral Eller: Yes. That summer we had *Albany*, *Wisconsin*, and *Missouri*—the three heavy ships—and had a number of destroyers, destroyer escorts, and minelayers. Each one carried some midshipmen.

John T. Mason Jr.: Quite a flotilla.

Admiral Eller: It was. We crossed the Atlantic as a group, training as a single task force. After rounding the Orkneys and entering the North Sea, we split up into three forces. One went to Copenhagen, which I had, one to Oslo, and one to Edinburgh.

John T. Mason Jr.: So as not to overwhelm the hospitality of the ports.

Admiral Eller: Yes, and also, to give a chance to visit more countries. Each group visited two ports. My second one was Rotterdam. One of the others went to Lisbon and one to Cherbourg. So we went to a number of different countries, a good diplomatic gesture.

John T. Mason Jr.: How many midshipmen did you accommodate on the USS *Albany*?

Admiral Eller: I could have accommodated more than I took, which was between 400 and 500; the battleships carried more and the smaller warships fewer. We had the youngster class and maybe the first class.

John T. Mason Jr.: Yes, those two classes because the other class had aviation summer.

Admiral Eller: Aviation, submarine and so on for the second class; the new plebes stayed at the academy. In addition to the midshipmen from the academy, we also had ROTC midshipmen.[14] We came to Annapolis the end of May, and on 2 June, which was Saturday, we embarked the midshipmen. On 4 June, we got under way to cross the Atlantic.

I've always been very much interested in leadership and training. I prepared these

---

14. ROTC – reserve officers' training corps.

two documents very carefully in the time that we had getting ready for the cruise. I'll read a short extract from each one. These are thick documents, but I won't read much. On the cover sheet of leadership—

John T. Mason Jr.: Was this distributed to the midshipmen?

Admiral Eller: No, to all the officers. The emphasis on all my ships—and I kept after it—was that this cruise was to train the midshipmen, to make them officers. Every person on board, officers and enlisted men, was responsible to help in the training. We had very good results.

"As we enter the midshipmen cruise with the mission of helping to shape and train our future officers, I can think of nothing more important than that we give them on board *Albany* a fine example. We have a splendid ship, clean, efficient, taut, well run. We have a fine crew. In you officers I have already noted the qualities of leadership that make this a top-notch ship. Therefore, I am sure that you who may not have seen the enclosure, will be happy to have it to help you become an even better leader.

"In reading the document, which came out in the latter days of the Pacific War, you will find a number of profound observations on leadership. If I had to single out the top ones, I would set down the following: "First, high example; second, thorough knowledge and preparation; third, driving will and energy to accomplish a goal; fourth, constant attention to the welfare of subordinates; fifth, pride in ship and pride in the Navy; sixth, a spirit of teamwork; seventh, a can-do attitude that seeks to solve a problem instead of finding difficulties and why it can't be done."

Then from one of several documents on training: "In peace or war, our primary mission is training. In conducting it, officers and petty officers inevitably not only shape the Navy for the future, but leave their mark on the lives of subordinates. With that responsibility in mind, you should take every opportunity to improve yourself, not only in performance of duty, but as an instructor. Some of the essential elements of teaching and learning are set forth here to assist us in *Albany* to improve our techniques of training.

"Training problems can be more easily understood if you keep in mind that any instructor must be a leader in all senses of the word. You are dealing with human beings who respond to example and wise direction. Your job is threefold. Not only must you pass on skill and knowledge, but you must develop certain attitudes in the students. Some are: pride and enthusiasm in the Navy, respect for authority, willingness to accept responsibility, ingenuity, drive, and determination to do a job well. These attitudes are taught primarily by example. You must be a good example, enthusiastic about your subject, and be a true leader by your appearance and actions, causing your men to respect authority and to develop pride. Treat all men equally. Give credit for achievement by pointing out work well done. Praise honest effort. Let each know that you are interested in his progress. If necessary, give reproof, but give praise for any good you can find. Most men want to learn. You must convince them that you have knowledge to impart that will be worth their while to learn. Interest, the desire to learn, is a major factor in learning.

"Men like to take part in the teaching-learning process. When they learn, they want others to know about it. They get great satisfaction out of supplying the correct answer to a question. Let them do more talking than you and more showing and more use of the hands."

Then I noted four ways to teach. Teaching by telling. First by doing it, then by telling them about it, then by letting them do it, and then by repetition of the example.

"Teaching by telling is the poorest of all and should be used only when conditions make it impossible to add showing and doing. Telling ain't teaching and listening ain't learning."

Then on another memo to the officer of the deck, I insisted that although his first duties were to operate the ship safely and correctly, he should ensure that the midshipmen on the watch keep busy continuously.

"Some of the duties they should carry out are: frequently check position by stadimeter, compass, and radar; work maneuvering board on all contacts and information changes; conduct maneuvering board tactical exercises drill; let each midshipman handle the deck; hold combined signal, tactical drills; instruct midshipmen in navigation and require them to fix and keep the position of the ship."

This was done pretty effectively on the cruise. I think it was the finest cruise I've ever been on, not only my own midshipman cruises, but also one while I taught at the academy.

John T. Mason Jr.: And now with the present system, it isn't possible to do this.

Admiral Eller: No. I think the summer cruises were a tremendous asset to our training. The best education I received was plebe summer, because you studied what you were supposed to learn the night before. And then the next day you did it. You were corrected if you didn't do it right, and you kept doing it until you did it right. You were busy all the time. And the next best training was the midshipmen's cruise.

Foul weather plagued our transit. Strong winds struck the second day out—45 to 50 knots and very high seas. I had the chief engineer list special precautions, and the under heads of the departments for the midshipmen observed and learned from it. Admiral Holloway kept us busy with tactical exercises all the way across. We cruised at about 12 knots, so we had plenty of time—nearly three weeks at sea—as we had when I was a midshipman. You had plenty of time to get to know the sea, and to know the ship, and to know your jobs.

When we got into the North Sea, as I mentioned, we divided into three groups. I took *Albany* and three destroyer minelayers, DMs, into Copenhagen. I was the senior officer in the group, in command of what was going on. Before our cruise, the naval attachés in Copenhagen and Rotterdam had made excellent arrangements.

In Copenhagen, Captain Bob Lockhart had arranged with the Danish CNO for a joint exercise with *Albany* and our three DMs, starting in the Skagerrak.[15] This was artificial to some degree in that I was limited in the area for maneuvering the force, but it was still a good-sized area, 60 by 120 miles. I had to be on a prescribed course and speed, although I could maneuver to avoid contact. I was to meet night attack by aircraft and torpedo boats, although they could pick me up in the day or late afternoon. The exercise started about 6:00.

Of course, in the summer it never gets dark there until about midnight. So we really had no night cover. Our plan was to send out a picket destroyer as a decoy. The airplane picked us up all right, but we shot it down according to the umpire after he had picked us up. But he must have gotten the report in, and the motor torpedo boats came out, but they were detected. They saw the destroyer and went after it. And meanwhile, we

---

15. Captain Robert G. Lockhart, USN.

had picked them up on our radar. We were able to evade their first attack, and, theoretically, again to destroy them before they could get in torpedo range. They realized that had happened and asked for a repeat, which we did without trying to evade them. Holloway was quite pleased, as were we. He wrote: "The *Albany*'s outstanding target designation and acquisition procedure on radar enabled her to acquire and lock on the air attack at 2,000 yards. The ability to identify and bring under fire the motor torpedo boats at a range outside of torpedo-effective range indicates excellent liaison between CIC and gunnery. The stationing of the radar picket for early warning and as a decoy proved effective. The commanding officer of the USS *Albany* displayed excellent ability and judgment in organizing and deploying his assigned forces. Employing imagination and enterprise were evident in the manner of entering into the spirit of the exercise despite limitations imposed by weather and artificialities."

We had a most pleasant visit in Copenhagen. On the way in we passed Elsinore and Kronborg Castle of Hamlet fame. As usual, on this trip, and in the Middle East for that matter, there was a press conference almost as soon as we tied up. I didn't get any sleep that night to amount to anything because of the exercise and conning the group through the Skagerrak and the Kattegat. Then we had calls most of the day and exchanged calls.

I liked, especially, Vice Admiral A. H. Vedel, the Chief of Naval Operations then, and for many years afterward, like Ruge in Germany.[16] He was a very fine man, smallish in stature, but large in mind. We became friends and stayed friends until he died. Like many well educated Europeans, he had a hobby in which he had become quite well known. He was one of the most noted botanists in Scandinavia. In his garden, which wasn't large, were many strange plants he had picked up in his travels over the world and had been given to him by the horticultural societies, because they respected his ability to take care of them. In fact, he showed me one tree of which there were only a handful of seeds brought back to Europe of the oldest known tree in existence, which they found in inland China up in the Tibet area. It's a conifer and is supposed to antedate the sequoia in origin. He had it growing very successfully.

---

16. Vice Admiral Aage Helgesen Vedel was Commander in Chief Royal Danish Navy. From 1950 to 1961 Vice Admiral Friedrich Ruge held the post of Inspector of the Navy, analogous to Chief of Naval Operations of the Federal German Navy

After the calls that day, we had a critique on Tivoli attended by most of the senior officers of the Danish Navy. They were very much pleased with our operations with them. The ambassador was a lovely lady named Mrs. Eugenie Anderson.[17] I was never much in favor of putting women in as ambassadors, but she certainly charmed the Danes.

John T. Mason Jr.: She was from Minnesota.

Admiral Eller: They wrote Ambassador and Mr. John Anderson in formal social language.

One of the most thoughtful gestures that I've seen anywhere was the Lord Mayor's reception at the city hall for the crew. He gave two of them for starboard and port liberty parties. They were very nice occasions. Of course, there were the usual rounds of luncheons and receptions. I gave one in each port the last day before sailing to thank the people for their courtesies. We had a most successful visit. I spoke to the crew as I did in each port, there and subsequently, on being a true representative, the only representation of the Navy that some of these people would ever see. They would get their impressions of the Navy from them for the rest of their lives. We had a fine ship, and they were a fine crew. And they should maintain the reputation.

We kept a list by month of liberty violations. Any division that had no violations was given extra liberty in the next port. In Copenhagen we had practically no trouble at all. The chief of police and the mayor said that in 20 years of their memory, no crew had acted as well as *Albany*'s. Mrs. Ambassador said, "Three thousand ambassadors of good will." And Admiral Holloway sent us a well-done dispatch.

John T. Mason Jr.: Now for purposes of this cruise, the crew of *Albany* was reduced somewhat, was it not?

Admiral Eller: Yes, somewhat. Most through sending men to schools.

John T. Mason Jr.: And then got them back again.

---

17. Helen Eugenie Moore Anderson was the first woman in U.S. history to be appointed chief of mission and ambassador. She served as ambassador to Denmark from 1949 to 1953.

Admiral Eller: Hopefully. Somebody else might grab them.

Our trip to Rotterdam, through fog and storm, was one of the wildest of my experiences. I've never had quite a night as the last night going in. En route, our DMs left us and went to another group, and we picked up a group of destroyers in the middle of the North Sea coming down from Edinburgh. It was typically misty as we passed through the waters of Jutland—foggy, heavy traffic.[18] The fog closed thickly, but we made contact with the destroyers just at the time designated, about noon. Then the weather, which was already foul, got fouler.

The North Sea and the English Channel still had extensive minefields that hadn't been swept. There were swept channels that had to be carefully followed. The one leading into Rotterdam must have run for 150 miles or so. We entered it at dusk in a thick fog, cold, rain, and a high wind that chilled to the bond. I've never been colder than I was in the North Sea that June. We couldn't see anything. We had to navigate by radar, and there was an occasional buoy that, hopefully, we would pick up and not get out of the channel.

We drove on all night. I wanted to make our arrival time. The destroyers wanted to slow down. They couldn't stand it. I had set 17 knots in order to get there on schedule. So I put them astern and let them get what protection they could from our wake, which was considerable. And we went on at 17 knots, and finally made it the next morning with everybody on the bridge frozen and sleepless. The entrance into the harbor was about the worst entrance I've ever experienced in any harbor. This is one of the mouths of the Rhine. It looked to me as if 10,000 vessels were coming and going. Many of those coming down were tugs towing barges, and they would hurry on at full speed, even though you were turning. You had to get out of their way, and at the same time, stay clear of those speeding upstream in the crowded harbor. We had to turn before going alongside our pier. So we turned with these ships coming at us. I got more gray hair that day, I think, than at any other time in handling a ship.

We had the usual calls and sports and recreation for the crew. I had met Admiral E. J. Van Holthe, the Chief of Naval Operations, as I had Admiral Vedel for that matter, when

---

18. The Battle of Jutland was the most significant naval engagement of World War I. Fought between the British Grand Fleet and the German High Seas Fleet, it took place 31 May 1916 in the North Sea, off the coast of Denmark. The British lost more ships in the battle but scored a strategic victory by maintaining control of the seas.

overseas with the Joint Chiefs setting up of the military side of NATO.[19] The Dutch were always very hospitable, doubly so this time. I forgot to mention that Admiral Holloway flew in for one day with me at Copenhagen, had a lunch for the top people, then flew out the same day. Again this time, he flew into Rotterdam, made his calls, had a lunch for the notables and then flew to join one of the other ships.

We sailed again with excellent performance ashore. The chief of police, who is a key figure, reported, "This is the best of any visiting squadron in my experience." The reason always is, I think, twofold: the officials ashore and your own people. We had excellent cooperation of the police there as in Copenhagen. We always carefully selected our shore patrol. We had this intensive indoctrination that I mentioned on the need to set an example and to hold up the good name of *Albany* and the Navy.

Then we also tried to make the port interesting, both with athletic events and tours. I would give them little talks. The chaplain and others wrote articles in the ship's paper. Then we put out tour information for individuals to carry with them. As a result, there was a great deal of traveling by the crew, which pleased me. And as I mentioned, we gave them a reward wherever a division was outstanding and urged the men to take care of their shipmates. Holloway sent us another fine dispatch of congratulations on exemplary conduct. "You have maintained the prestige and good will of the United States among the fine people of Denmark and Rotterdam."

From Rotterdam we sailed down the English Channel and joined up with the Cherbourg force and later the Lisbon force. We crossed the North Atlantic at 10 to 12 knots. The slow passage gave time for constant drills and exercises with the other ships, and maneuvers, and other midshipmen training, particularly in gunnery.

John T. Mason Jr.: That was the purpose of the extended trip?

Admiral Eller: Yes, that was the purpose. Training went on day and night. Even when we didn't have a special night exercise like general quarters at 3:00 or 4:00 in the morning, those on watch, and often others, continued day training through the night. The drones we carried were in demand all across. Going over and coming back we frequently refueled. The heavy ships usually refueled the destroyers and other lighter ships, though our tankers did

---

19. Vice Admiral Jonkheer E. J. Van Holthe, Commander in Chief/ Chief of Naval Staff, Netherlands Navy.

at times. In one complicated exercise off the Azores, *Albany* re-provisioned from *Missouri* on one side and on the other side refueled from *Elkomin*, our tanker. Holloway was pleased with that. He said, "Beautifully executed, a source of pride and inspiration for all hands." When you did anything right, he promptly told you. If you did wrong, he told you also, but in a very elegant way.

That's the first time, I think, I'd been in the Sargasso Sea. There it was, much as you might read in the Ancient Mariner. There was the drifting seaweed, great masses of seaweed, like islands almost. There were drifting timbers, parts of ships, barnacle encrusted. It was very impressive.

John T. Mason Jr.: It's part of the Bermuda Triangle.

Admiral Eller: Yes, I guess it is. Gunnery training was continuous, star shell firing at night and drone firing by day. Usually on Saturday nights, we had happy hours. The midshipmen and crew competed with each other in excellent performances.

John T. Mason Jr.: That is happy hours without alcohol?

Admiral Eller: Yes. That's right. True happy hours. Some very fine acting and singing and music. We got off Guantánamo on 16 July, and conducted firing exercises by the midshipmen and also the crew. We had some of our own scheduled gunnery exercises and the midshipmen joined in. Holloway's report noted, "Gunnery firing was the climax, and rightly so, to the midshipmen's training. Great are the demands on the young and inexperienced men in precise performance of duty under the stress and shock of gunfire. It is a great developer of fiber in discipline and steadiness. The sobering effect upon NROTC midshipmen was particularly marked." I believe the NROTC was, in a sense, really more devoted learners than the academy midshipmen, maybe because they realized that they had inferior experience.

From Guantánamo we returned to Norfolk and debarked the midshipmen. The NROTC midshipmen went on their way and the Naval Academy midshipmen boarded AKs to come up to Annapolis.[20]

I haven't mentioned that we had on board four Midwestern publishers. I made it a point to give them double training. The officers and enlisted men showed them all over and through the ship. We had them handle the wheel, take different jobs on deck, and in the engine room and elsewhere. They turned to with enthusiasm.

John T. Mason Jr.: Were they reservists?

Admiral Eller: No. We had a program under way when I was in Public Information, of sending journalists on cruises to try to give them an understanding of the Navy. They would be influenced all their lives by what they learned. If they found the Navy not doing a good job, they would tell it as they saw it, but we were hopeful that we were good enough that they could see it and understand the importance of the Navy to the country.

I don't think anybody can understand anything unless he experiences it. Really understands it. You can read about it, you can study it, but until you actually do it, you don't understand it, because it's always different in practice. This is particularly true in the Navy. Citizens can understand military operations ashore because they not only see them, but they can walk over the ground just as the soldiers walk over the ground or ride on it. And they can understand airplanes, because they fly in them. But they can't understand the intricate interwoven work of a ship unless they actually experience it. It's very intricate, all the different functions of the ship combined together.

John T. Mason Jr.: I was smiling a bit, because I thought you must have had a difficult time in McNamara's day when experience was down the drain.

Admiral Eller: He was ruinous, he and Johnson before him.[21]

I wrote a little article for the midshipmen and put it in *Sea Breeze*, the ship's paper. We gave each one of them a photograph of the ship and said, "The photography in after

---

20. AK – the Navy designation for a cargo ship.
21. Robert S. McNamara served as Secretary of Defense from 21 January 1961 to 29 February 1968.

years will recall to you who now leave us the events of those brief two months, which have inevitably shaped you for the future. The Navy has been forged more deeply into you, the Navy and the sea as viewed from USS *Albany*. I am proud of the Navy, of its fundamental purposes, and of its value to the country. I am proud of this crew who strove to live close to these purposes of integrity, efficiency, faithful and loyal service to the United States. I am proud of your midshipmen, who by your superior efforts have demonstrated that you will keep for the Navy in the future the same great purposes without which the Navy is valueless." We included the publishers in the message.

John T. Mason Jr.: Did you get any repercussions from this among the midshipmen?

Admiral Eller: I have seen midshipmen as officers years later who were enthusiastic about the cruise.

John T. Mason Jr.: That's what I mean.

John T. Mason Jr.: And I have letters from the publishers too. Here's an extract from James Benham's letter who was publisher and editor of a paper in Terre Haute, Indiana:[22] "Back home in the more ordinary pursuit of trying to get out a newspaper I find it difficult to adequately express all that I feel about my recent sojourn on the *Albany*. It was one of the most enjoyable experiences in my life and one that will provide pleasant memories as long as I live. I should add that all officers of the *Albany* were extremely kind and considerate. I'm sure that some of them must have thought at times, 'What manner of men are these jackasses?' I particularly appreciate your kindness to my family in inviting them to be board as your guests on the last day. My little girls got a terrific wallop out of it, as did my wife. I'm sure you will hear from her. You cannot imagine all the superlatives she used. [She did write. She turned out to be a radio announcer and public speaker. She, like her husband, now understood and became good advertisers of the Navy.]

"In going back over all that I have just said, it seems rather weak because there is

---

22. James R. Benham was editor of the *Terre Haute Star*.

a certain spirit in the Navy, of which I am deeply appreciative and proud, and which my weak ability finds no way to put into words. I enjoy contact with it. For my money, I will go along with the Navy any place, any time."

He was a man of contrasts, a very hard-nosed newspaperman and at the same time, a man of very sympathetic and human spirit. For example, he was especially fond of books like *The Wind in the Willows*, "a superb book."

And we got a "well done" from Holloway at the end of the cruise, the second one for *Albany*, "You handled the drone exercises throughout the cruise with great dispatch and effectiveness." So we had a successful cruise that, I think, affected people for a long time.

Agnes and the boys came down and took a house in Norfolk for a month, while we prepared for the next deployment. In August *Albany* headed for the Mediterranean with a large task force of relief ships for those in the Sixth Fleet rotating home. Vice Admiral Felix Stump, Commander Second Fleet, flew his flag in *Albany* on the way over. Holloway stayed in Norfolk.[23] We had a regular expeditionary force, and the crossing was conducted as a war exercise.

We sortied with two attack carriers, three cruisers, 14 destroyers, and we picked up en route a hunter-killer group, a mine group, an amphibious group, a submarine group, and a logistics group, a total of around 50 ships. This would have been a regular expedition in World War II, and was very similar to one in the conduct of the operation. We cruised in war formation and conducted battle exercises all the way across—ASW, AA, anti-surface. General quarters blasted day and night. Then we refueled and reprovisioned at sea. Our excellent radar in *Albany*, which I believe was the best in the fleet, helped us to recover, with our helicopter, two pilots from the USS *Franklin Roosevelt*, which Admiral Pride rode as the OTC.[24] Her skipper was Fitzhugh Lee, an old friend of mine from the academy.[25]

---

23. Vice Admiral Felix B. Stump, USN, commanded the Second Fleet from March 1951 to June 1953.
24. OTC – officer in tactical command. Rear Admiral Alfred Melville Pride, USN, commanded Carrier Division Two, 1951–52. The oral history of Pride, who retired as a four-star admiral, is in the Naval Institute collection.
25. Captain Fitzhugh Lee, USN, commanded the USS *Franklin D. Roosevelt* (CVB-42) from 28 July 1951 to 26 July 1952. The oral history of Lee, who later retired as a vice admiral, is in the Naval Institute collection.

We crossed in only ten days this time to the Straits of Gibraltar, which we transited and engaged the Sixth Fleet as the "enemy" in the western Mediterranean. After several days there of battle exercises against the fleet and shore air from Port Lyautey and from bases in Europe, the two fleets joined and proceeded to different ports. We took into Lisbon four carriers, six cruisers, and 24 destroyers.

John T. Mason Jr.: Going into Lisbon. You filled up the Tagus.

Admiral Eller: We certainly did. I talked to the crew again before liberty, "You come from the finest country on earth and the finest Navy. Live up to them. Be ambassadors of good will." And they did again. In all talks I tried to make them see the broad picture. "We are the hope for the world. Portugal is a small country, but a firm ally with a glorious past history of the sea by such men as Prince Henry, Vasco da Gama, Magellan, and others. The Navy brings you to many countries. Learn about waters, weather, ports, lands, and people. See as much of Lisbon and its marvelous seashore and mountain castle country north of the city as you can. It will help you. It will help the Navy and the country. The more you know, the better off the Navy will be." We had only a few days there—two or three, maybe four.

As relief for *Columbus* we transferred from her special ciphers, special codebooks, and special Mediterranean instructions while in Lisbon. I had a little time to see Sintra again and went to the ambassador's reception, Lincoln MacVeagh.[26] Then I had him on board ship. He was the only diplomat, in fact, one of a handful of civilians that was interested in seeing everything about the ship. He went from keel to maintop and wanted to have everything explained. He tried to understand it. I was quite impressed with his interest.

John T. Mason Jr.: Well, he was one of the outstanding diplomats that we had in that era.

Admiral Eller: The more he knew, the better he would be able to handle every situation.

From Lisbon we then sailed back into the Mediterranean and went first to Augusta

---

26. Lincoln MacVeagh was U.S. Ambassador to Portugal from 1948 to 1952.

Bay. We passed north of Sicily into the Tyrrhenian Sea. There I saw a striking sight. Along about 11:00 at night, I was on the bridge and all of a sudden there was a light flashing high in the sky seemingly a half mile or a mile up. It puzzled us until we studied the chart and realized it was the volcano on Stromboli.

John T. Mason Jr.: I thought you were going to say it was a UFO.

Admiral Eller: I expect it was taken for that by many people. It was just like a window closing and opening into heaven. That's exactly what it looked like, a golden-red flare, then darkness and then flash again. We sailed on through the Straits of Messina. All of this area, of course, is filled with legends as told by Homer, Scylla and Charybdis and the Aeolian Islands. That's where the Sirens charmed Ulysses's crew, wasn't it? The Aeolian music.

John T. Mason Jr.: Oh, yes, their music.

Admiral Eller: We went into Augusta Bay on the south coast of Sicily. Nearby is Taormina, an ancient resort of Roman emperors Nero, Augustus and others. It's filled with Roman ruins. It has a beautiful resort hotel in an old monastery. Right under Taormina, or off to the east of it, is the rock Cyclops is supposed to have thrown after they put out his eye with a hot coal. We were busy preparing for combined operation, but I did take time to go to Syracuse where the Athenian overseas expedition in the Fifth Century B.C. had been destroyed because of lack of leadership, of delay instead of attacking when they arrived. The most poignant and dramatic narrative in history, I believe, is Thucydides's account of the failure of the Athenian expedition to capture Syracuse. I have read that many times, and it always fills me with sorrow, because it meant the beginning of the end of Athens's greatness. And it all depended upon leadership, just two men in a divided command.

We went from Syracuse into Naples conducting war exercises with allied warships, including the cruiser *Tromp* of the Dutch Navy. It was a sleepless voyage all the way because we had foul weather and operations carried us through restricted waters. We transited the Straits of Messina again. We replenished. We always replenished at dawn it seemed to me, which meant getting up an hour before dawn after late maneuvers in order to start replenishing.

John T. Mason Jr.: Is there any significance attached to that?

Admiral Eller: I think the significance is it gives time to do other things. Actually, you have a number of ships replenishing and it takes time, and the heavy cruisers usually led off.

John T. Mason Jr.: Oh, I see.

Admiral Eller: The trip into Naples was quite interesting with Vesuvius dead ahead. About 4:00 a.m., a black mass loomed in the night—we'd always get to port early in the morning. Soon it turned dark blue in the mist. Then it became volcanic rose at dawn.

I was the senior Navy ship captain in the Mediterranean at the time. So whenever there was an independent job to be done, I became the OTC, officer in tactical command. In the forthcoming exercises, I was OTC for various segments. Hence, proper preparation left little time for sightseeing. But I wanted to see Capri. I went with my executive officer, a very fine man, Dwight L. Moody—named after the great evangelist—his wife, and my navigator, a reservist, who was superb. We rode the gig across the bay to the mouth of the Blue Grotto, took one of the guide's boats there into the Blue Grotto and then came out again. The navigator said, "Let's go back."

They had already stopped the visiting, because high tide closes the entrance. The guide said, "With this low boat, you can go in briefly. So he and I went in with the guide. No one else was there, so we swam in the Blue Grotto, just blue as you swam in it. We had to lie flat in the boat to get out before the entrance closed. Also, I wanted to see the landing beaches at Salerno. So I took the marvelous drive down the Amalfi coast. At the south end of the bay where the landings took place are the tremendous Greek ruins of Paestum. I believe they are the most impressive Greek ruins in Italy.

John T. Mason Jr.: They weren't destroyed by this.

Admiral Eller: No, happily the landing was above them.

As I did in all ports, the last day or so we had a party on board for orphans. A group of very lovely sisters brought them. They were true Christians revealed by their kindness and the happiness of the children.

Now we were having a NATO exercise out of Naples. Admiral Carney was then CinCSouth.[27] And General Eisenhower had just come over to head NATO. He brought down many of his staff, and Carney came out with his staff and distributed on the various ships. I had some of them, but most were in *Des Moines*, flagship of Commander Sixth Fleet.

Part of the exercise was a shore bombardment and landing exercise on the northeast coast of Sardinia. As OTC, I was in charge of the bombardment. *Des Moines* and *Macon* with Eisenhower and Carney and Gardner followed astern of *Albany*.[28] It was one of the foulest nights I've ever seen, high winds and heavy seas, almost like a hurricane, constant rain and fog. I was up all night being sure that we didn't run aground. We got into the firing position and conducted our firing. Carney called off the simulated landing because it was too rough. But we had a very good exercise. We maneuvered all day, then sailed up past Corsica and Elba. About 1:00 in the morning, we broke off from the rest of the ships and conducted USS *Des Moines* into Cannes harbor where Carney and Eisenhower and staffs disembarked by helicopter and boat.

Then we went out again for several more days of exercises. After refueling, again, at dawn we came into Cannes for a rest period. This is the only place that we stayed any length of time in my Mediterranean tour.

John T. Mason Jr.: Well, it was a pleasant place to stay.

Admiral Eller: It was. The crew deserved some rest and recreation. For nearly two months with very brief breaks we had conducted constant exercises day and night. We were there about eight or ten days. I took that time, again, to learn something about the roads and

---

27. Admiral Robert B. Carney, USN, served as Commander in Chief Allied Forces Southern Europe from June 1951 to July 1953.
28. Vice Admiral Matthias B. Gardner, USN, served as Commander Sixth Fleet from 19 March 1951 to 27 March 1952.

the beaches. I went west nearly to Toulon to see the landing beaches at Saint Raphael and Frejus. It's a beautiful drive with umbrella pines along the coast and cliffs above it.

Then I went east through Nice to Monte Carlo and north to Grasse, the center of the perfume industry. It's marvelous country in the spectacular mountain range. On the third trip, I got up before dawn and went inland up the Maritime Alps to the Italian border about where Hannibal crossed on his march into Italy. We reached the snow line, about 7,000 feet. It was a land of deep gorges, plunging waterfalls, heavily forested, and little towns hanging right on precipices, or on mountain peaks. These mountain peak towns, like the old fortified towns in Italy, were still very much as they had been for 1,000 years or more. The next evening a terrific storm struck the port, the worst we had in the Mediterranean. About midnight it calmed. I guess we were in the eye of the storm and didn't realize it. In the middle of the midwatch it struck again with fury. Gusts of wind reached 50 knots within no time. Boats broke loose. We had a supply ship alongside who lost her anchor. She was banging so hard we had to let her go. She had to go to sea. The destroyers had to go to sea, and others did too. Some fouled each other.

We had our boats well secured but as I watched, about 4:00 a.m., two just snapped loose. We were able to recover one of them when the wind calmed a few hours later and our whaleboats could navigate. The other one hit the beach. We got it off and to the repair ship but we lost it there, because the ship couldn't lift it on board in this heavy storm.

John T. Mason Jr.: It sounds like a description of something in the Aleutians.

Admiral Eller: Yes, the williwaws. They have a name for these storms that come up suddenly in the Mediterranean, which I've forgotten. One minute it's calm and the next minute you're in a major storm.

From Cannes we sailed to Piraeus, another busy and interesting trip. We conducted battle exercises all the way across, including a shore bombardment exercise off Algiers. We had a night surface action and, again, *Albany* was OTC after we'd passed Malta and were in the eastern Mediterranean. And we had dawn submarine torpedo attacks, dawn replenishment, and so on. The dawn approach into Piraeus was fascinating. I had never seen the Parthenon. In fact, I'd never been in Athens except to fly in and out.

Miles at sea, as the sun rose, I saw this beautiful marble edifice seemingly floating in the clouds like a dream of the past. It was a most glorious sight in the rising sun. I had been fascinated with ancient history and Greek history, especially since youth. Hence, Greece was a particularly interesting place. Since Commander Sixth Fleet was along in *Des Moines*. I didn't have any real responsibilities in diplomatic functions and was free of calls. One of our officers had to go to the airport. We sent him in our helicopter and I went along. After we had dropped him, we flew east over the battlefield of Marathon, then west over Salamis and down across Corinth to the Peloponnesus.

Of course, there were constant functions. I knew several people, including Rear Admiral Richard Glass of our mission and Captain Don Wilber, the naval attaché.[29] In the embassy I had met Ambassador John Peurifoy before, a very able man.[30] He later went to Southeast Asia and was killed in an automobile accident. He was another hard-nosed, clear-thinking—

John T. Mason Jr.: He was in Vietnam, wasn't he?

Admiral Eller: Yes. It is believed that the accident was contrived. We lost a very fine diplomat in him, a very fine American. And his wife Betty was equally so.

Declining functions arranged on Sunday when I did much of my traveling after early church, I took three of the ship's officers in our car and headed inland. We went over the low mountains that ring Attica and Athens, then turned northwest and drove up Mount Parnassus, a tremendous mountain, mostly barren. We got up close to the top where snow was beginning to accumulate, and then came down the flank to the west to a plateau where Delphi sits. The Oracle of Delphi held audience there. There are extensive ruins and an ancient amphitheater where they still play games. Here ended or began one of their races.

Delphi sits in a very spectacular site. The cliff seems to drop straight down from it. We had lunch at a little restaurant sitting right out on the edge. You could look down to the west and see the Adriatic Sea. Corinth was far below you and the Corinthian Canal.

---

29. Rear Admiral Richard P. Glass, USN; Captain Donald T. Wilber, USN.
30. John E. Peurifoy was U.S. Ambassador to Greece from 1950 to 1953. In 1955, while serving as ambassador to Thailand, he and his son were killed when the car Peurifoy was driving collided with a truck. Another son survived the accident.

Peloponnesus was to the south. To the east lay Athens and the Aegean. It's an outstanding spot in natural beauty. You could see why they believed in the Oracle of Delphi up there close to God.

I tried to see the Parthenon the night of our arrival, but the guards wouldn't let me. I went to the ambassador's for a function later that night. The Prime Minister was there, and I mentioned that I would like to see the Parthenon at night sometime. Right on the spot he gave me a special pass. So when we came back from Delphi, we stopped and saw the Parthenon at night in all of its beauty with the lights glowing from the city below.

Then Admiral Gardner had King Paul and Queen Fredericka for dinner one night, which I attended. They were both personable.

I became very fond of one of the retired Greek naval officers. The head of the Navy was Admiral P. Antonopoulous. He came on board for dinner one night, bringing his brother-in-law retired Admiral Constantine Alexandris, who was a very nice gentleman, an author and historian. My second prize essay was printed in 1950 or 1951. After reading it in the *Proceedings*, he had translated it into Greek and had published portions of it.

From Piraeus *Albany* separated from the main fleet and proceeded with destroyers to Souda Bay in Crete. At dawn, again, I saw a fine sight. It's worth getting up at dawn for these port approaches.

John T. Mason Jr.: It's worth getting up at dawn any morning.

Admiral Eller: Yes, it is. Mount Ida, over an 8,000-foot peak, rises almost straight up from the seacoast. I saw it emerging from darkness into the high mountain of daylight. We were there a couple of days for a goodwill visit, and, as in all the countries, we used our welfare fund or contributions from the officers and crew to provide something for the orphanages and the schools. In this case, we gave athletic gear to the schools of Crete, received with great appreciation.

I was anxious to see the old Cretan ruins. We weren't too far from Knossos and the restored palace of King Minos, site of many of the Greek legends. The bull played a dramatic part in it. I went through the museum and was amazed at the beautiful work in gold and silver and pottery, and their tools and the artistry of their painting—all this before 1,500 B.C.

John T. Mason Jr.: Their designs are really outstanding.

Admiral Eller: Yes, they are. They had great talent. There was the labyrinth of the old Greek legend. You could see how one could get lost in it. And portions of a 3,500-year-old road, which impressed me. It was built as well as ours are now, maybe better.

We sailed in a north gale and heavy seas again and joined up with the Sixth Fleet to operate in the Sea of Crete. Then we sailed north and west to Istanbul, Constantinople. Threading through the Greek islands was quite an interesting experience, and the transit of the Dardanelles even more so with the fortifications the Turks had built there in World War I and World War II. The ruins of Troy are near the south entrance. We passed through the Sea of Marmara at night and anchored early at Istanbul, fairly close in. There, as in other ports in the Mediterranean, we held tight security. We kept two 3-inch mounts and directors manned day and night, two 5-inch/38s manned at night with condition watches. And kept a boat patrolling around the ship, a picket boat. We illuminated the waterline, and had armed sentries forward, aft, and amidships.

John T. Mason Jr.: It's interesting that in that period you were doing that. I assume we do it now with even greater vigor.

Admiral Eller: Yes. Well, that was, of course, the Korean War, and some are not talking very peacefully at any time.

I had known Ambassador Wadsworth from our conference in Istanbul the year before.[31] And I was several times with the CNO, Admiral Ridvan Koral.[32] He was the head of the Turkish Navy. I'd known him and others there, too, from the February conference. This was in late November, only about nine months since the conference. There also was another friend from the National War College, Fred Merrill, who I think was commercial attaché. He wasn't a State Department type. On Thanksgiving Day, he invited Captain

---

31. George Wadsworth II served as U.S. Ambassador to Turkey, 1948–52.
32. Admiral Ridvan Koral, Turkish Chief of Naval Staff, 1950–52.

Fitzhugh Lee— who had been at the War College, too—and me and others to lunch. I took my intelligence officer and Fitz Lee and drove along the coast road, which runs either right on the beach or on a cliff, east to the Black Sea, and then inland up into Thrace. I usually took an intelligence officer on these trips, because we would write a report of visits in which we would give information on the roads and the coast.

Much of the time on Sunday I had conferences getting ready for the next operation. I had to be up that night through the midwatch again. A sudden storm blew up and we had to work to keep *Albany* from fouling *Des Moines*, which was anchored close aboard. We were in Istanbul nearly a week. Happily, I had part of a day to go through the town. One of the sights that impressed me was St. Sophia, which is now a museum, with its 200-foot dome. I believe it was built originally by Constantine I, wasn't it?

John T. Mason Jr.: Yes, Constantine I.

Admiral Eller: The Blue Mosque is one of many in the old city with its blue tiles. It is beautiful. You either took off your shoes or put on socks over your shoes, a slipper sock. The massive city walls are there, or were then. They are four miles long. The old city was on something of a peninsula between the Golden Horn and the approach form the Sea of Marmara. On it were watchtowers and castles. It's an impressive sight if it's still there. With the fleet it held off invaders for 1,000 years. So it was a pretty good wall. Then the Grand Bazaar, the old souk, is grand. It had everything in the world and covers many city blocks. One of the sights that struck me was the massive underground cistern built by Constantine. It has huge arches and cavernous pools.

We sailed for fleet exercises shortly after Thanksgiving, again in foul weather. The 28th Amphibious Group joined us in the Aegean and we conducted an assault landing on Souda Bay. Again I was in charge of the fire support group. After these exercises I separated with *Leyte* and destroyers and headed for Algiers. I believe that was the first fleet visit to Algiers since the war.

We piloted by radar all along the coast of North Africa. The Atlas Mountains are very rugged. There are two ranges, the lower Maritime Atlas Mountains and then the Sahara Atlas rising high in the background. Greek and Roman ruins abound all through there. This was the granary of Rome, of course. Now it's mostly desert.

We had separated from the fleet with very nice commendations from Commander Sixth Fleet and from ComCruDiv 6, my cruiser division commander: "USS *Albany*'s performance in this Mediterranean tour has even bettered previous high standards. Examples are yesterday's performance in MedLantEx. [This was the amphibious exercise.] The international goodwill created by *Albany*'s gift to the children of Athens, well done, and Merry Christmas." That was CruLant/ComCruDiv 6.

We went into Algiers for just two days. Our schedule was tight to get home. There I became quite fond of Vice Admiral Leon Marie Sala, Commander in Chief of the French Maritime Forces in the Mediterranean. There we had a type of mooring that I've never had anywhere else and would just as soon not have. We moored stern to. When you came in, you turned and dropped your anchor.

John T. Mason Jr.: Why is this? Current?

Admiral Eller: That was their system. I can't remember why they did it. Maybe it was because of the current. It might have been the wind, but there is no real reason for it. You can moor, anyway. But we dropped the anchor, brought it astern, and let it out until the stern was almost touching the seawall. If your anchor dragged, you would have been in a sad state. It gave me gray hairs.

Of course, Algiers had changed since Decatur and Preble were over there attacking it.[33] The French had made it a beautiful city, much of it like a city of southern France with the trees, the flowers. That was the French modern part of the city. The old Arab souk and Arab town were just the way they had been, probably when Preble was there.

We did the diplomatic parts of it as fast as I could since our visit was short. The consul general was Tom Lockett, and Boise Hart was a very fine young assistant. I wanted to see the road inland and the wild Atlas Mountains. So I got up early and drove south across the Atlas Mountains. First you cross the Maritime Atlas Mountains to an area which

---

33. Stephen Decatur (1779–1820) was a noted American naval officer of the early 19th century. He fought against the Barbary Pirates in the Mediterranean. Edward Preble (1761–1807) was a U.S. naval officer who fought with distinction during the First Barbary War.

they call the "tell." This is a verdant area of Algiers that provides a great deal of fruit and grain and much other food for the country. I think they are about self-sufficient. Then we went on into the higher Atlas Mountains that are very rugged and forbidding. You can understand why the Berbers were so difficult to conquer in these wild mountains.

We drove to Bou Saâda right in the edge of the Sahara, where there is nothing but a world of sand in all directions. It's arid, dry, hot, dusty. We came back a little different route and drove through numerous Roman and some Greek ruins, orange groves, and flowers. It's an attractive country along the coast. From Algiers we went to Gibraltar. I took *Leyte* and four destroyers along. The flag officer of Gibraltar, the admiral commanding the area, was Vice Admiral Lord Ashbourne whom I'd known in the Pacific before he became a peer.[34] He was a younger son's son and had no chance of being a peer, but then the others died off and he got the title.

John T. Mason Jr.: He was down around Manus, wasn't he?

Admiral Eller: He probably was. I knew him in Pearl Harbor. He had a cruiser and came in there.[35] I've forgotten the name of the cruiser. He was a very fine person. He's still alive. In fact, I've seen him since. We were in Gibraltar just for three days, but we were several times in his home. Both he and Lady Ashbourne were delightful persons.

I took time to go through the fortifications. They are quite impressive. There is an amazing labyrinth under that rock, all woven through it. Of course, there are water systems through there too, and food, and ammunition. The second day we were there Tom McKnew, secretary of the National Geographic Society, who was the Secretary of the Navy's guest, flew in to ride home with me.[36] He was anxious to go over to Tangiers where Kent Loomis, a classmate of mine, later with me in naval history, was the attaché.[37] So we took our helicopter and flew there for a few hours. The next day we drove into Spain to see the roads. Then you could go in and out from Gibraltar without any real

---

34. Rear Admiral Edward Russell Gibson, Royal Navy, Third Baron Ashbourne, Admiral Superintendent of the dockyard at Gibraltar, 1950–52. He was promoted to vice admiral in 1952.
35. Ashbourne commanded the minelayer *Ariadne*, 1943–45, and the light cruiser *Mauritius,* 1947–48.
36. Thomas W. McKnew.
37. Captain F. Kent Loomis, USN (Ret.), served as Director of Naval History from January to July 1970 after taking over from Admiral Eller.

difficulty. Now Spain has closed the border. The only way you can get to Spain is to go from Gibraltar to Tangier and then fly back to Spain.

The last part of that cruise was to Norfolk. Again I set 17 knots, because we had a date of arrival just a couple of days before Christmas. And, again, we exercised constantly. Again we had weather so foul that the destroyers couldn't beat into it and screen us as they ordinarily would. Hence, about half the trip I had two of them astern of me and two astern of *Leyte*, so that they could get the benefit of our wakes. And we made it on time.

Tom McKnew was very much like Lincoln MacVeagh. He wanted to see everything. So I made it a point for him to go from the chain locker to the steering engine room, with guides and on his own. He liked to talk with the crew, ate in the different crew messes, the CPO mess, and the wardroom.[38] He rarely ate with me because he wanted to see the ship and learn about it.

We had *Elkomin* as our oiler on the way across. Her skipper wrote me one of the nicest letters I've ever received. We got a number of commendations after the cruise. But this letter of his is something that makes the heart feel good: "Dear Captain Eller. Ordinarily I'm not much of a letter writer, but I feel compelled to write and thank you for a pleasant trip and for your understanding treatment of our shortcomings. I particularly felt I had to tell you so, because I realized that on several occasions I was unnecessarily argumentative, and I am very sorry this chip on the shoulder attitude has developed, because I felt that when operating under the tactical command of competent combatant units, the tanker boys were always getting the wrong end of the stick. I realized early that in this case it wasn't necessary. But I'm afraid that this argumentative trait has developed into a habit. I wish to thank you again for a most pleasant trip and also for showing me the error of my ways in screaming before you are hit. Moon Mullins."[39]

John T. Mason Jr.: Oh, Moon Mullins.

Admiral Eller: I don't think I'd known Moon before.

---

38. CPO – chief petty officer.
39. Captain Henry Mullins Jr., USN, commanded the fleet oiler *Elkomin* (AO-55), 1951–52.

Tom McKnew got a very nice write-up on there in our ship paper, *The Sea Breeze*. They came to love him because they said, "Our Best Guest: On the return trip from Gibraltar *Albany* has had the great good fortune to have as our fine passenger Dr. Thomas W. McKnew, Secretary of the National Geographic Society. We have enjoyed his daily inspection throughout the ship from chain locker to the steering engine room and from keel to sky forward. He has tried our chow from the mess line soup and platter to the brass of the wardroom and has drunk good Navy coffee in many messes. He has been interested in every part and activity of the ship. We, in turn, have found him so tour friendly and intelligent and so much of a good shipmate that we would like to have him sign up for a full tour in *Albany*. Doctor, we have enjoyed our cruise together and regret to see the finest passenger yet leave our fine ship."

I wrote a little homecoming editorial, as I often did, in the paper. Some of this might go in: "We return home filled with understandings that our home lies in the most wonderful land on earth. However useful to the world's peace has been our tour in the Mediterranean, we're happy to come home.

"Each of us has a clear understanding of why we serve this fine country of ours. Each of us is more ready than ever to defend her and the great blessings she has given us. I have been proud of the finest example as Americans you as a crew have set abroad. It is an example reflected in the numerous letters and dispatches of commendation we have received. No group of 1,400 Americans could have set a finer record. Few could have done as well."

Here is some evidence of the quality of this fine group of people. The country is blessed with men like these. On 13 January I got an unexpected letter from a lady. She says, "You've never met me and I've never met you, but I and my daughter, Ruth, were on board your ship January 11." This was after we were home, of course. "We had such a wonderful time that I felt I should thank you and your entire crew. We fell in love with the *Albany* and her crew as well. Everyone did his best to make us comfortable and to show us all over the ship. It was indeed a thrilling experience for us and one which we will never forget." Signed, Dorothy Doutill.

We had a little time in port again to prepare for the next operation, which was a lulu. This was a cold weather battle operation exercise. The objective was to learn how to operate in cold weather, cold weather battles, if necessary—to learn the different problems, how to overcome them, and to train the crew to be ready under any conditions. We were simulating resupplying a base in southern Greenland. In preparation we started school for all hands. First I had the heads of departments break out all publications that we had on Arctic operations, including especially the fine Arctic Operations Handbook. Each one of them then prepared a one-page list of hints for his men. Also lists of special materials and items to get, for example, though experimental at that time. We obtained heated clothing for the lookouts, and they used them with great approval.

If you go out in cold weather, several light layers are better than a few heavy, or one heavy. If you can wear two or three pairs of socks, large shoes so there is plenty of looseness there for air and warmth. Otherwise, you'll get frostbitten, masks for men exposed. You are supposed to keep dry and your clothes clean. I didn't know this before, that body oil clogs the little pores in your clothing, and you should keep it clean and washed at all times. We got special cold weather lubricants and coatings. With plywood we built some protection around the bridge. Using different kinds of lubricants for our gun mounts and directors, we were able to operate them all during the cruise.

Another thing that I didn't know was that you needed more food. So we gave not only three meals a day with meat at each meal, bacon and eggs at breakfast, steak or pork for lunch, and something else at dinner. But we had hot soup and coffee 24 hours a day in the galley for all hands. And for those on watch we gave them another full meal every two hours. The crew was quite happy with that. They came through in good shape.

We were conducting this at the worst season of the year, of course, in January and February. We had constant high winds and heavy seas and fog for three weeks. And three weeks of condition watches, a good part of it general quarters. We had two forces. Our force was the blue. The black opposing us included shore-based air, submarines, and surface ships. We usually had in our force up to 27 vessels in formation, including CVLs, CVEs. *Albany* was the heavy ship. I had APAs, and AKAs for the reinforcement and replenishment, and tankers—one or more.

The second day out we met our first opposition. We had surface raids all night. Our good radar and our tactics in maneuvering helped us to destroy the surface raider. We did that two other times. We escaped all surface raiders all right. Our CV and CVL and the destroyers were quite efficient, too, and we sank several submarines, theoretically. Umpires made the decisions.

John T. Mason Jr.: Were you attempting to try out any particular ordnance?

Admiral Eller: We had nothing new in ordnance that I know of. Of course, the 3-inch/50 was relatively new. I don't remember anything. We probably did have some minor pieces, but no important ones.

John T. Mason Jr.: What about the area of communications?

Admiral Eller: We were testing our communications as well as gunnery under these conditions, our radar too. We had to use special lubricants. One of the chemical companies had put out a new product with which we coated our antennas. It made them more effective under ice and snow conditions. After the first few days, we had ice and snow encrusted on the ship almost constantly. The heavy sea spray broke high up and it was cold enough in the bitter winds that even the saltwater would freeze on the ship. So every day we had to chip and keep the directors and guns operating, moving them, rotating them. We had to chip and scrape constantly to get the snow and ice off decks and bulkheads. This is particularly important high up topside, because it makes the ship top-heavy. You might have very serious trouble in a storm, and we had plenty of storms.

En route and all during the cruise we had constant schools, part of each day every division went to school in its own particular area on precautions and actions to take in the cold weather operations. And we came through very well. We didn't have any casualties of importance or anybody with frostbite or other suffering from the cold.

About the third night out, in fog and heavy sea and high wind, two of our AKAs collided. I can't remember the circumstances, but USS *Mellette*. I think, may have had her steering gear jam. She swung into *Vermilion*, hit her well forward, and cut a hole 40 feet wide in the *Vermilion* from the deck almost to the waterline.[40] So she was in much danger of sinking, of course, which would have been quite a disaster.

John T. Mason Jr.: Yes, it would be hard to rescue anybody under those circumstances.

---

40. The collision of the attack transport *Mellette* (APA-156) and the attack cargo ship *Vermillion* (AKA-107) occurred on 23 January 1952.

Admiral Eller: Yes. Holloway was riding in *Albany*; he wisely undertook to escort the two damaged ships to port. *Mellette* had some flooding and some damage forward and continued to have much trouble steering, though she wasn't in the precarious situation of *Vermilion*. So we escorted them up off Halifax, creating an oil slick. It didn't take too much oil. I think about 10,000 gallons in all, which is about 250 barrels. Just a little oil calmed the spray down so *Vermilion*, by keeping the wind off her bow, could prevent too much water from flooding into the part that was open. Of course, she had her collision bulkheads well shored, and they were not leaking.

The collision happened in the middle of the night, so we went all that night and all the next day. When we got fairly close to Halifax, the winds had moderated a little. We sent the two ships on in with a destroyer escort. They got in safely. Then we turned and started back for the force at 21 knots. Well, 21 knots in the seas we were hitting had effects on the ship. We finally had to slow down, but until we did, the seas sheared away stanchions forward. They lifted the barbette of number one turret about a half an inch and sheared life rafts and other items from the deck just as if somebody had come through with a great sickle and swept them away. You would feel as if the ship had run aground every time you hit into the giant waves. It was as if you had hit a solid wall. Spray swept over the bridge up to the topmasts.

John T. Mason Jr.: You were tempting fate, weren't you?

Admiral Eller: We should have slowed sooner. We went ahead with our resupply operation and got up right off Greenland. This was about ten days now that we had been under these sorts of conditions. It was as miserable weather as I've ever experienced and the most miserable for that length of time. We were in floating cakes of ice, with icebergs about. We got the real training; there is no question.

The exercise wasn't over. We got through safely having sunk the enemy submarines and surface raiders and beat off the air. Then we had to battle our way back again against air and submarine opposition. And the storms—we still had our 25- to 30-foot waves. We finally got to Halifax. As we were going in, I spoke to the crew and I was wrong in what I promised, because it didn't work out that way: "As you approach Halifax, I want to congratulate all hands on another splendid job. All of us are better men now by having overcome the problems of cold and rough weather. We are better trained to serve the navy and our country. You will find Halifax a splendid city. We are arranging bus tours, dances, skating and so on. I know you will keep up *Albany*'s good name ashore that has brought you commendations from Copenhagen to Istanbul. We had nearly a perfect record last month in the Med; let's make it perfect here."

Then I gave them extra liberty. Actually, I say I was wrong about the dances and so on, because as we were coming in the approaches to Halifax, King George VI died. That was on 6 February 1952. So our stay was shortened from a four-day goodwill visit to a two-day sympathy visit and all functions were called off. But the people were very appreciative of our coming. The papers were filled with pictures of us and the appreciation of our coming.

I had another experience here that one hopes never to have again, the most difficult departure from a dock that I've ever experienced. I had a ship ahead of me and a ship astern, both not many yards away and the wind and the current each driving us onto the dock. The line from the tug that was helping to get my stern out broke, and I was left with no help in an almost impossible situation. That's one of the times my prayers were promptly answered. I manipulated the engine and got ahead a little. The stern wouldn't go out, but then finally it started to ease out and I finally got clear. But it was the most difficult ship handling I've ever had. Holloway was standing on the flag bridge above me looking down, strained. He was feeling it just as much as I was, I know. I was afraid for a time that I wouldn't make it, would have to give it up and wait for better circumstances.

After we got back to Norfolk, I wrote up the report of the operation and Holloway did also. I might read a little from mine: "During an active year of widely varied operations, all profitable in improving the readiness of the ship, none has been more valuable in its training of *Albany*'s crew than Micowex. Actual experience is not only the best teacher, it is the only way to fix knowledge permanently in many people. *Albany* is decidedly a more effective unit because of this northern operation, the first for most of her crew in cold waters where our next war may have to be fought. The enclosures cover the various features of preparing for and carrying out this operation. The following comments, taken from our detailed report, give the highlights of the cruise. Excellent information on the Arctic exists in various publications, especially our Arctic Operations Handbook. Based on these and discussions with people having Arctic experience and on early planning conferences, each department of the ship obtained material, conducted training, and took precautionary action. As a result, no unforeseen difficulties were encountered and all cold weather problems were measurably lessened. Increased rations and frequency of issue helped maintain high morale and efficiency. Plenty of nutritious hot food is required to replenish energy in northern latitudes, not only from cold weather, but from loss of sleep as a result of condition watches and operations."

Then I said in addition to three meals we had the two-hour schedule for exposure of the crew: "The general efficiency of the crew. Because of multiple layers of clothing, gloves, ice, and slowing-down effect of subfreezing temperatures, topside operations proceeded at a more leisurely tempo in northern waters. However, with adequate warm clothing, high energy food, frequent replacement of watchmen, the ship's duties were carried out with usual effectiveness. There was no increase in accidents. Health, except for numerous colds, was excellent. No frostbite or other impaired health due to low temperature was experienced. Preventive measures were emphasized in ship-wide training several weeks before the crew started and continued during it.

"Special measures for ship and gun control. Because of special need for alertness and quick effectiveness of these men, care was taken to ensure their comfort and efficiency. The bridge was fitted with double awnings, numerous heaters, temporary wooden sidewalls, various ceiling materials, wind shear defrosters and wipers, aviation clothing including electrical heated suits for lookouts. As a result there was no lessening of efficiency.

"The operation of guns and topside machinery. Employment of low temperature lubricants and emphasis on water-tightness of fittings helped to ensure that gun and fire control equipment and all topside machinery operated with the usual dependability.

"Firing guns. The non-firing performance of guns and associated equipment was gratifying. It is recommended that in subsequent operations, target practices be conducted in order to obtain maximum experience and tests. In this connection it would be useful to include shipborne drones for 3-inch and automatic weapons practice.

"Ice removal gave no particular problems. Slippery deck ice could be most bothersome. The decks and ladders along frequented routes were kept passable by liberal applications of rock salt, which melted most of the ice, and with sand. [It gave us rust problems too.] This procedure and the provision of numerous lifelines made passage, even in heavy seas, possible."

And so on. That's enough from that.

John T. Mason Jr.: Judge, you say that this made the *Albany* so much more in a state of readiness for warfare in that area, but I can't but observe that it is temporary, this state of readiness. Because of the crew, it's dispersed.

Admiral Eller: That's true.

John T. Mason Jr.: And you have new ones that don't know.

Admiral Eller: And you have to do it all again.

John T. Mason Jr.: You have to do it all over again.

Admiral Eller: Yes, but suppose we had gone to war that year.

John T. Mason Jr.: Well, yes, the immediacy of it.

Admiral Eller: And all training is that way, for that matter, because you have this constant rotation. The real benefits come from the old hands that served there. Well, take my officers. I suppose on that ship, maybe a third of the officers didn't stay in the Navy. Maybe some of them were in the reserves. But those that did stay, as they went along, they have the experience, they have the knowledge, and above all, if looked at, they have these reports which they can refer to and train the people in the same way over again. But training is a constant need and a constant practice in the Navy, if you are going to have an efficient ship.

John T. Mason Jr.: And also, I suppose one might say it's an occupation?

Admiral Eller: It is an occupation. In fact, I've often said that a naval officer is above all things a leader and a teacher. These are two things he has to do. He has to know his profession and do it, of course. But training is constant. Every duty I've ever had in the Navy was always training. And you didn't have the continuity of experience, except maybe in a few individuals who helped to carry it along.

I'll try to finish up on *Albany*. On our way back from the midshipman cruise, something had happened that I'm sure changed my life and probably for the better. I didn't realize it at the time. Admiral Sherman died as we were coming back from the cruise. I forget what date it was, but, as you know, he was in Spain and then in Italy and had a heart attack.[41] The pictures I saw of him when he was in Italy showed that he had changed tremendously even before his heart attack. His face didn't look like him at all. He was drawn and haggard. He had been working too hard. And I guess the same thing could happen to anyone. He never took any time out. He was always working.

In my last days in the ship before I was relieved in March, I tried to get the memos in shape to help maintain *Albany*'s excellent performance. One was a memorandum for the officer of the deck, in which I summarized the experience and actions that we should take in order to ensure that we have a well run ship and a safe ship. Let me cite a couple of parts: "Try not to do it all yourself. Organize your watch and leave yourself to supervise so when the going gets heavy you take over the conn. Always have somebody at the conning station looking ahead. Never leave your bow and the ship's ahead unwatched. Always have somebody looking astern.

"When you give an order, your responsibility does not end, it just starts. See that the order is carried out. Follow through until the action desired is completed. In a simple helm command, for example, you must: require a repeat back; check rudder indicator to ensure that what is being repeated is being done; check compass repeater to see that the change of heading is correct; continue helm order procedures and check until steady on course; be sure someone is looking over and, in particular, on the side to which you are turning. Use thumb rules whenever possible." I found thumb rules extremely valuable to me.

---

41. Admiral Forrest P. Sherman, USN, the Chief of Naval Operations, arrived in Paris on 21 July 1951 after a tiring week of negotiations in Spain and Italy. At 10:40 the following morning he had a mild heart attack, then died in Paris at 1:05 that afternoon after two more heart attacks.

"As an example of this, in column changes, to turn in the water of the ship ahead, bring his kick under the ship between the bridge and turret two, before giving rudder orders. You have two checks: first the time interval from the instant the ship ahead starts turning." I always used a stopwatch on that. "Second, the turning bearing on the guide. By using all three every turn should be a good one. "

Then I put out some more information on training and another memorandum on that. I'll read a little from it: "In previous memoranda and discussion, I have emphasized some of the important qualities of leadership that each of us should strive to possess: enthusiasm, determination to get a job done despite any obstacle, alert eagerness to improve, and achieve are some of the qualities we all need and we all can have. Two of the noblest traits of a leader are integrity and a high standard of example. Another worthwhile trait is full-handed preparation, whether it be for a specific job or in long-term development of our naval knowledge so that each of us may be of increasing value to the Navy and our country.

"A good leader is also a good instructor. Among others, the qualities of enthusiasm, drive, preparation, and example are inspiring elements in teaching, which help to stimulate interest and drive home knowledge. As you have well observed, much of an officer's and petty officer's life is spent instructing others. It is the nature of our job that we must always be training ourselves and others to be ready when we are needed. The foregoing are essential characteristics for the foundation of successful training. To them can be added certain basic principles which experience has proved sound, such as ensuring that in all training there is active physical participation by the learner under conditions stimulating his desire to learn."

Then I gave them a long summary again of very much the same things that I've said before, learning to do by doing. Another thing that was very close to me was trying to get the sailors close to their named community. The original USS *Albany* was named after Albany, New York, and we carried on the name. So we organized a good citizens ship award. I wrote the mayor. We ran a program to encourage the crew to contribute and raised $1,000 to set up as a trust fund in Albany, which would give a $50.00 bond every year to the high school senior who most emphasized the development of good citizenship by displaying moral integrity, strong religious example, and leadership in promoting these characteristics among his schoolmates. This was not only good for the community, but it was good for the crew on board to be supporting something like this.

John T. Mason Jr.: To focus on something like that.

Admiral Eller: Yes. So we got that under way. Some years later I checked and it was still operating.

In March Captain E. S. Hutchinson relieved me.[42] I'll end this by reading extracts from the two fitness reports. I wouldn't do this except that it applies to something that follows:

"Captain Eller continued throughout the period to show the same outstanding leadership in skill and command as was evident in his initial months on board. The Albany operated with distinction as Second Fleet flagship during the three weeks of September and then again for three months in the Sixth Fleet, and finally turned in a distinguished performance as flagship of ComCruFor Atlantic Fleet in recent cold weather exercises.

"The Captain not only lives up fully to all standards required by regulation and service custom, but he has, in addition, a nice sense of the added touch, which lends distinction and prestige to an action or operation. As I moved about in the Mediterranean, I picked up his trail from admiring remarks from American ambassadors and foreign flag officers.

"From my observation in operations and inspection I made of *Albany*, I consider that Captain Eller has maintained a very high standard of morale in all-around performance and has peaked the alertness and efficiency in radar and other elements of air defense. He is recommended for accelerated promotion."

Then Holloway, who could be either a good or a bad marker, wrote in another report, "During the past five years I had opportunity to closely observe some 60 outstanding captains in the academy classes of 1924 to 1926. I place Captain Eller in the small group of some 10% at the top of the foregoing that I consider particularly outstanding and capable of distinguished service as flag officers in our Navy. He is a gentleman of highest personal integrity and an outstanding leader as indicated by the tone and morale in *Albany*, a ship without peer in these categories. He possesses and exercises controlled imagination and enterprise in the best sense. He is particularly suited

---

42. Captain Edward S. Hutchinson, USN, commanded the *Albany* from 8 March 1952 to 28 February 1953.

to represent his country and his service, either in professional conference or in public capacity. An outstanding ship handler and a bold seaman undaunted by adverse conditions at sea and always enthusiastic and confident. These attributes, together with his strong sense of values and cooperation and loyalty, have made him particularly valuable as a flag captain. In addition, he has shown unusual competence in creating a high order of battle efficiency in the *Albany*. The ship stood first in the cruisers of the Atlantic Fleet in gunnery performance in fiscal 1951 and continues to indicate the same high efficiency. Fully qualified for flag rank now, I strongly recommend him for selection for accelerated rank promotion with the first of his kind. I would particularly desire to have him serve with me in war or peace."

John T. Mason Jr.: Now, that is quite a fulsome praise from Holloway.

Interview Number 18 with Rear Admiral Ernest M. Eller, U.S. Navy (Retired)
Place: Annapolis, Maryland
Date: Thursday, 29 May 1980

John T. Mason Jr.: Well, Judge, it's lovely to see you this morning on this beautiful spring day.

Admiral Eller: It's lovely to see you always.

John T. Mason Jr.: Are you going into the realm of international affairs? You had concluded your tour with the USS *Albany* last time.

Admiral Eller: I had been ordered to OP-35, our political-military section that reviewed plans and dispatches, any action of the department, trying to consider the State Department view. And we had a great deal to do with both OP-30, the Strategic Planning section of CNO, and with the State Department. We had frequent liaison with them, constant liaison.

John T. Mason Jr.: Now, you took over this assignment in 1952.

Admiral Eller: Nineteen fifty-two. I was deputy to Admiral B. L. Austin and was supposed to succeed him within the year.[1] At this time we were in the middle of the Korean War with negotiations.

John T. Mason Jr.: You could say that now too.

Admiral Eller: Yes, I think we could say so still. They had been willing to come to terms after suffering such severe losses in 1951. So we, unfortunately, instead of going ahead and

---

1. Rear Admiral Bernard L. Austin, USN, served from 1952 to 1954 as director of the International Affairs Division of the Office of the Chief of Naval Operations. The oral history of Austin, who retired as a vice admiral, is in the Naval Institute collection.

winning, accepted their desires for negotiations, thinking that we would have an early end. In fact, I read that correspondents were betting that the negotiations would end in six weeks and that there would be a treaty.

John T. Mason Jr.: Certainly that was Burke's understanding, too, you know.[2]

Admiral Eller: Is that right? I didn't realize that. He was there, of course. Well, it had lasted a year already when I came in the late spring of 1952. The Communists had gotten worse and worse in negotiations. Meanwhile, they built up strength and maintained a constant series of crises, constant derogatory propaganda against the United States, and constantly increased their demands until they were outrageous.

We got all the dispatches related to the negotiations and had to work with the State Department on them. That was a very frustrating job to me, because it was a continuous battle over words and phrases. The State Department men would want to tone down anything that we did; they were always ready to give in. The Joint Chiefs of Staff in time got so tired of the negotiations that they would agree to a concession, thinking that would be the last one and the Communists would be satisfied. But they were the typical bullies; once they got one concession, they would demand another bigger one.

I talked to Admiral Turner Joy about it when he came here as superintendent. I think the trials there helped to kill him. You didn't get a chance to interview him, did you?[3] Arleigh Burke's ideas would be quite similar to his.

John T. Mason Jr.: Yes, I have got Burke on Korea.

Admiral Eller: Syngman Rhee saw the issues more clearly.[4] He understood the

---

2. In 1951–52 Rear Admiral Arleigh A. Burke, USN, was part of the United Nations delegation in the Korean War truce talks at Panmunjom. The oral history of Burke, who retired as a four-star admiral, is in the Naval Institute collection.
3. Vice Admiral C. Turner Joy, USN, served as Commander U.S. Naval Forces Far East from 27 August 1949 to 4 June 1952. In 1951–52 he was also senior U.N. delegate in the Korean War truce talks. He covered that experience in his memoir, *How Communists Negotiate* (New York, Macmillan, 1955).
4. Syngman Rhee was the first President of the Republic of Korea when it was established in 1948 and held that office until 1960.

Communists, which is an Oriental way of thinking too. If you're soft and give in, you are susceptible to greater demands. He wanted no compromise. He was particularly adamant against what I think was one of the most outrageous things the country has ever done, which was returning the prisoners who didn't want to go back to China. We did that with the Russians, of course, in Germany.

John T. Mason Jr.: Condemning them.

Admiral Eller: Condemning them to death.

This was 1953. The negotiations neared an end when in June 1953, Rhee engineered the escape of about 25,000 prisoners who didn't want to go back. Rhee was condemned bitterly by the Joint Chiefs of Staff and State and by most people in this country. But I was rather exultant over it myself. At the time, this editorial from Memphis, Tennessee, expressed, I think, the views of any American who really understood what was going on out there.

It says, "Brave South Koreans, a patient and honorable lineage. They have been conquered by Japanese, subverted by Russians, invaded by Chinese, and rescued, at considerably more pain to themselves than to us, by the Americans and the United Nations. Yet they say we will fight on for what the United Nations promised but forgot, the unified independent democratic government in the sovereign state of Korea.

"Syngman Rhee is wrong in his wish to carry on the war at this time, but the only reason he is wrong in his position is that at this time there aren't enough people in the world who are like him and will make it stick. All two billion of us ought to be like him, then the world situation would be different and the lies, the terror, and evil of communism would be gone."

But we went ahead with the armistice.[5] We were quite happy to do so, of course, by then. I think Russia had made up her mind that she had got everything she could out of it,

---

5. On 27 July 1953 negotiators for the United Nations and the Communist North Koreans signed an armistice agreement at Panmunjom, Korea, to end the Korean War. It took effect at 10:00 that same date.

and, therefore, was willing to have the negotiations come to an end.

John T. Mason Jr.: May I ask one question?

Admiral Eller: Yes.

John T. Mason Jr.: Based on what Arleigh Burke told me, did you in your division have any knowledge of the incident involving—I guess it was Burgess in Washington who apparently was sending information by way of London to the Communists—and they knew, on the North side in advance of the South side negotiators, what they were going to get in the way of communication?[6]

Admiral Eller: We suspected something was going on, but that's a long time ago and I don't remember whether we knew anything about that or not. It may have come out later. I don't know whether Arleigh knew it at the time of the negotiations.

John T. Mason Jr.: No, they suspected it, but they didn't really know. They were just amazed at the instructions they got and, also, at the fact the Northerners obviously knew.

Admiral Eller: Knew in advance.

John T. Mason Jr.: And were taking advantage of that.

Admiral Eller: Well, this has been true, unhappily, in the State Department, I guess, all this century. There are always some there who don't agree with the national policy, usually too many, and they don't hesitate to pass out the information. I told you in a previous tape when I was in Public Information about my experience with Drew Pearson and a State Department man handing him a document. I'm sure they did that with others,

---

6. Guy Burgess was a Briton who served in the Foreign Office's Far Eastern Section and later the British Embassy in Washington. He was a spy on behalf of the Soviet Union and in 1951 accompanied fellow spy Donald Maclean in escaping to Moscow.

and I'm sure there were Communists there, as there are everywhere—or Communist sympathizers, extra liberal thinkers who are used by the Communists. Besides Korea, we had crises of every sort from most parts of the world. Vietnam then was in the early stages of being taken over, the whole of it, by the Communists. They had organized during World War II, formed cells throughout the country to take it over. And, of course, we had agreed to the division of the country, like Korea, which ensured in the end disaster.[7]

We hadn't agreed to the division yet. That came later. The French had come back to take over, and the Communists had organized a resistance throughout the country. This had increased until the fall of 1952, when Giap went on the offensive.[8] He said later on that he didn't hope to defeat the French in military operations as such, though he might win some battles, but his strategy was a long-term resistance war depending more on propaganda and politics—just as against us in Vietnam—and more on erosion of national will than on fighting. Also on murder and terror in South Vietnam. The atrocities of the Communists were never properly reported by the press in this country. They were unbelievable.

I don't know whether you've ever talked to Wally Greene, General Wallace M. Greene Jr.[9] He would be marvelous. He was Commandant of the Marine Corps from 1964 to 1968, and was the best-informed man in Washington on the Vietnam War. I think in many ways he had the deepest understanding of the men, of world events, of anybody I knew then. In naval history, I saw much of him in preparing our war reports on Vietnam and was impressed by his outstanding steps to get the truth about Vietnam, which I will cover later.

Then there was, of course, Formosa. There were rumblings of China invading, and we were always getting dispatches and acting on problems that might erupt there. In Europe during this period, there were Stalin's purges in 1952 and 1953, which were about

---

7. The Geneva Accords of 1954 brought an end to the First Indochina War. Included were a ceasefire and France agreeing to withdraw its troops. The agreement divided created the nations of North and South Vietnam.
8. General Vo Nguyen Giap, Vietnam People's Army, was the principal military commander during the First Indochina War (1946–54) and the Vietnam War (1960–75).
9. General Wallace M. Greene Jr., USMC, served as Commandant of the Marine Corps from 1 January 1964 to 31 December 1967.

as brutal as any he'd ever made. As he got older, he became much more suspicious and vindictive up to his death in March of 1953. I was one who believed that there would be a breakup in leadership, hoping it mostly, I guess. This has astonished me that after quite a bit of murder and shuffling, they came out again with their same brutal system, as they have through several changes, without a division of power. This is contrary to history, because in the past a tremendous dictator's empire is usually broken up. It may be the power of tanks and airplanes, the immense capability of killing that is present today.

We introduced into our plans the thinking from our section, tempered by the political viewpoint. It was very interesting to be in the center of world affairs information. But it was the most frustrating job I've ever had: the constant quibbling over words and phrases, which could change the meaning of something good into something that was wrong. I could never get adjusted to that.

During the year, my disc got worse from long hours sitting in the chair and commuting. We usually left home before 7:00 A.M. and got back home after 7:00 P.M. Count and I drove together.[10] He lived at the corner below us. I had little exercise or sunlight, and the riding in the car was bad for me. So I got worse and worse.

John T. Mason Jr.: When had it begun to develop?

Admiral Eller: I had my first disc, in my lower back, in 1949 and I was laid up for a long time with that. It never has recovered. It gets bad and then gets better again. And I had the next one in the Middle East in a crash landing of an airplane that got my neck. So I had both of them. And I hadn't learned to use braces yet. They hadn't been tried.

John T. Mason Jr.: Were they using braces as a medical expedient?

Admiral Eller: They were, I think, for the back; I don't know when they got the one for the neck. But I got them later.

Then I had another job thrown at me, in late 1952 or early 1953. The proponents of a general staff in unification had got their nose under the tent in 1947 just as some of us

---

10. "Count" was Admiral Austin's nickname.

expected. And when the camel gets his nose under the tent, that's the beginning of the end, unhappily. The proponents were very strong in Washington and elsewhere; *The Washington Post* was their chief mouthpiece. Phillip Graham, who married the boss's daughter had been in the Air Force during the war, and he was completely sold on the need for a single chief of staff.[11]

There had been a steady series of changes increasing the authority of the Secretary of Defense and building up his empire since 1947. But in 1952, when Eisenhower was elected in the fall, Truman immediately had Secretary of Defense Robert A. Lovett develop his ideas on what changes should be made in the Defense Department.[12] Truman favored centralization. Eisenhower favored it. Secretary of Defense Lovett's paper came out urging centralization and a single chief of staff of all the services under the chief of staff and a single military.

Eisenhower, having this paper, then appointed a loaded committee, really loaded. Lovett was on it. General Bradley, Nelson Rockefeller, Milton Eisenhower, Vanevar Bush, who was an empire builder, an able man—well. most of these were able men—and General David Sarnoff, a reserve general.[13] There was no Navy voice on it. So there wasn't much doubt what would come out. The Navy Department was concerned about this. I expect it was Admiral Duncan because he's wise and farseeing.

John T. Mason Jr.: Wu Duncan?

Admiral Eller: Donald B. Duncan.[14] They decided to form a team to examine the plan that was certain to come out from this group and to propose a Navy plan. And instead of

---

11. Philip L. Graham was publisher of *The Washington Post* from 1946 until his death in 1963. In 1940 he had married Katharine Meyer, whose father Eugene Meyer was the owner of the *Post*. She ran the newspaper after her husband's suicide.
12. Dwight D. Eisenhower served as President of the United States from 20 January 1953 to 20 January 1961. Robert A. Lovett served as Secretary of Defense from 17 September 1951 to 20 January 1953.
13. Nelson A. Rockefeller, who had careers in both business and public service, was at that time head of the President's Advisory Committee on Government Organization. Milton S. Eisenhower, the President's brother, was president of Pennsylvania State University and advisor to the President. David Sarnoff was a businessman and pioneer in radio and television. He headed the Radio Corporation of America (RCA) from 1919 until he retired in 1970. He became an Army Reserve brigadier general in the Signal Corps in 1945.
14. Admiral Donald B. Duncan, USN, served as Vice Chief of Naval Operations from 10 August 1951 to 1 September 1956. His oral history is in the Columbia University collection.

fighting it, the thought came—I believe from Struve Hensel, Assistant Secretary of the Navy in 1945 to 1946—to propose an alternate. He was a very personable man. I knew him and liked him when I was in Public Information. He had already left, I guess, when I took over Public Information, but he was around the department a great deal. He was a very ambitious and scheming man, unknown to me at the time and perhaps unknown to Duncan. He sold the Navy and I expect Wu on the fact that instead of fighting the plan as we had in the past and losing much, that we propose a plan ourselves that they could accept and we would lose less. Struve Hensel's view was that we develop a system for the Secretary of Defense like General Motors, which has a lot of vice presidents in charge of different areas of responsibility in policy, not in direction of operations.

Our team consisted of Admiral Tommy Robbins—known as Lord Plushbottom behind his back according to the way he was built—myself as his second and who handled most of it, three other officers and some yeomen.[15] So we followed Struve Hensel's suggestion. He was around quite a bit, coming down from New York and talking about it. We developed this proposal, which looked good, of several assistant secretaries under Secretary of Defense in different areas of policy responsibility.

The basic plan was accepted, but Secretary of Defense took the bad part and left out the good since each of these areas of policy responsibility increasingly provided a chance to build an empire and to enter into direction of operations. Struve got one of the jobs.[16] He was looking for it. And he, like all the others, began to build up power and overhead. As planned, each assistant secretary was to have two or three people on his staff, but soon every one of them had a flag officer from each service and the flag officer had captains and colonels and others under him. Now I expect that each of the assistant secretaries of defense has 50 to 100 people working for him. The system has really grown into a monster. Someone has said, "A growing octopus that sends out a strong cloud of ink that hides it and beclouds every issue."

One of the serious effects of this is that the deputy to the Secretary of Defense and nine assistant secretaries with their staffs, plus the great horde of people in the Joint

---

15. Rear Admiral Thomas H. Robbins, USN.
16. H. Struve Hensel served 1952–54 as General Counsel of the Department of Defense and in March 1954 became Assistant Secretary of Defense (International Security Affairs).

Chiefs of Staff have grown into a top-heavy mass. If you ever saw an overhead that killed initiative and action, you have it there.

John T. Mason Jr.: It's what Forrestal anticipated would happen and which he feared.

Admiral Eller: Which he feared would happen. He said, of course, he would keep the number down to a handful, but it got away from him and worsened after he left. One of the most vicious results is that the departments lost people to go to Secretary of Defense. Then they have to expand their numbers to answer the questions and handle the paperwork imposed upon them by this tremendous group topside.

A professor called in for consultation by the Secretary of Defense's office came down to Rotary a month or so ago to hear our speaker from Washington, whom he knew. Now this professor was a good man in his field of research. He knew nothing about military affairs, but he was called in by the research and development section of the Secretary of Defense. I asked him, "Why do you have to review what is put out by the experts who know something about it?"

"Well," he said, "they may make mistakes." So anything that the Navy wants, or the Army, or the Air Force wants to do in the field of research after going through intensive study and evaluation in the service, and budget battles, has to go to the Secretary of Defense. And he either approves it or disapproves it, or sends it back for further evaluation, further comment. It's a killing system.

In 1952 I was not on the selection list that would have had me relieve Austin, which was what Sherman had planned.[17]

John T. Mason Jr.: Which Admiral Sherman had planned?

Admiral Eller: Yes. He had died, of course. I learned afterwards that there were two aviation admirals who were foes of Sherman and whom I had offended in a minor way over the years. One of them was very good; the other was a mediocre man. They were both very strong willed.

---

17. This refers to selection for rear admiral.

John T. Mason Jr.: They were on the board?

Admiral Eller: They were on the board and were the veto members of it. They wanted someone else, saying I had not had enough experience in combat and should be in better health before selection next year. Admiral Nimitz wrote a letter, and I'll read part of this into it, because he expressed what a number of people wrote about it, and many wrote to BuPers:

"I noted with disappointment that Captain Eller was not among those selected by the last board. I've known this capable and devoted officer for many years and selected him for my staff early in the Pacific War. On the possibility that some of his accomplishments, especially in the field of active participation in combat may not have been fully covered, I request that this letter be placed on his record.

"When Captain Eller was ordered to my staff in 1942, his practical experience in peacetime training and war experience in England made him particularly fitted for his work in gunnery and training in the development of fleet gunnery procedures. To his long experience in peacetime, he had added a year and a half of combat operation, including nearly a year with the British fleet and gunnery officer on the USS *Saratoga*.

"On my staff he contributed to a marked degree to the combat readiness in the fleet by his analytical powers, his keen mind, his courage of opinion, and his sound judgment backed by aggressive and forceful initiative. His many common sense contributions benefited from his persistent efforts to keep them within the experience of the fleet by his participation in combat operations.

"He was on Guadalcanal and ships in the area in November-December 1942. In 1943 after playing an important part in the development of AA readiness, amphibious tactics, underwater demolition teams, and shore fire control support, he rode Admiral Turner's flagship in the Gilbert Island operations and participated in the assault seeking improvements in fleet readiness.

"He participated in subsequent operations and in the Okinawa assault with the special purpose of seeking improvements in gunfire support and in combating the kamikaze.

"Admiral Lee, Admiral Shafroth, and Admiral Blandy at different times asked for the services of Captain Eller on their staffs afloat.[18] But members of my staff considered that until a command was available, he would contribute more to the war effort in the larger tasks of training, operations analysis, and improvement in armament.

"Captain Eller sought to get various other afloat jobs. He was delayed for various reasons. Among these was the fact that the end of the wear did not seem imminent, and it appeared there would be ample time to give him a full sea cruise. Eventually, when he had acquired sufficient seniority in the spring of 1945, he was relieved from my staff to take command of an APA and ample time to train for and participate the contemplated assault on Japan. I understand his record in that ship was excellent.

"His wide range of abilities, his sound judgment, his industry and integrity, and profound understanding of the many complex facts of our modern Navy make him a uniquely valuable officer for flag rank." Then there were others I won't go into.

John T. Mason Jr.: Well, that certainly refuted the contention that you hadn't had enough experience in the war.

Admiral Eller: One little thing I did that year was work for the Moravian Church in a major reprint of the *Houses of Peace*, my book on the Moravians. Fleming Revell, the publisher, had destroyed the plates, and it would have been too expensive to set them up again. But I found in New York a lithographing company that would facsimile reprinting at a low cost and that was done.

My back steadily worsened with daily commuting, and the work didn't let up in the office at all. After we got out the reorganization plan, there were other major things, one being an important study on the freedom of the seas.

Then I had some major speeches I had to make. One of the most important I've ever made was Naval Operations in the Mediterranean. I was in early 1953, as I remember, in Constitution Hall. And it was, I guess, the biggest audience I ever had. I was amazed. It

---

18. Rear Admiral Willis A. Lee Jr., USN; Rear Admiral John F. Shafroth Jr., USN; Rear Admiral William H. P. Blandy, USN.

wasn't good weather, but a tremendous crowd came to hear it. We were quite interested then in conditions overseas, I guess, more so than I knew.

John T. Mason Jr.: Weren't we fearful of another war?

Admiral Eller: Yes, we were. It was in 1950 when I went to the Middle East. I might read just a couple of statements from this to show the nature of it.

"Naval Operations in the Mediterranean. When we read of Rome and Greece and other great peoples, it is difficult to appreciate in the rush of events in this second half of the 20th century, that we live in Rome of today. Tonight in this coliseum we are in the capitol, not only in the Rome of today, but of the strongest nation of all times. Destiny has given the United States leadership of the world in the 20th century. If we survive our struggle with the Soviets, the world can see a golden era surpassing the greatest of the past. It is appropriate, therefore, to be discussing naval operations which are the manifest evidence of sea power and of national power. Every great and free civilization has been founded on sea power. The other elements of national power must, of course, be present, but strength at sea stimulates and combines all of them. It is also appropriate to be discussing the Mediterranean. Steaming through the Med, I often thought of empire that held sway there. In a sudden storm off Attica, like that which wrecked Xerxes's fleet, it suddenly came home to me that most of the decisive naval operations in history before the United States became a leading power took place in and about the Mediterranean.

"Someone has said that the Mediterranean is the heart of history and sea power is its artery. G. K. Chesterton added, 'If nothing remained in the world but what was said and done and written and believed in the lands lying around the Mediterranean, we would still have all the most vital and valuable things of our world in which we live. Our philosophy of government, our laws, our arts and sciences, our alphabet, our religion spring from the shores of the Mediterranean."

Then I go on and pick up the history of sea power in the Mediterranean from the time of Egypt and Crete. Crete I especially stress because it was a first-rate sea power.

"It reached magnificent splendor when its navy was strong. It declined in invasion, disaster, and death 3,000 years ago when its navy declined."

I go up into Mahan, to Napoleon and the British struggle. First Carthage, of course, and Rome.

"Carthage lost to Rome and disappeared from history because at the peak of Hannibal's achievements she gave up the sea. It is the irony of destiny that Napoleon also lost the empire of the world, because he lost that of the sea."

It was a long speech—I thought it too long—but they wanted an hour's speech for the Naval Historical Foundation.

John T. Mason Jr.: I see.

Admiral Eller: They had a major speech about once a year in those days.

"In the titanic struggle between East and West, not unlike the classic ones that decided the fate of the world in the past, the vitality of the Mediterranean has thus reasserted itself. Today we find many reasons for bringing back the Mediterranean as a center of power conflict, some old, some new. Note a few of them:

"It is an open highway toward the heart of Eurasia. A free sea route to the Middle East, bridge between continents. The open road to the world's largest petroleum reserves. The means of protecting the Suez Canal. The open route to all nations of the Moslem Crescent. It is the connection between the West, via Suez, and South Asia's vast populations still uncommitted in the world's struggle between slavery and freedom.

"It is the protection of U.S. and NATO bases in North Africa as well as South Europe; the support for Turkey, the eastern buttress of NATO; the means to prevent Russia's rolling up the flank of NATO; the guard to Europe's coastline, the back door to NATO."

Then I discussed the Sixth Fleet and some of the tremendous activity there and its outstanding value in encouraging the people of the area. I quoted a couple of the diplomats. One of them said, "In the powerful gray diplomats of the Sixth Fleet we see the guarantees of small people's independence for we know that you command them for the freedom of the whole world. I feel certain that wherever there is free consciousness your presence in the Mediterranean waters brings steadfastness and hope."

Our Navy not only averted war, but it gave heart to the allies, as I pointed out. Then I brought in the fact that Russia has pressed for the Mediterranean for centuries. There was the so-called "Last Testament" of Peter the Great that may have been merely Napoleon's propaganda, but it's quite interesting. It says that Peter the Great stated, "Work toward Constantinople and India. He who holds them will rule the world. Wage constant war against Turkey and then Persia. Europe will be conquered when powerful fleets manned by Asiatics passing through the Mediterranean will attack France from one side while Germany is overrun from the other."

There is quite a bit more on that. It's significant that the problems we faced then in the Mediterranean are even greater problems now. I mentioned that the Middle East oil would give Russia her logistic needs when she broke out into the Persian Gulf. I didn't have to be a prophet then to see what oil was going to mean, but it didn't sink in to the mass of the people.

"Keeping the sea open to the Middle East would permit us to maintain and increase the flow of life-giving petroleum, which is essential to the industrial and military power of the Free World. Few in our country realize the importance of the oil fields in the Middle East to us and our allies. No one can quite realize the quantities involved."

I gave the production—two million barrels a day then. It's astonishing how much it has increased in three decades since. I pointed out our decline in reserves and our increasing need for it.

"Back of the shield of the sea we have been able to send out power to all the world to strengthen and rebuild freedom. You hear much pessimism as to our progress and the prospects for freedom's victory. If matched against hoped-for goals, there could be warrant for discouragement. If, however, we compare our strength, our measure of unity and the recovery of our lives from the destruction of the greatest war in history the advances in a few years are striking. We have not gone as far as we would have liked to have gone, but we have gone far."

It did look very promising them, too, of course, because we'd saved Europe; we'd saved Japan and brought it in on the side of freedom. It appeared that we were on the way to handling the Soviets.

John T. Mason Jr.: They were not so formidable at that point.

Admiral Eller: They weren't.

"Sea power is the cement of our alliances today. What would happen to NATO and ANZUS and our other allies if we lost the sea? What would happen to our basic strength of our nation, its tremendous manufacturing capacity?"

Then I point out what we have to import: "Without a navy, alliances have no meaning. A thin line of ships holds the Free World together. It is sobering to realize that the hard-won fabric of NATO, our national effort in Korea, the United States influence throughout the globe are a delicate framework hanging together on less than three score large fighting ships and a few hundred small ones, which, with the aid from the allies, must control a hundred million square miles of sea. By this handful of ships, it has been possible to project far overseas the total power of our national purpose, our wealth, our industrial might, our united military strength in the struggle to check Communism."

Then I concluded with a prophecy that if we kept our Navy strong we would have a golden age. If we didn't, it might be disastrous. And we didn't, I'm sorry to say.

John T. Mason Jr.: You read a statement the other day by a Britisher to the effect that their great success as an imperial power was not based entirely on the Navy. It was the fact that the Navy and their Foreign Office—the whole government worked as a unit.

Admiral Eller: Yes.

John T. Mason Jr.: And the Navy had relatively few ships, but still the fact that they were a unified effort, the comment was, contributed to their success as an imperial power.

Admiral Eller: That is correct.

Paul Stillwell: And in contrast, we haven't done that.

Admiral Eller: We haven't done that. And furthermore, the British always managed to keep their Navy superior. As you say, they had relatively few ships, but they always managed to keep superior, except temporarily in the American Revolution. At certain period, they let the Navy decline, and then when they did, it was disastrous for them. A stick isn't worth anything unless it is strong, unless it has a strong national purpose back of it, just as he said.

During this time, I kept working on my newspaper friends. I had a tough one out in Arizona, William R. Matthews, editor and publisher of the *Arizona Daily Star* in Tucson. He was very anti-Navy when I met him in Public Information. He was a nice man, but he just looked the other way. He had said, "We don't need the Navy. Other things are more important." Now, in June 1953, he wrote, "As a Navy man, you will see that I am more and more coming around to the conclusion that he who controls the sea lanes will be masters of the Free World in contrast to what H. J. MacKinder said, 'He who rules the heartland rules the world.' He who rules the heartland cannot rule the world unless he controls the sea lanes." This is just what the Russians have realized.

At my annual physical in 1953, the doctor put me in the hospital for treatment and possibly an operation. By then I had almost constant pain and numbness in the neck and the arms and in the lower back and right leg. From this I had a queasy stomach. So their treatment as to put me to bed, stretch my neck with weights, which almost killed me. It helps some people. Moist heat and deep electronic heat, massage and whirlpool helped. Not sufficiently, but they helped quite a bit. I think rest is more important than almost anything else.

John T. Mason Jr.: They decided against an operation?

Admiral Eller: The orthopedic surgeon wanted to operate. The neurosurgeon said to hold off. Naturally, I agreed with him, especially when I saw some results on people who were there. Some had operations and came out all right. However, one man that I knew well had a neck operation and had semi-paralysis from then on. That's what they all feared, of course. The neck is especially dangerous to operate on.

Another, a Marine colonel, was having trouble in the back. One way of trying to see what was wrong in the back was to inject a dye into the spinal cord. That is called a milogram and is crucially painful. It nearly killed him. He was half decrepit for weeks on account of it. So I resisted the milogram. Another one had a back operation, and his miseries were worse. This is what a fine doctor told me when I had my first disc trouble. He said that he had operated on hundreds of them and some got better and some got worse. So he recommended to hold off as long as I could tolerate it. Right now mine are worse. I can just tolerate my leg. It's the other leg now, curiously.

Sometime during the period I was there, the neurosurgeon put a neck brace on me. It looked like a medieval instrument of torture, not like the little one I have now that just wraps around the neck. It was exactly like a horse collar with the very heavy braces down to pads on the chest and pads on the back. Then a cupped brace under the chin pushed it up so that you were almost rigid in the neck. For the lower back I got a heavy torture contraption with steel braces all around much more rigid and severe than the one I have now.

Finally in early 1954, a medical board surveyed me, and I retired at the end of March. About then I heard of an osteopath in Washington, an elderly man who had helped some in the Navy, and they swore by him. I spoke to the neurosurgeon, a very fine gentleman, Lieutenant Commander Emil Thelen.[19] He said that it would be worth trying. So I began to go to him even while I was in the hospital and continued there intermittently for years until he died, Dr. Johann Pastorius. He was worth the cost of admission, even if he hadn't done any good, just to hear his stories. He was a marvelous narrator.

He was the son of a Prussian Army officer and had been sent to military school in his father's footsteps. It was so brutal and harsh that he ran away to sea. On one voyage his ship got to America, and he jumped ship and joined the Marines. In those days—of course, this must have been in the 1890s—a great part of our Navy and Marine enlisted men were foreigners. In fact, in the Navy, I think at one time a little earlier, practically all enlisted men were foreigners. He joined the Marines for a tour, then went into the Army Medical

---

19. Lieutenant Commander Emil P. Thelen, Medical Corps, USN.

Corps. He claimed that he wrote the *Army Pharmaceutical Manual of Medicine*. Later on I saw one and his name was on it, so that authenticated that story.

Some of his most delightful stories were about the Spanish-American War. He was at San Juan Hill, where he said Teddy Roosevelt's Rough Riders met only scattered and wild shooting and walked up comfortably.[20] But the news accounts of Hearst papers and others made him a world hero. I guess that's one case where newspapers bombasticism did our country much good, because he was one of our great Presidents. He saw the emergence of the United States as a world power and built up the sea power needed.

John T. Mason Jr.: He certainly was.

Admiral Eller: His duty at San Juan Hill was to go with General William R. Shafter, who he said weighed 300 pounds, as I've also heard from Army officers.[21] He couldn't walk up the hill. It was too hot and he was too heavy, so he rode on a mule and Pastorius's job was to fan him as he rode up the hill.

And another story concerned President William Howard Taft.[22]

John T. Mason Jr.: Another fatty.

Admiral Eller: Another fatty. When Taft was President, Pastorius's Army assignment was to go to the White House and give the President osteopathic treatments for his back. He always carried a black satchel and in it, by the President's command, had two bottles of bourbon. That was all the medicine required.

Just after I retired, General Bedell Smith asked me to be Secretary of the National Security Council.[23] This would have meant more haggling over words for six days a week

---

20. Colonel Theodore Roosevelt commanded a group of Army troops in the Battle of San Juan Hill on 1 July 1898. The battle, near Santiago de Cuba, was a decisive action in the Spanish-American War. The soldiers of the 1st U.S. Volunteer Cavalry had the collective nickname of "Rough Riders."
21. Major General William R. Shafter, USA. He received a Medal of Honor for his actions in the Civil War. Fort Shafter in Hawaii is named for him.
22. William Howard Taft served as President of the United States from 4 March 1909 to 4 March 1913.
23. Lieutenant General Walter Bedell Smith, USA, served as Under Secretary of State, 1953–54.

and more commuting, ruinous for my back. So I declined, as I declined civilian jobs offered in Washington. I needed to stop commuting and get in better health.

While in the hospital with nothing particular to do, I did considerable that had been put off. But one thing I had to work on first was a major speech at the National War College, which was scheduled before I was hospitalized. I hope someday to put this into something more than just notes. Ordinarily I speak entirely from notes. I go over it so much that I never say the same words exactly, but I know the points and what to say. It's harder, I guess, to do it that way, but it makes a better speech.

This speech was on sea power. In essence, I compared Alfred T. Mahan's viewpoints on sea power with today's. I read again his *Influence of Sea Power Upon History* and other of his writings, and picked out what I thought were his basics.[24] One is geographic position; two is physical conformation; three is extent of territory; four is population; five is national characteristics; six is government attitude and action toward maintaining a strong Navy, with supporting elements such as merchant marine, shipbuilding, and overseas bases.

The values of sea power are the destruction or containment of enemy forces at sea; the defense of homeland, preferably by overseas operations; control of the sea for your own communications; blockade and denial of sea communications to the enemy; the free movement of our armies, providing advantages of maneuvering, mobility, surprise, concentration of force, offensive operations; and naval and amphibious attack limited to unfortified or weakly fortified areas. This was in the time of Mahan before we developed the awesome striking power of World War II.

John T. Mason Jr.: Yes.

Admiral Eller: I spoke to the National War College, and they also brought in the Industrial College—another large audience. I used an interesting allegory early in the speech: "Some of you gentlemen who have been in the Middle East, as were Red Stroh and I

---

24. Alfred Thayer Mahan (1840–1914) was the United States's most influential naval historian and philosopher. His lectures at the Naval War College led to his greatest work, *The Influence of Sea Power upon History, 1660–1783*, published in 1890. His writings stimulated the growth of a large Navy and the nation's overseas expansion.

together—captain of one of my flagships—may have heard this ancient legend. King Solomon one day leaned on his staff looking out over the golden city of Jerusalem and his empire beyond. He seemed all powerful. Not a cloud was in the sky. But even as he leaned, a tiny worm in the heart of his staff ate it away silently, invisibly, inevitably.

"This is an allegory on the life of man. The minute he is born he begins to die. It is an allegory on his empires. Their crumbling ruins cover the earth. In the middle of January 1954 how far has inevitable destiny eaten away the strength of the United States, and in particular the strength of sea power? Exploring this question, we will cover two broad points: first, what are the factors in sea power evidenced so remarkably in history as recorded by Mahan and others; second, how has our jet propelled atomic age changed these."

So then I examined each point against operations in World War II and came out with the conclusion that although developments like aviation, electronics, and atomic energy have had their effect upon sea power, they have basically not changed the fundamentals of sea power and its benefits.

In the hospital I was treated only part of the day. I began to write on the meaning of sea power under the changes of atomic energy, guided missiles, the electronic age. This speech was basically part of that. The speech, incidentally, was taken down by a stenographer, not by a tape recorder, because they didn't get it exactly. Then the National War College had it reproduced, and what I am reading from is a pamphlet of which they had a number of copies printed and used in the curriculum.

Of the articles that I wrote or started in the hospital, three appeared in the *Naval Institute Proceedings*. The first, completed in late 1953, appeared in November 1954, "Troubled Oil and Iran." I might read the start of that.

"If today, the United States had to select one key area overseas that she ought to make stronger for her future safety, which would it be? Indochina? Western Europe? Korea or Turkey? Japan or Greece? Or would it be Iran?

"A powerful case can be made for the ancient kingdom of the Medes and Persians. Throughout the fearful length of the Iron Curtain frontier that runs many thousands of miles by sea, and by land reached by sea, no section can exceed Iran in raw materials and strategic benefits, and none is weaker. Part of the weakness comes from Iran's unique position between our sea power represented by only a token on her southern sea frontier."

That's when we had just a little Middle East force and practically no ships.

"Soviet sea power is second to ours in the world and overwhelming on the Russian-Iranian sea frontier, the Caspian. This part of Iran's chain of straw lies in geography and can be improved only to the extent that the United States is willing to commit larger naval forces in the Middle East command."—which we finally are doing a generation later, at a time of crisis.

"But most of Iran's other weaknesses need not exist. Indeed, this land of ancient world empires could and should present one of the strongest barriers to the Soviets: in her lofty and rugged mountains; in the stout fiber of her average citizen; in her potential wealth, which surpasses that of our stouthearted ally Turkey. In her heritage of culture, leadership, and pride of greatness Iran has no equal in the Middle East-South Asian area. It is a tragedy of our generation that she has not measured up to her potentialities."

This is partly so because of the Soviets, the United States, Iran, and Great Britain. In 1953, I said—and I would, unhappily, say differently now—"At this writing it appears that the United States, Iran, and Great Britain have realized their responsibilities in this major historical blunder of the 1950s and have taken the first steps to correct it by renewing oil production in Iran."

That was when Mosaddegh had come in and the Shah had temporarily fled the country. Then we had helped put him back in power.

I agree with what the Shah recently said, and have always thought this, that he was wrong in giving up the leadership of Iran this last time, in large part because of pressure from the United States. We didn't realize what we needed in Iran. We don't need a foe there. We need, above all things, a friend and an ally, because this is the route where the Soviets can break down from the Caspian to the Persian Gulf and take over the oil. The Russians have been trying to get to the Persian Gulf for centuries, and time after time, have taken away land from both Turkey and Persian in their progress toward it.

John T. Mason Jr.: Well, as usual, we were swayed by ideals rather than practicalities.

Admiral Eller: We should be swayed by ideals, but we should temper them with practical understanding. We knew that the Shah's regime employed oppression, but largely upon those who deserved it—Communist agitators and intriguers, and the priesthood, of whom very few, I think, are dedicated Moslems in the sense that they live by the dictates of the Koran. Most are out for what they can get out of it for themselves, and they want to keep the power that they have.

Another article started in 1953 was "The Soviet Bid for the Sea." Each article points up the dangers of the growth of Soviet sea power and the importance of the Middle East. I might quote a bit of it, which the Naval Institute well illustrated.

"Why do Soviet shipyards work day and night building warships? Is it a sudden decision? Is it simply fulfilling the 'demands' of the Russian people, that Stalin stated on the first Red Navy Day after the war, for 'a stronger and mightier navy'? Or is it a specific step in a long-range plan? In the correct answers to these questions lie the foundations of grave decisions for the United States security."

We, as a nation, had not then, in 1954, realized what was happening in naval development in the U.S.S.R., and apparently haven't realized it until it's almost too late. I went into the swift advances going on in the U.S.S.R. in all phases of naval development. I showed how the empire had expanded historically from a small area and now was trying to take over the world.

Then I ended with, "Resolution without strength to back it can also fail." This came from the President's saying that we would put a stop to the Soviets. "In fact, a sure breeder of irresolution is weakness. We will need all the strength we can muster in this struggle for civilization. Of all military strength, none is more important to us than the Navy. If we let the Soviets surpass us at sea through their aggressive building or our inaction, we assure disaster. If we fail to be ready at sea, we fail everywhere."

The third article, published in November 1956, was written partly in 1954 and finished sometime in 1955—"U.S. Destiny in the Middle East." In it, I show the current importance of the Middle East in detail and briefly discuss its importance in the past:

"It is a strange twist of fate that the Middle East has become decisive to our own future. Here a great part of the history of the world has been written. Here empires, almost without number, have flowered to greatness only to die. For some centuries now, we have considered the Middle East a land of the past. If this was ever true, why is it not still true? Why, in particular, does the Middle East become a key to the destiny of the United States far away? These are important questions with complex answers."

Then I went into each question to try to point out answers. In the discussion, I quoted Admiral Burke, then CNO.

"As Admiral Burke recently said, 'The threat from the Soviet Navy alone is grave. In terms of new ships, submarines and aircraft, and in terms of weapons progress, it is far more serious than the threat we faced in World War II.'" He was correct, and the threat has grown monstrously.

The Kremlin rulers know the Middle East is valuable and intend to prevent its becoming strong before they are ready to move in. They want unstable governments, mob rule, issues that inflame nations against nations, and family against family." Just what we have today exactly.

They foment trouble and feed those fires they don't start. The Soviet leaders themselves tell us what value to place on detente. Nikita Khrushchev says, 'If anyone believes our smiles involve abandonment of the teaching of Marx, Engels, and Lenin, he deceives himself poorly, those who wait for that must wait until shrimps learn to whistle.'"[25]

And I had one article in the *National Geographic*, not because of my skill in writing, but because, I think, of Dr. Thomas McKnew. You probably know Tom, don't you?

John T. Mason Jr.: No, I don't know him.

Admiral Eller: He was for a long time secretary and then became vice chairman of the board. He urged me to write something on the Middle East. So they published an article entitled, "Troubled Waters East of Suez." This was a summary account of my Middle East tour with beautiful illustrations.[26] It was, I guess, one of the most frustrating articles I ever

---

25. Nikita S. Khrushchev served as First Secretary of the Communist Party, 1953–64, and Premier of the Soviet Union, 1958–64.
26. Captain Eller's article appeared in the April 1954 issue of *The National Geographic Magazine*, beginning on page 483.

had printed because they have a staff dedicated to making the language sound the way the *National Geographic* articles have to sound.

John T. Mason Jr.: Well, they do.

Admiral Eller: They all sound the same in a way. They chopped up everything I wrote, but they kept the essence of it. One little girl, when I spoke of flying over the lava wastes of Eastern Saudi Arabia, said, "Why they have never had any volcanoes there." It took me six or eight letters to get that straightened out. They research everything, but she hadn't done enough research.

While I was in the hospital and writing, friends on magazines and papers from Public Information days asked me to write articles. Others picked up material from the *Naval Institute Proceedings* and condensed it or quoted it. So there was quite a bit of publication in that period. Somehow I got in touch with the editor of IBM's magazine. *Think,* a superb, slick-cover magazine. He asked me to write some articles on the Middle East. I think the assistant editor came to the Mediterranean speech.

I ran in *Free World Security* and *Think* in February 1955. These dealt with the same theme:

"The issue between Communism and freedom is joined around the world, but vital areas where the decisions rest are few. One of these is Iran. She is weak today. One can see there much, however, of the greatness of her past. We in the West should hope so, for Iran is the key to the strategic Middle East, perhaps the key to peace in our time."

Then I touched on the strategic importance of Iran, which is obvious: the road to India; the center of the weak Moslem dike against communism; the means to outflank Turkey and Pakistan; the way to Suez; the sea door to Europe.

American Ordnance was the publication of American Ordnance Association, which had developed with my assistance while I was in Public Information from the small Army Ordnance Association. Colonel James Walsh, a West Point graduate and an officer in the Army for a time, had got out and gone into business and made a fortune. He had supported the Ordnance Association financially. A very fine colonel, Leo Codd, as executive secretary, had run it through good times and bad. When unification came along, they had the inspiration to change it into *American Ordnance*. So I helped them bring the Navy into it and to make it representative of all the services. They were appreciative as long as they lived, invited me to all their trustee special meetings and their executive group meetings. A number of my writings had appeared in the magazine. They now asked me to do an article on Midway.

John T. Mason Jr.: The Battle of Midway?

Admiral Eller: The Battle of Midway, which I term "a crossroads of history."[27] It was one of my better analyses of the steps taken by both sides and the errors made, though very few errors by the United States fleet. I came to the conclusion this was one of those battles that was directed by the Lord, because it couldn't have gone that way otherwise. Victory was one in a million chances.

Also, I had articles in the Navy League magazine, then titled *Now Hear This*, and in a very fine magazine on the West Coast, *The Argonaut*. W. W. Chapin was the publisher. I'd gotten to know him in San Francisco on Public Information duty, and became close to him. Some have called this fine publication the best weekly in America.

One of the great men I've ever know was Wheeler McMillan, editor of *Farm Journal*. A very wise and a tremendous supporter of free enterprise.

John T. Mason Jr.: That was published in Philadelphia?

Admiral Eller: In Philadelphia. And *The Pathfinder*. Graham Patterson was publisher of both magazines, and Wheeler McMillan was a powerhouse for him with the *Farm Journal*. He had a broad mind and a broad philosophy that I've not seen in many people.
On the *Buffalo Evening News*, I had a good friend in the editor, and he picked up practically anything that I published.

---

27. From 4 to 6 June 1942, U.S. and Japanese naval forces fought a battle northwest of Midway Island in the Pacific. After Japanese bombers had struck the island, carrier-based U.S. dive-bombers attacked and sank the Japanese carriers *Hiryu*, *Soryu*, *Kaga*, and *Akagi* and the cruiser *Mikuma*. U.S. ships lost were the carrier *Yorktown* (CV-5) and the destroyer *Hammann* (DD-412). The battle was both a tactical and strategic victory for U.S. forces.

Walter Annenberg of the *Philadelphia Inquirer* published a number of things, as did the *San Diego Union*. E. F. Hofer's *Industrial News* distributed nationally from the West Coast, where I'd gotten acquainted with the publisher, picked up parts of many articles—which many of the over 10,000 papers he reached—in turn, reprinted. More on this organization later.

After I retired, an organization in the Defense Department that prepared talks asked me to write some articles. They called them talks, but they actually are studies on different aspects of defense to be used for instruction of enlisted men and officers. These were periodic talks that commands would give weekly or monthly. I was asked to redo two that I didn't think much of, "Tools for Fighting-Men Ships," and "Tools for Fighting-Men Guided Missiles," both of those being appropriate for me. So I did.

Then BuPers asked me to prepare a pamphlet on the U.S. Navy. These were maybe 2,000 or 3,000 words. Enough for a brief talk. The contract for each must run about 15 or 20 pages, much longer than the article. They put out equal opportunity, all of this paperwork just to say, "Will you write such-and-such a paper?" I didn't even read the contract but went ahead and wrote it.

At the same time, I had long had in mind two or three books. One was on public speaking. I had started speaking early in high school as a debater and always felt nervous, and wasn't sure that my way was the best way. So at some time I started reading books on public speaking and still have some scattered around the house. Then I studied more and more the methods and I got down to a formula that I feel has been most useful for me. When I have a speech coming up, as quick as I get it, I start thinking about it and at some odd time—on an envelope usually—jot down three points as the rough frame of the speech. Then, as many people have said in different ways: start with something that matters; say something about it built around the three points; say what was said in a summary; and then end strong with an appeal, a quotation, a prophecy, or a warning.

Having got the rough outline—it's very rough because I've never been able to do a detailed outline—I then read extensively to build up the points with significant data. Having done this, I always go over it several times, the real work, and try to add to it examples full of life, humor, references to the audience, powerful apt quotations. I collected several notebooks with these.

Soon after I got out of the hospital, I completed a manuscript for the book since much of it was already assembled. I made it more lively with a large number of appropriate cartoons primarily from *The Saturday Evening Post*, which had superb cartoons in those days.

John T. Mason Jr.: That was in its heyday.

Admiral Eller: In its heyday, yes; and I knew the editor then. One citation was St. Paul's speech to the Athenians on Mars Hill, an example of keying a speech exactly and aptly to a situation. He composed it in his mind as he passed the objects of their devotion. The manuscript was religious and idealistic. I sent it to one publisher who said it was too idealistic. Just then I got involved in other activities and didn't have time to work on it and launch it again. Maybe I will one day.

I also have always collected quotations. I've got a drawer full of them here and I have a large subject notebook made up while I was in Naval History. From my youth, apt quotations, inspiring ones, humorous ones that are keyed to the point have appealed to me.

We always read in my home from a Baptist daily text I think it was. Of course, we now read the Moravian daily text, which I started learning about when I got to know Agnes. I began to use inspirational quotations in my *Log* and *Trident* writings during midshipman days. Then when I was assistant editor of the *Naval Institute Proceedings*. in spare time, while teaching at the academy, I began to put them on the page at the end of articles. I think this may have been the first time this was done with any consistency. I remember one of the first was Mahan's "Tenacity of purpose and untiring energy in execution can baffle deeply laid plans."

Captain George V. Stewart, who was the editor first, and then Rear Admiral Albert T. Church let me have a free hand. I began to use those in the magazine and also began to use more photographs, which the editors have far surpassed now in quality and volume.

John T. Mason Jr.: Well, they have such a collection.

Admiral Eller: Yes. And they have more people working on it.

I had the idea that I would make up a daily reading volume, something like the church ones, but with other quotations in them as well. My idea was to have a page for each day of the year with a number of illustrations. Each page would have a New Testament and an Old Testament quotations, a hymn quotation, a quotation from a classical philosopher like Pericles or Thucydides, outstanding quotations of the past few centuries like Shakespeare's, Goethe's and so on. I divided it into 12 sections, each one for a month and each emphasizing a quality of the soul: faith, hope, love, service, courage, patience, and so on.

The first part of the summer of '54, I typed thousands of quotations and began to assemble them into 12 main sections. Then time ran out. By autumn, rest, freedom from commuting, the braces and osteopathic treatment had eased my disc trouble to the point that I considered taking on one of the jobs offered. Friends in the E. F. Hofer organization asked me to be the eastern representative for their free enterprise publication service that had published many editorials based on my writings—at times picked up by as many as 2,000 to 3,000 newspapers. This seemed worthwhile, so I tried it for a few months but found it not suited to me. One benefit was I occasionally had to spend a Sunday in New York for an early Monday conference, and I always went to hear Norman Vincent Peale's magnificent and inspiring sermons.

At this time, Bucknell University was having trouble with its engineering departments, and was about to lose accreditation for some or all of them. Most had stayed in a rut. The pay was low; laboratories and some courses needed updating; research was negligible, partly because of poor labs; morale was in the bilges. In 1955, the president and trustees asked me to take the new position of Director of Engineering. I didn't want to leave our home, but my back was better; I was well along in planned writing and the challenge appealed to me.

While my agreement to go to Bucknell still pended. Admiral Freddy Boone, then Superintendent of the Naval Academy, was pressing to build a memorial stadium.[28] Appropriate funds were not available. He asked me to prepare a brochure and to head up

---

28. Rear Admiral Walter F. Boone, USN, was superintendent of the Naval Academy from August 1954 to March 1956.

the committee that would fund it. So I did and made extensive preparations, but the project was turned down by the alumni association trustees. They didn't feel they had the staff or the money to run the drive, which they probably didn't. Admiral J. F. Shafroth, a good friend, was one of those who turned it down, and another friend, Admiral George Hussey, was president of the association.[29] So that died, but they used much of what had been prepared in the drive a few years later when we built the stadium.

The last group of writings that I did in that period was on the Moravians, in whom I had been interested long before writing *Houses of Peace*. The first book was *Whispering Pines*, put out in 1954 by a publisher in Winston-Salem, who asked me to do an introduction to evaluate John Henry Boner, a Moravian poet, and to put his poems in context. The book was a reprint of a very rare volume of Boner's *Whispering Pines*. In that I said, "Man's life gains power and inspiration from rhythms. Before history he began to understand the changing cycle of day and night, of the moon, the tides, the rising and setting of the sun, the majestic sweep of the seasons from the death of winter to rebirth and growth into full-blown summer.

"Our century has brought further knowledge of rhythmic forces extended from the heart of the atom to infinity, but the farther science reaches, the vaster the mystery becomes. All of us feel the effect of these forces upon the hours of light around us. All of us reach with conscious wonder or with vague unknowing ache to the unfolding surge of eternity.
"Some speak in scientific formulae, some with machines, some in weighted tomes, and some in poems, as did John Henry Boner. He wasn't a first poet of the world, but he was, nevertheless, the first poet of his own assigned part of the world, and some of his poems rank high. He drank of the same elixir as his towering contemporaries Tennyson and Browning: 'quickness to see through the conflict of life, the melody and beauty of nature, and overlaying all the eternal goodness.'

"Most of us are best when we speak of what we know best. We know best what we love, are warmly interested in, and deeply feel. Boner was best in recapturing amidst city turmoil, the magic of his youth: the green, rolling hills of Piedmont, North Carolina; the forests with the oaks and whispering pines; the swirling Yadkin River; the misty distances

---

29. Vice Admiral John F. Shafroth Jr., USN (Ret.); Vice Admiral George F. Hussey, USN (Ret.).

of the Blue Ridge, the most beautiful of mighty mountains I have known; and especially, best of all, his hometown of Salem, the city of peace and his people, the Moravians. Their lives and history were filled with proof of the power that directs our days. It is love of God's green handiwork and expression of God's power above all else that give magic to most of Boner's best poems." He had some very good little poems. I had been brought up in the same general area, so it was a work of joy for me.

John T. Mason Jr.: To relive it.

Admiral Eller: When I was writing *Houses of Peace*. I got interested in John Amos Comenius.[30] He is one of the world's great men and author of many works. Agnes's father had collected Moravian books and had, perhaps, the best private collection in the country, including two not in the Library of Congress. One of these that I liked especially was quite rare; it had been published in England in 1858 by Daniel Benham. I believe it was the first translation of Comenius's *The School of Infancy* into English. I borrowed it and then began to read everything I could in the Library of Congress by and concerning Comenius.

He was a late contemporary of Cervantes and Shakespeare, and Francis Bacon. He thought very much like Bacon and Shakespeare and Cervantes, too, in their broad view of humanity, but he had a deeper religious conviction than any of them. He was a man of incomparable energy. He suffered the trials of Job. He lost his father and his mother and a couple of his sisters in his youth, but he had an unfailing, unyielding faith in God's designs, despite all his sorrows and his losses. I wrote an introduction about as long as the book itself in order to present him. It's really a synopsis of his life. I might quote what he said when he was a youth.

"In the spring of 1614, a young man of 22 walked along the dusty roads of the Holy Roman Empire bound from Heidelberg to Prague. His long, slender face was that of a dreamer. In his eyes burned a purpose that foretold that he would do more than dream great dreams before he reached the end of this troubled *The Labyrinth of the World*.

---

30. John Amos Comenius (1592–1670) was a Czech philosopher, teacher, and theologian.

On the long foot journey, Comenius had time to think thoughts he probably spoke to a companion, of his own problems and the problems of the world that lay large in his heart. They were a burden that could have been unendurable to a man without Comenius's philosophy that the object of 'life is to be prepared for eternity. Unless you look forward to this, you lose your life entirely.

Comenius lived in a time of upheaval, like us in this second half of the 20th Century. His own era was to crumble about him. Most of all that he treasured on earth would disappear in the Storm of the World. He had already suffered deeply. What he would yet suffer was to be far worse than he could dream—just as the catastrophes of our era have been more far-reaching than anyone alive today sensed in the fragrant spring of 1914. They may be worse still in this age of atoms."

This is a fine quotation of his: "When I attained that age," Comenius writes in *The Labyrinth of the World*, "at which the difference between good and bad begins to appear to the human understanding . . . it seemed most necessary to me to consider what group of men I should join and with what matters I should occupy my life."

He decided to go into teaching and into the church. In his words, "We are born to do; therefore, an active life is truly life. Idleness is the sepulcher of living men."

He started to write as a youth. He began to make a tremendous dictionary of Czech-Latin, transferring Czech into Latin and Latin into Czech. He worked on it most of his life and had it destroyed in war several times.

The Thirty Year War broke out in 1618—this was the plague of his time. It ended in 1648, but was followed soon thereafter by other wars. Seventy-five percent of the population of Bohemia and Moravia died. It shrank from three million to under 800,000.

Comenius lost his first wife and his two babies, his church, school, library, and manuscripts—everything that he had. With most of the other surviving Protestants, he was exiled from his homeland. Comenius established his church's headquarters in Poland. He was elected head of the church and ran it. At the same time he devoted himself deeply to education, because his philosophy was that if you could educate a man properly in a religious environment, you could remake him and remake the world. He himself ran a school. He revised the educational system in Sweden and Hungary, hoping he could raise money and support for his church. And he wrote extensively on education, including textbooks that spread through the world. He said that education had three foundations: the Bible, related to the soul; nature, the physical world around us; and reason, science accumulated wisdom of the mind. And he divided education into four parts: zero to six, the school of the mother or the school of infancy; then six to 12, 12 to 18, and 18 on—very much as we still divide it. He has been called the father of modern education. In fact, there are several quotations I have in here, including one by Nicholas Murray Butler, which point him out as being the great forerunner of our educational system today.

Early in his exile he wrote a book that became world famous, *Janua Lingruarum Reserata* (The Gate of Languages Unlocked). This swept through the world and was translated into many languages including four in Asia. It was a textbook in our country, including at Harvard, according to Samuel Eliot Morison's history of Harvard. Cotton Mather says that Comenius was invited to come there to be its president. The Latin school was for ages 12 to 18. He wrote a simplified version of the *Janua* for this age group called *Orbis Pictus, The World in Pictures*. This was for teaching Latin. It and the Janua are said to be the finest books ever written for transmitting knowledge of languages.

Here is an example. He had a picture on a page, usually one devoted to philosophy and right living. Then he had the local language on one side and the Latin on the other. Comenius was fluent in Latin, Czech, and German, and he wrote in all three. Latin, of course, was the universal language at the time.

I found *The School of Infancy* so full of wisdom related to the period of life, which Comenius says is the most important period in shaping a person. "The first care," he says, "ought to be of the soul," the principal part of man. "The next care is for the body that it may be made a habitation fit and worthy of an immortal soul. Regard the mind as rightly instructed, which is truly illuminated by the radiance of the wisdom of God." And why is it so important to bring proper education into the baby's life? "Everyone knows that whatever disposition of the branches of an old tree obtain, they must necessarily have been so formed from its first growth. Man therefore in the very first formation of body and soul, should be molded so as to be such as he ought to be throughout his whole life."

I borrowed the book from Agnes's father and then read extensively in many books on the Moravians and Comenius. I got a German copy of it—Comenius wrote different versions in Czech, German, Polish, and Latin. Then I hired a St. John's tutor to translate the German so that I would have that to compare against this text, which was done by Daniel Benham in England, who greatly loved the book as I came to. Then I checked the Latin. I'm poor at Latin, but was able to check certain passages that needed to be checked. And I edited the final version to leave out some of his lengthy examples but so indicated where they were left out, examples that today would not be appropriate. I then sent it to the University of North Carolina Press and they sent it to a couple of Czechs in this country, authorities on Comenius. It was finally published by the university. I gave quite a number of copies to the church to be used as wished.

The reason I was so much interested in it is the same reason that Benham gave. In 1858 Benham said that he had a twofold purpose in translating this great book on education. First, he was convinced of the vast importance of the subject. Second, he believed that "although multitudes of books have been written since it was originally published in 1633, yet nothing has appeared at all comparable with it, much less superseding it as a work of inestimable value to a faithful Christian mother."

In essence, Comenius showed throughout the book that a mother was not only the most important teacher, but she could teach a child the beginning of everything, the beginning of religion, the beginning of philosophy, the beginning of geography, the terrain around him, astronomy by pointing out the stars, the moon, and the sun, and could, in fact, shape his character and his interest in life in the maternal school, which would shape him for the rest of his days.

My work on Comenius's *The School of Infancy* had unforeseen early benefits. By the grace of God, it took me to North Carolina for my last visit with my father, who died that fall, and next to last with my mother, who died of heartbreak in a few months. It also enriched my commencement address at Salem College on 30 May 1955—one of my more significant talks.

Part of the beginning included this quotation from Comenius's Rules of Life, a booklet he prepared for a favorite student's departure from his school. "The object of this life is to be prepared for Eternity. Unless you look forward to this, you lose your life entirely."

Not long after the commencement address, having finished *The School of Infancy* manuscript, we shifted homeport to Bucknell. As always, Agnes had gone along helpfully with my decision, though I know she did not want to make the move.

At the university, where conditions were worse than expected, the new broom started sweeping hard. This stimulated the dedicated old-timers, especially, who were eager for leadership and direction. All people want to excel. It's easy to slack off; most will, but they want to do well. A busy and productive year followed. Flying visits that summer took me to some of the best engineering schools from MIT to Johns Hopkins, North Carolina State, Penn State, and Ohio State. Also to various research and development centers like Applied Physics Laboratory, Naval Ordnance Laboratory, and Naval Research Laboratory; and to visit leading Bucknell graduates. From my work in missiles and radar, and duty on the Joint Research and Development Board, I knew leading men at several universities and labs. Many useful ideas resulted.

Re-accreditation was coming up in eight months, so it was necessary to work fast. A few alumni had formed an ad hoc engineering council that had spurred the establishment of the Office of Director of Engineering. With them we now developed a formal organization of all engineering graduates as a division of the alumni association. My visits included leading certain of these for ideas and support, equipment and funds.

With these funds and a grudging grant from the university comptroller, it was possible to pay the department chairman to stay on for the summer to get new programs under way. We met as a committee weekly, with me as chairman, to take up needs, to work on joint projects such as publications, and to approve my actions.

I knew it was unwise to order them to accept anything. Academic freedom ruled. Teachers, whether good or bad, were free agents— witness the Marxists that infest our colleges today. Engineers who had to deal with proven laws and facts were easier to lead than those in liberal arts and so-called social sciences, which are not so social and certainly not science. But even with engineers, it was necessary to persuade and let them make decisions affecting their departments, or to think they did. I did go counter to one university rule that each department select its chairman. In engineering, existing ones stayed on. They were old hands, good men who needed someone to handle their problems and to spearhead moves to solve them.

The committee early agreed to prepare lists of what was needed to prepare department equipment and curriculums, and to draw up a tabulation of research projects teachers could undertake. From them, with my modifications, resulting in part from visits to top engineering schools and research labs, we developed several little brochures—a chairman can usually steer the deliberation of a committee to accord with his views. My drafts of the roughs generally ended up basically the same.

One of the brochures tabulated by departments, "Equipment and Machinery Needed." Another summarized research proposals. In the Navy League and American Ordnance Association, I had made friends with many executives in corporations. Visits to them and to laboratories, and personal mailings to alumni and to 30-40 corporations who recruited at Bucknell, brought good results. We received as donation, scores of large and small items, new and used, with a value of thousands of dollars. General Electric, for example, gave us one machine worth over $10,000.

The research brochure also had favorable results. It included a list of fields of special capabilities and interests not only of engineering professors but also of those in math and science. In a few months, we more than doubled research contracts and grants. The most important benefit was stimulation of enterprise and enthusiasm in professors.

Having learned from Secretary Forrestal the value of a high-level advisory committee, I promptly set one up, of top engineering educators and leaders in industry. Most were friends, some of long-standing in the Navy like Admiral Cochrane, now retired and vice president of MIT.[31] They were of much value in pressing our needs.

A heavy speaking load locally and afield consumed about an evening a week. There were some major speeches, such as at Ohio State University on the Middle East, to the Foreign Trade Council in New York. And there, also, to the annual meeting of the AIME on the strategic importance of Middle East oil. This talk was printed in AIME proceedings and picked up by various publications.

---

31. Vice Admiral Edward L. Cochrane, USN, was Chief of the Bureau of Ships during World War II. After his retirement from the Navy in 1947, he was on the faculty of the Massachusetts Institute of Technology.

There were also several important national engineering society meetings to attend with the appropriate professors. The interchange of ideas helped, and I got to know some of the finest men in the teaching profession. Another facet struck me—that a high proportion of the professors were narrow specialists. At the American Institute of Electrical Engineers meeting, I lunched one day with a group of senior professors. One said his field was generation of electricity. Another's was long-line transmission, another's radio. It was easy for me with my general theoretical knowledge and detailed experience in radar, influence fuzes, and gunnery, to hold my own.

A happy by-product of the meetings was the chance to help a number retiring from the Navy, and some from the Army, to go into teaching or to prepare for it. Anyone with a long career in the service, of course, has a splendid foundation. Training, teaching, is a constant part of his job.

That winter, two part-time assignments infrequently took me to Washington. One of them—although I had no realization of it then—would steer me out of education to a second career in the Navy, moored in Washington. It was my longest single tour and, perhaps, my largest contribution to the Navy and to the nation's understanding of the giant role of sea power in preserving freedom. The tour would also see the Navy's beginnings in oral history, pioneered by Allan Nevins and Jack Mason.[32] I will cover this duty separately, closing this series, now years old, with this interview.

The first assignment was to the staff of the President's Disarmament Committee. Harold Stassen, whom I had known in the Pacific, headed it up with cabinet rank as special assistant to President Eisenhower.[33] While spending an occasional day or two in Washington to review Soviet proposals and to work on U.S. position papers—usually I could also cover Bucknell business at the National Science Foundation, NRL, and elsewhere.[34] At one time, with Stassen, I developed plans for a visit to the U.S.S.R. by a committee from the engineering societies that would, by chance, include me, but it fell through. Experience on the disarmament committee reinforced my realization that

---

32. Joseph Allan Nevins was an American historian. In 1947 he created the first institutional oral history program at Columbia University. Dr. John T. Mason Jr., the interviewer for much of the Eller memoir, worked in Columbia's oral history program for a number of years before joining the Naval Institute.
33. Harold E. Stassen served as governor of Minnesota from 1939 to 1943. As a Naval Reserve officer, he served in World War II and afterward was president of the University of Pennsylvania, 1948–53.
34. NRL – Naval Research Laboratory.

it is impossible to negotiate with the Soviets and come out with a fair resolution—as has been demonstrated in the decades since by their constant intractability, violation of agreements, and buildup of arms.

The other assignment, requested by CNO, led to a few short sessions in Washington. An internecine war had erupted in the Navy Department between John Heffernan's Division of Naval History and a group of writers in Public Information—all friends of mine—supported by Robert Albion, well-known professor at Harvard and Princeton, speaker and consultant who demonstrated in my experience how much a man could fool the world with a good education, glib tongue, and big front.[35] The issues between the two divisions need not be narrated. The committee of three appointed to investigate charges and countercharges consisted of: Allan Nevins, dedicated American, noted historian, indefatigable workers, "Father of oral history," cheerful and interesting companion; Walter Whitehall, Director of Boston Athenaeum, able historian, ghostwriter for Admiral King's autobiography, super speaker, Elizabethan in talents, wise and witty conversationalist; and myself, one-time Director of Public Information.[36]

The meetings with these two repaid many times over the time consumed. Airing the charter revealed that most were blown-up gossip. A few changes by Naval History, and a few changes in the charters of responsibility by both organizations straightened out the issues in gray areas, where duties of the two meshed.

While in Public Information, I got to know Watson Davis, a fine American who headed a science education organization that published *Science Digest*, a periodical tailored to high school students, public-spirited and farseeing, he had initiated science fairs and prepared kits covering procedures for holding them. Youths undertook projects of interest and developed working models. Many showed remarkable perception and skills. They were exhibited at a regional fair sponsored by an appropriate institution. Winners received prizes and went on to state and national fairs.

---

35. Rear Admiral John B. Heffernan, USN (Ret.), served as Director of Naval History from July 1946 to October 1956.
After teaching at Princeton University, Dr. Robert G. Albion served from 1943 to 1950 as Assistant Director of Naval History for the Navy Department. In 1948 he was appointed Harvard University's first professor of oceanic history.
36. Ernest J. King and Walter Muir Whitehill, *Fleet Admiral King, a Naval Record* (New York, W. W. Norton, 1952).

The science fair idea interested me because of its benefits to youths, to their schools, and to the prestige of Bucknell if we sponsored it. Visiting my friend, I got the kit and his support in starting a fair in our area. Two professors outside engineering agreed to handle the large administrative load. Some funding was needed, which I obtained at an address before the West Branch Manufacturers Association in Williamsport, a small city some 20 miles from Bucknell. The fair held next spring stimulated wide interest. It was a rousing success that became an annual event.

The dawning age of computers had not yet reached Bucknell. The university had no money to buy one. We learned of a simple knockdown kit from which a teaching computer could be assembled. From my meager engineering fund, I allocated $1,000 to each head of department to use as he wished. The dedicated head of electrical engineering, Professor George Ireland, put his in on one of these kits. Aided by grants, we soon got a kit. With student aid, Professor Ireland assembled it in office hours and computer instruction got under way.

On my visit to North Carolina State University, I saw a large impressive teaching nuclear reactor—perhaps the first such used in a U.S. college. One like it was far beyond our capabilities and means, but from the Atomic Energy Commission, headed by my friend Lewis Strauss, I learned of a simple "pickle barrel" reactor that could be used to teach the rudiments of atomic energy.[37] One enthusiastic professor took courses preparing for it. He and I attended a nuclear engineering conference at Gatlinburg, Tennessee, in early autumn 1955. We were housed in an old-fashioned rambling, summer resort hotel sitting over a stream running through town, a rustic, delightful place. We also visited Oak Ridge.[38] In the following weeks, we got the teaching reactor, and the nuclear age had dawned at Bucknell.

With advance permission from the professors, I sat in on classes now and then. Also, periodically we assembled as a group to discuss ways to improve instruction. On one occasion, I proposed consideration of a teacher evaluation to be filled out by students for the teachers' own guidance, passing around copies of a rough questionnaire for the

---

37. Lewis L. Strauss was a member of the Atomic Energy Commission, 1946–50, and chairman, 1953–58.
38. Oak Ridge National Laboratory, Oak Ridge, Tennessee, which has long been involved in research and development in the field of nuclear energy.

professors' modifications and return. The proposal was greeted with limited enthusiasm, but they worked on my draft. Including changes that seemed appropriate, we had a useful sheet that the teachers could pass out to their classes, or not as they pleased. The points emphasized were: knowledge of subject, in practice as well as theory; enthusiastic presentation—enthusiasm generates enthusiasm which speeds learning; relate lesson to the real world and students' interests; cite examples that sparkle with drama, emotion, humor, etcetera; and bring in high ideals and high purpose when appropriate. Ample copies went out to each teacher. Several, if not all, used them, apparently with favorable results. Only two chose to show results to me.

A pressing need was finding relief for the chairman of the mechanical engineering department. He was a splendid, dedicated, old stalwart who had been kept on a year beyond the age of 70. The university had been unable to find a replacement because of its declining prestige in engineering and low salary scale. We got through a salary increase, then began to bring in candidates from as far away as Colorado. Part of the selection process included interviews with our committee of department chairmen.

Admiral Earle Mills, then retired in New York, heading up a large company, gave me the name of Captain Herbert F. Eckberg, U.S. Navy.[39] He was an excellent officer scheduled to retire in 1957, but to be retained in an interesting post in Washington. Getting his agreement, I put his name on a list of candidates. For one reason or another, candidate after candidate was brought to Bucknell for an interview and rejected or dropped out. Studying the resumes, it was clear to me that Captain Eckberg stood head and shoulders above the others in teaching experience under various circumstances, in practical experience, in leadership, and in management ability. The committee, however, still leaned toward theoretical academicians. Finally, when the list had dwindled, they followed my recommendation and brought him in. His visit won them over unanimously and enthusiastically. We got an excellent replacement in him. Later on, he would fleet up to head the engineering school.

In the spring of 1956, the accreditation team gave us a thorough working over for several days. The positive steps we had taken pleased them. We passed with flying

---

39. Vice Admiral Earle W. Mills, USN (Ret.), had served as Chief of the Bureau of Ships from November 1946 to February 1949.

colors, much to all hands' satisfaction and relief—a sensation something like passing annual admiral's inspection.

About the same time, Admiral Wu Duncan telephoned asking me to return to active duty to relieve John Heffernan, soon to retire, as Director of Naval History. The desire to stay on at Bucknell conflicted with the realization that I might be of special use in the Navy Department. The challenges of education appealed to me. President Merle Odgers of Bucknell wanted me to stay on as vice president for development of all the university as well as engineering. We had bought a home with a lovely view close to the engineering building, and had many good friends in the area. Furthermore, it seemed to me that Secretary of the Navy Charles Thomas would not want me; some of the functions of the Office of Naval History came directly under him.[40] At a recent small gathering in Washington, I had strongly intimated to him that he wasn't pressing the necessary buildup of the Navy to meet the growing Soviet threat. He disagreed with me on the importance of the Navy. He was one of our lesser SecNavs, did not understand the importance of sea power, and worked more for his political career than for the country, as too many do in Washington. I told Admiral Duncan that Thomas wouldn't want me, but he said he could work that out.

We had achieved accreditation and revival of engineering at Bucknell. Hence, it seemed feasible to leave it to others and to go on to the larger field of developing Naval History and emphasizing the vital importance of the sea to America. In his skilled way, Admiral Duncan did work out any problems with the Secretary of the Navy. I got Rear Admiral Elliott B. Strauss for relief, and in September we set course for the Navy again.[41] This long tour of 14 years will be covered separately, so I now drop anchor on this extended series of interviews.

---

40. Charles S. Thomas served as Secretary of the Navy from 3 May 1954 to 1 April 1957.
41. See the Naval Institute oral history of Rear Admiral Elliott B. Strauss, USN (Ret.).

Interview Number 19 with Rear Admiral Ernest M. Eller, U.S. Navy (Retired)
Place: Admiral Eller's home, Wardour, Annapolis, Maryland
Date: Friday, 28 December 1984

Paul Stillwell: Admiral, the purpose here is to follow up on your post-retirement career, which really was not a retirement at all. You returned to active duty as Director of Naval History.[1]

Admiral Eller: Yes, I took over in September 1956 from Rear Admiral John Heffernan in a short turnover, a couple of days since he lived in Georgetown and I could call on him. Also, he had an experienced small staff headed by two people that were very knowledgeable. One was rear admiral (retired) but serving as a captain, F. Kent Loomis, my classmate who knew the Navy intimately. The other was Miss T. I. Mertz, Timmy Mertz, who had been with me in Public Information and knew not only the intricacies of the Navy Department but the whole complexity of the bureaucracy in Washington. So with them and by my tendency to take shortcuts and do things directly, we were able to bypass most of the bureaucracy—which too often says it can't be done, or we don't like the idea, or we can't find the money, or whatever—and we would go right to where we could get some help to do it.

I had unhappy living conditions the first couple of years. Because of my bad back and neck, I couldn't travel every day, and my wife wanted to stay here with our younger son, who had two years yet before going to college. He was at Severn. So I lived in a little apartment and commuted on weekends. As a partial compensation I could work in the office after closing time and get twice as much work done.

Paul Stillwell: What was the basis of your being chosen to fill that billet? How did you get to be picked?

---

1. The Office of Naval History was established in July 1944. It merged with the Office of Naval Records and Library in March 1949 and became the Naval Records and History Division. In 1952, it was renamed the Naval History Division, and in December 1971, it became the Naval Historical Center. In 2008 it became the Naval History and Heritage Command, the current title.

Admiral Eller: I suppose it was because of my writing and interest in history. A dozen or so of my articles had appeared in the *U.S. Naval Institute Proceedings,* three being prize essays. I think I mentioned that Admiral Duncan called me at Bucknell, where I had a very interesting job, and asked me. I was reluctant at first, but on reflection thought I could do a great deal of good in the job.

Paul Stillwell: What is the rationale for having a retired officer on active duty in that billet?

Admiral Eller: He can stay on a long time, is the main reason, I think. I was there over 14 years. You gain the experience. And second, if you're the right man, you can do much. I was interested, really, not only because of history, but had been disturbed for decades by the threat of mushrooming Soviet sea power; and had written and spoken about this since V-J Day.[2] A recent report by the secretary of the Naval Institute states that my article in a 1956 *Proceedings* on this grave problem led the way for many others in later years. Also, since the 1930s, I've felt that the country didn't understand the Navy and our need for sea power. Hence maybe there was the possibility that in the job we could do something about that.

We had a relatively inadequate staff, some ten sections, each with just a handful of people, a total of about 60. I might mention them. The library was our basic unclassified source. It had a good experienced staff, especially Mr. Fred Meigs, who was dedicated, of high integrity (always an honest answer) and had a memory that would recall almost anything. It might sometimes take several days, but he could always find an answer to what you asked him. This was one of the largest staffs of seven or eight.

The classified operations archives, with a similar-sized staff, was another basic foundation. It held about four million documents, most of World War II, with little effort made to get any since. Loretta McCrindle was then heading it and was retiring in a year or so. She was replaced by a splendid young naval reservist who reverted to civil life, Dean Allard.[3] He came to the division about the same time as I. And he developed, I'm sure, the

---

2. V-J Day – Victory over Japan Day, marked the end of the war in the Pacific on 15 August 1945. Because of the time difference it was 14 August in the United States when combat ended.
3. Ensign Dean C. Allard, USN, served on active duty from 1955 to 1958 and then joined the Naval History Division. He headed the operational archives section from 1958 to 1982, when he became senior historian. He was Director of Naval History from 1989 until his retirement in 1995. He earned his Ph.D in history from George Washington University in 1967.

best archives in the United States. He was superb, of high integrity, intelligent, honest, and hard-working, always dependable, an able writer.

Paul Stillwell: What are the qualities that make for a good archivist?

Admiral Eller: Those are, plus leadership, helpfulness, and ability to organize. Also the classified archives would acquire some very sensitive files and demand high security.

We also had an early records archives, or rather a staff of two to three who worked at the National Archives in the old naval records transferred there some years earlier. I tried to get everything documented that I could, because there is a lot of fabled information passed around in history. Once it gets into a history book, then it passes on forever, and it's hard to get rid of it.

Paul Stillwell: Are there any examples of those fables that you might mention?

Admiral Eller: I might as well speak on that now. One would be the origin of the Navy, for which we celebrate Navy Day. We celebrated it for years based on George Washington's birthday. Then early in this century we adopted Theodore Roosevelt's birthday.[4] The Marines had their birthday on 10 November, and in protocol took precedence ahead of the Navy. Now, that didn't make sense to me.

Paul Stillwell: From 1775.

Admiral Eller: 1775. It didn't make sense that Congress would provide for Marines before authorizing ships in which they would serve. So I started research on that question and finally got the document that showed the day Congress authorized the first ships for the Navy, 13 October 1775. So we started using that as Navy Day and trying to get everyone else to do so; within a couple of years, it became official Navy Day.[5]

---

4. Theodore Roosevelt was President of the United States from September 1901 to March 1909. He was such a strong advocate of naval power that for many years his birthday, 27 October, was observed in the United States as Navy Day.
5. Navy Day was observed on 27 October from 1922 to 1972. Since 1972 it is called Navy Birthday, celebrated on 13 October.

Our small research section, headed by Bill Morgan, that did in-depth studies, dug out the document.[6] Bill was completing his Ph.D. thesis relating to the American Revolution. A hard worker, he became quite knowledgeable on the early period.

Then we had the ships' history section with various functions. Besides ship histories it chose the names of ships and recommended them to the Secretary of the Navy—usually they were accepted—and selected sponsors for the ships. This took a tremendous amount of time, because congressmen and relatives of people, including many in the Navy who were interested in certain names of ships, worked on us all the time. Usually our selections went through and were signed by the Secretary. Occasionally, somebody up the line decided differently, and in the case of the name for the Polaris submarine, the decision went to the President. Eisenhower named the first one.

Paul Stillwell: What had been the plan before then, before it went up to the President?

Admiral Eller: This function didn't go up to the President before. Ships were named in the department. But the Polaris submarine was such a phenomenal advance in sea power that everybody got interested.

Paul Stillwell: What was the intention to name the submarines before you got into naming them for famous Americans?[7]

Admiral Eller: Some wanted to name them for fish, of course, as in the past. Others wanted to name them for different other reasons. I wanted to name them for cities and states. We were phasing out the battleships, and there is a great benefit to the country to have ships named for cities and states. Because of local interest and pride, different people wanted different names. Finally the President came in and chose *George Washington* for the first one. Nobody would disagree on that. Later on, naming got political, and presidents chose names that they wanted for political purposes, like *George Washington Carver*. Although he was a great scientist, he did not fit the name

---

6. Dr. William J. Morgan, who took part in the collation and editing of *Naval Documents of the American Revoltion*.
7. "Forty-one for Freedom" was a motto for the 41 Polaris/Poseidon-armed ballistic missile submarines of the *George Washington* (SSBN-598), *Ethan Allen* (SSBN-608), and *LaFayette* (SSBN-616) classes. All were named for distinguished Americans and allies. The first was commissioned in 1959, the last in 1967.

source, which was great Americans who participated militarily, preferably employing sea power. George Washington was a great seaman at heart.

Paul Stillwell: He went across the Delaware River.

Admiral Eller: He went to Bermuda, too, as a young man, though he got seasick. He still wanted to join his half-brother and be in the British Navy, but his mother wouldn't let him. He did understand sea power better than almost any other President, I think.

Paul Stillwell: You eventually got your wish, because the current Trident submarines are being named for states.[8]

Admiral Eller: I know they are. The wheel turns.

Paul Stillwell: Just to pursue that a little further, how much impetus did you have on naming a number of different kinds of ships for cities, since cruisers were not being built much any more?

Admiral Eller: We didn't at that period because we couldn't, lack of appropriate new construction.

Paul Stillwell: Did you have a hand in that business with the LSTs being named for counties?

Admiral Eller: It had started before me, but it just had started. We worked on it and kept it going. Some people wanted to change back again to just numbers, so the struggle never ended.

Paul Stillwell: In the '60s, the process got into naming things for cities. I remember a number of amphibious ships, for example, the LPDs.[9]

---

8. USS *Ohio* (SSBN-726), the first of a class of nuclear powered submarines armed with the Trident ballistic missile, was approved in the early 1970s. She was laid down 10 April 1976, launched 7 April 1979, and commissioned 11 November 1981.
9. LPD is the designation of an amphibious transport dock. The lead ship of the type was the USS *Raleigh* (LPD-1), commissioned on 8 September 1962.

Admiral Eller: Yes, when we got the larger ships, we got city names again on ships of various sizes, assigning the smaller ones to smaller cities. I remember one incident on that. We named one for a community in North Carolina of some importance. A congressman wrote his constituents how he had gotten this adopted for the only city in the country of that name; actually there are about 18 other small ones.

A main function of the ships' history section was developing ship histories. It had only a few less than 5% of the total ships that had served. And most of these had been prepared hastily during the war in Public Information; they were transferred to Naval History just before I got there Most weren't very accurate. Admiral Heffernan had started a *Dictionary of American Naval Fighting Ships* publication project to curry statistics and a very short history of each ship. This had not gotten anywhere for lack of staff, and was little more than an idea when I arrived.

The curator section was woefully undermanned, only three men. The section had a number of photographs but most lacked identification and weren't catalogued, and we had no systematic input of new ones and had very few relics or memorabilia. In fact, the requirement when a ship was scrapped was to retain only the bell, besides the items that could be used again like anchors and chains and disposable equipment, and, of course, the silver service when a ship had one.

Paul Stillwell: Was there a museum at that point in the Washington area for displays of relics?

Admiral Eller: No, except for the small Truxtun-Decatur Museum of the Naval Historical Foundation.[10] The man in my job was automatically elected curator of the foundation, and our small curator staff did most of the work setting up displays when at long intervals they had been changed.

---

10. The Truxtun-Decatur Naval Museum opened in 1926 in a house in Washington's Lafayette Square, not far from the White House. It was named for its first owner and occupant, Stephen Decatur, a hero of the Barbary Wars at the beginning of the 19th century. It remained in operation by the Naval Historical Foundation until 1982 when that organization turned the house over to the National Trust for Historical Preservation. By that time the house had been superseded as a naval museum by the Navy Museum opened in the Washington Navy Yard in 1963.

Paul Stillwell: Where were your headquarters? Were you still at Main Navy?[11]

Admiral Eller: Main Navy all the time I was there. That was very convenient. Of course, we were still separated from much of the department on the other side of the river, and our documents, what exhibits we had, and those of the Naval Historical Foundation, which we took care of, were stored in different parts of the city, some in old Fort Washington, down the Potomac, with no real care of them. Happily, all the documents of the Naval Historical Foundation collection, the private collections, had gone to the Library of Congress for care and retention, although still under the control of the Naval Historical Foundation.

There was also the Morison history section. Management of S.E. Morison's great series came under us.[12] We had a section of two, a historian, Roger Pineau, followed by Jack Bauer, and one ex-chief yeoman who had been with Morison from the start, and was reputedly the only man in the Navy who could read his handwriting.[13] Morison wrote on long yellow paper in ink. He would underline, cross out, insert, and write in different colors, and he had execrable handwriting to begin with. Morison also had a good secretary at Harvard. She and Martin typed all of his material.[14] Then it came to me to read. Morison was adamant in his views, but if you could prove something was wrong, he would change. I adopted a policy of sending pertinent parts of the manuscripts to different ones mentioned in it, like Carney and Conolly and Barbey.[15] Often they disagreed with some part of the manuscript, but he wouldn't change until we could produce documents, and seldom changed his opinions. So the conclusions are his. We also had another small staff at the Naval War College with him, I think three people, headed by Rear Admiral Bern Anderson, retired. This section did the charts and some of the research and also commented on his writing, with little effect.

---

11. Main Navy was the popular name for the old Navy Department building at 17th Street and Constitution Avenue in Washington, D.C. The building remained in use from its opening in 1918 until the early 1970s, when President Richard Nixon directed that it be demolished. The adjacent Munitions Building was long occupied by the War Department. In 1943, with the opening of the Pentagon, the Army moved out and transferred the Munitions Building to the Navy.
12. Rear Admiral Samuel Eliot Morison, USNR, was a noted civilian historian at Harvard University. He received a Naval Reserve commission as a lieutenant commander in order to collect material for what eventually became the 15-volume *History of United States Naval Operations in World War II*.
13. Captain Roger Pineau, USNR; Dr. K. Jack Bauer.
14. Donald Martin.
15. Admiral Robert B. Carney, USN (Ret.); Admiral Richard L. Conolly, USN (Ret.); Vice Admiral Daniel E. Barbey, USN (Ret.).

Paul Stillwell: I'd be interested in your opinion of the Morison series, the quality and thoroughness and so forth.

Admiral Eller: Written in haste when we didn't have everything, despite errors I think it's outstanding. In fact, I wrote the introduction or foreword to the last volume, number 15, and spoke highly of the series because he wrote brilliantly and had limited errors.

Paul Stillwell: Very readable.

Admiral Eller: During the 1920s I first read him in his *Maritime History of Massachusetts*, before I knew him. I thought then we had a real historian. He went to original sources seeking to get the facts. He didn't try to modify them, but he did draw some longbow conclusions in most of his works.

Paul Stillwell: Are there any that you remember specifically?

Admiral Eller: No, I don't now, but I told him at the time; sometimes he would change and sometimes he wouldn't.

Paul Stillwell: I wonder why the Navy didn't have an official history of its part in the war comparable to the Army series?

Admiral Eller: Staff, I imagine, and money.

Paul Stillwell: Why would the Army be more adept at getting money than the Navy?

Admiral Eller: The Army didn't have ships to operate. The big problem in the Navy is everybody needs more than he has, or thinks he does. We have never had too many ships, usually too few, especially in peacetime. The Army probably got accustomed to spending more on staff and support. Until World War II, the Navy had small staffs. Fleet staffs on board ship had to be kept to a handful. Now we have moved too much to the Army system. When I went on Admiral Nimitz's staff in May '42, not counting the intelligence section and the communicators, we had 20 or 25 people in the mess; we all ate together. Admiral Nimitz came in occasionally to eat with us as on ship. As the war grew, the staff grew some, but it greatly changed when the Army forced us, through the Joint Chiefs, to adapt the Army system. We added a joint logistics section that in time outgrew headquarters. Now, in gunnery, we continued to handle everything with four officers, and three or four yeomen, without passing through a logistics section. But Army has to have a big staff. I've gone into that in my various statements, I think, so I won't repeat here. It's a system that kills initiative and prompt action in staff work. With the old Navy system we could make a decision almost instantly, see the chief of staff, and admiral if necessary, and get it approved at once.

Paul Stillwell: Do you plan to talk more in your outline about the *Dictionary of American Naval Fighting Ships*?

Admiral Eller: Yes, I haven't come to that yet.

Paul Stillwell: I hope to hear more about that one.

Admiral Eller: I wanted first to mention all of the sections.

Paul Stillwell: All right.

Admiral Eller: I've about covered them. We had a classification and declassification section, just one officer and an enlisted man, and we were charged with declassification. If somebody wanted a special document, it had to be declassified or the sections cut out that couldn't be declassified. Then we also had charge of the change of classifications as years passed, downgraded by groups. This required care since there were hundreds and maybe thousands of documents in a file. You had to be sure to go through it and not leave something in there that would be troublesome.

Paul Stillwell: Where did you get the expertise? Whom did you call on to know what should still be classified?

Admiral Eller: We went to this appropriate section in the Navy Department. We had close working relationships with the various officers.

Paul Stillwell: There was such a mass of material. How could the operational sections spare people to do this work?

Admiral Eller: Well, they wouldn't. We would take single documents to the office for review.

Paul Stillwell: I see.

Admiral Eller: We also had a mailroom. We had to have, because we received some 20,000-25,000 letters a year. Of these about 10% came to me direct because they involved matters that I could handle. There matched at least an equal number of communications by telephone. The mailroom always amazed me. The two people there weren't ones that seemed highly able to do this, and yet they were able to get these to the different sections very capably. Miss Mertz was partly responsible for that, because she looked at anything that might have to come to me.

Paul Stillwell: What sorts of things did you ask to have come to you?

Admiral Eller: First of all, anything that I knew, any person I knew, anything that involved several of the sections or that might involve a "no" answer. I set up early in the game a requirement I had adopted in other jobs that any letter had to be answered in a couple of weeks, if possible. It wasn't always done, but that was the goal.

Paul Stillwell: Certainly desirable.

Admiral Eller: And if you couldn't give a full answer, give an interim answer. And if you couldn't give the answer at all, try to find out the source that could and send it there, or else refer the writer to it.

Paul Stillwell: Was that the bulk of the mail, people asking for information?

Admiral Eller: Yes. Any complex or partial answers would come to me in draft. For a very involved one, I would send appropriate parts of it to different sections for research. Most of this 10% were people with whom I communicated or projects that I had under way.

Paul Stillwell: That's a pretty heavy correspondence load. I figured on the average, probably, you were handling ten letters a day personally, if you divide 250 working days.

Admiral Eller: Yes, I probably was. But I had good secretaries, usually three. Also, I had a pretty wide experience in a number of facets of the Navy and could supply background answers that the others couldn't. That is why I had anything complex come by me to sign, often adding to the final draft.

Also I asked all hands (and this was something very dear to my heart) when answering something about an error of the Navy, to try to put it in context and show what it amounted to in comparison to what was being done, what was being achieved. Too many books and opinions of people are based upon a little narrow point. Something I read in newspapers, and watched in speeches the other day, said the Navy paid $100.00 apiece for a little item. As SecNav states, that was true for two of them. Then we found out the dishonesty, forced the company to recompense, and then bought 100,000 of them for four cents apiece. It is a constant battle to correct error. I tried to do that in our letters, not to hide errors but to put them in context. Also, where possible, I sought to put in something to build up inspiration and pride in the Navy.

Paul Stillwell: I've talked with individuals who worked at Naval History and said they were impressed by your great loyalty and devotion to the Navy, and that came through in your work.

Admiral Eller: To me the country would be lost, there's no question about it, if we didn't have a Navy, if we hadn't had it in the war. That was one reason I started some of our projects, which I'll come to.

Now the deficiencies, I think I've named most of them; they were largely in ships' history, the curator section, and inadequate research studies. A number being used for standard answers hadn't been researched thoroughly. On a questionable issue we now adopted the system of finding the document and following it, not somebody's book.

Another weakness lay in our classified archives. We weren't getting current classified reports. Ultimately certain groups of CNO and other sensitive files should have been retired to our classified archives, but this was not being done properly. In a few years, though not without persuasion, we were getting everything. Admiral Radford, a friend of World War II, put his files there and worked on his book.[16] This and other special groups encouraged others. Anyone who had contact with Dean Allard gained confidence.

Paul Stillwell: A requirement was started for each command to submit its annual history at the end of the year. Did you have a hand in establishing that requirement?

Admiral Eller: Yes. Most of the things we did I started early in the game, but it took a while to get them under way. As for the annual command histories, we gave first priority to accurate ship histories. We needed them for the Navy's work, for all the Navy as well as for us for answering questions. We also needed a good history on all other commands. Many shore commands, if not most, didn't have these. In fact, they would come to us occasionally for something on their past and we didn't know either. So we got a directive signed requiring a command history, the first one going back to the origin of command, and then an annual supplement.

Paul Stillwell: Over the period of 14 years that you were there, were you satisfied that it was well established by the time you left?

Admiral Eller: It was well established early in the game. Now, I didn't follow up on them, of course, all the time, but once you got a good original command history, you were pretty well off. Then commands began to understand why it was necessary and did it.

Paul Stillwell: I would think that the quality of those would vary, depending on the amount of interest the individual writer had.

---

16. Admiral Arthur W. Radford, USN, served as Chairman of the Joint Chiefs of Staff from 15 August 1953 to 14 August 1957. Stephen Jurika, editor, *From Pearl Harbor to Vietnam: the Memoirs of Admiral Arthur W. Radford* (Stanford, California: Hoover Institution Press, 1980).

Admiral Eller: It did, of course. It does always. But as they began to realize what it meant to the command in prestige and morale, somebody would take an interest and would improve the history. I would say of the officers in the Navy, a high percentage wanted their command to have a good record of the command, but maybe only 10% of commanding officers really took an active interest to make it so.

In that connection, besides the Navy birthday, one of my first moves was in the curator section. For example my shop had few good oils. Practically all the Navy's fine old paintings belonged to the Naval Academy Museum, where Captain (later Rear Admiral) Harry A. Baldridge had done a superb job in getting donations of paintings, documents, and relics from all over the country. The New York Historical Society had those in the old Naval History Society Collection of last century, and the Naval Historical Foundation had a number, but we had practically nothing.

Happily, the Naval Photographic Center could use a dye transfer process which gives a reproduction far better than a lithograph. Some almost equaled paintings. We started the naval heroes series using these. John Paul Jones led off. We got a beautiful dye transfer reproduction of a good painting of him and matted it with a window in the bottom through which stood out "I have not yet begun to fight." In a frame alongside we put one of his stirring letters. This process started a series, first of only half a dozen, but ultimately 25 or 30. In time the demand for these became great enough that we developed a set of lithographs from them for sale by GPO.

Paul Stillwell: Did they prove to be pretty popular with the public?

Admiral Eller: Yes, especially with members of the Navy League and similar Navy-related groups. They like especially the dye transfers, but these were expensive compared to lithographs. Also, we couldn't furnish them, to any degree, to the public except where we wanted a Navy display as in a school. In the Navy itself they became very popular.

Our real deficiency, of course, was lack of help, and there wasn't much chance, with the competition elsewhere, to get any increase in complement. There were sources, however. The first was somebody like you, a naval reservist, who must do active duty somewhere. We got BuPers to send anybody who was qualified to us for short tours. One outstanding man was Professor Neville Kirk at the Naval Academy.[17] He knows ships of the last century like old friends. He also is a good historian. Neville was a great help to us several times, and there were quite a number of others like that. These fine workers contributed importantly, especially in the curator section, the ships' history section, and the research section. In fact, some of them would get so interested that they would work overtime beyond their reserve duty as unpaid volunteers. For example, a chief petty officer reservist, who was a schoolteacher in South Carolina, got so interested in helping us arrange our photographs, captioning them, and putting in a good retrieval system that he took the summer off and came back here year after year. Finally we got him to replace somebody who was retiring, and he stayed on for a long time.

Paul Stillwell: What was his name?

Admiral Eller: I don't remember. These people were all a great help to us. In 1956 we figured we had about 10,000 photographs, many of them not captioned, and 14 years later we had, I think, 150,000. One thing we started, which we hadn't been doing, was to go out aggressively to get photographs of current operations. In this period there were great developments in scientific technology, such as the moon shot and the space shots. We went after these photos, and those of other operations, as in the Antarctic. We went after everything we could. Whenever anything was coming off, a letter would go to the commanding officers asking for photographs, reports, and memorabilia. For example, when the first Polaris missile was fired from operations at sea off the *George Washington*, we got the original copy of the message the captain sent. Also we induced the communicators to turn over the first moon relay message. Thus we began to collect a great deal of useful information that would have been lost or gone into private hands and then lost. Since I knew most of the admirals, I could put special pressure on them.

Besides reservists, there were some short-timers due to leave the Navy in months or a year, in fact, the first commanding officer of the Naval Memorial Museum was scheduled to retire in a year, and BuPers didn't know where to send him, I guess, so they sent him to help us get started, which I'll come to. Besides these, there were volunteers. You'd be interested to know the number of people who have such loved hobbies that they're willing to do anything to get into their hobby deeper. Some of our short studies and many of our fine activities in the division were made possible by people like this,

---

17. Professor Neville T. Kirk, chairman of naval and diplomatic history, taught for many years at the Naval Academy.

who would volunteer and go. There was a psychiatrist from New Jersey who wanted to write up airships in World War I. He had seen the *Hindenburg* fly over the country when he was a boy and became absorbed.[18] He came down and worked with us in research. He did all the work and finally got his manuscript published in England. Another example is Sam Morison's grandson, Samuel L. Morison, who's in trouble now.[19] Eager to work in our office, he got into the NROTC, came up to us for reserve duty in the summer and when the duty ended, he stayed the rest of the summer as a volunteer to work on ships. He's a bug on ships.

Paul Stillwell: Yes, he is.

Admiral Eller: He went into the ships' history section, of course, and worked on the *Dictionary of American Naval Fighting Ships*. There we used anybody who could write and was honest in his research. He became very skillful. After he got his commission he wanted to come direct to us, but I told him to go to sea first and then try to come. Usually we would get young officers for their last year of required duty. He came and stayed on after separation, stayed on as a civilian without pay. Later we were able to get a small sum on contract to purchase say five completed histories for $100.00. Finally a vacancy opened up and he went on to the staff for years. I think he was still there when I left.

Paul Stillwell: I think he was. Did you make an effort to increase the size of your staff? What were the things that went into the annual budget considerations?

Admiral Eller: Well, that was just like trying to move a mountain, and I had little heart for it, knowing the Navy's greater needs. Where essential we tried and did get the curator section slightly increased as the museum got under way. However there was another

---

18. The German *Hindenburg* was one of the largest airships ever built. Completed in 1936, it was 812 feet long and 135 feet in diameter. It created an international sensation on 6 May 1937 when it exploded and burned while approaching its mooring at the naval air station in Lakehurst, New Jersey. That event ended regular airship service between the United States and Germany.
19. Samuel Loring Morison, the grandson of Samuel Eliot Morison, worked at the Naval Intelligence Center in Suitland, Maryland from 1974 to 1984. During the course of his work there, he leaked classified material to *Jane's Defence Weekly*. In 1985 he was convicted of espionage and theft of government property and served in prison. In 2001 President Bill Clinton pardoned Morison.

source that was highly valuable, especially for working parties at the museum. The receiving station, located in the Navy Yard, always had officers and men waiting for a school to start or for a ship to come back.[20] We could get dog help from there. This source speeded our progress with the museum, which I might take up now.

I wanted a museum in the Washington area from the start, and happily, two very fine gentlemen wanted it, too. One was Arleigh Burke, who was CNO when I came, and he kept pressing me to do something about it. We didn't have men or money or location. Thomas Gates was Secretary of the Navy those first years; he was one of our finest secretaries.[21] I put Forrestal first, then Gates, and then our present one. Those in between varied in quality.

Paul Stillwell: I'd say you certainly had a leg up with two individuals like Burke and Secretary Gates supporting your efforts.

Admiral Eller: Yes. Not only did Arleigh Burke support it, he pushed it. He kept pushing me. First he talked of getting the *Constellation* from Baltimore, which of course we couldn't; then of an active ship. One is finally in the yard, but not for what he wanted a big ceremonial ship with a good display area. He went to Europe in '59 on an official visit, so I asked his aide, Commander Ray Peet, to put Greenwich and the Swedish naval museum on his agenda, and any other large maritime museum.[22] When he came back, Arleigh was all the more fired up. He said, "Let's start a museum." This kept going on. Finally one day when Ray called up and talked about it again, I said, "Ask him to give me a memo that we need to start a museum." That afternoon it came over by hand, just a memo, not a formal directive that provided men and money; however it gave me a lever of sorts.

We set up a committee from different offices in Naval Operations, in BuShips, and others that were involved. I acted as the chairman. Of course the chairman always does the work, but usually gets what he wants. At that time, fortuitously, the Naval Gun Factory was being phased out. Buildings were being allocated to different departments of the government

---

20. The Washington Navy Yard is on M Street in southeast Washington, D.C. For many years it was an industrial facility known as the Naval Gun Factory. Since the late 1970s the residence of the Chief of Naval Operations has been in the Washington Navy Yard.
21. Thomas S. Gates Jr., served as Secretary of the Navy from 1 April 1957 to 7 June 1959.
22. Commander Raymond E. Peet, USN, served as aide to Chief of Naval Operations Arleigh Burke from 1957 to 1959. The oral history of Peet, who retired as a vice admiral, is in the Naval Institute collection.

as well as to the Navy. We prepared a communication to the Secretary asking for one of the buildings. Actually, in order to be sure we got the right choice, we said, "We have this proposal to start a museum. Here are the possibilities." And we named the old Naval Observatory—then occupied by BuMed—and other sites that would require expensive construction, and last the Navy Yard.[23] We specified that we needed a large building with ample storage and display area. We couldn't call it a museum at the time because the Smithsonian was then building the big new armed forces museum and many objections would be, "Why do you need that? They're going to have a very fine naval display," as they do have, which we helped Mendel Peterson with—he was in charge there. You may know him.

Paul Stillwell: No, I don't.

Admiral Eller: He was a naval reservist who did reserve duties with us in our curator shop and was a great help.

We wanted the display space first of all to help build esprit in the Navy through visible evidence of its achievements, so we called it the Naval Historical Display Center. We hoped it would instruct and inspire.

Secretary Milne, Assistant Secretary for Material, buildings, etc., would make the decision.[24] We learned he was descended from a midshipman who had served with Nelson in the Battle of Trafalgar.[25] We happened to have a very fine painting of Trafalgar hanging in one of the offices in the Pentagon, and we had some good paintings in Milne's office, loaned from the foundation or from the academy. So we swapped the painting of Trafalgar one day when he was out of his office.

Meanwhile to avoid long delay we carried the rough of our request by hand to the different people who would have to initial it, such as JAG, Supply, comptroller, etc. Incorporating their modifications (which were never large, but enough to make them want to initial the final pager). Putting it in smooth, we pushed it through for initialing in a

---

23. BuMed – Bureau of Medicine and Surgery.
24. Cecil P. Milne served 1957 to 1959 as Assistant Secretary of the Navy (Installations and Logistics).
25. Lord Horatio Viscount Nelson (1758–1805), British naval hero of the Battle of Cape St. Vincent, 1797, Battle of the Nile, 1798, Trafalgar, 1805.

very short time. Then I went to see Secretary Milne, talked to him for about an hour. He wouldn't agree yes or no at the time, but we got the building. We had the building—now to get people and money.

Paul Stillwell: Was it a building you had specifically asked for, or had you—

Admiral Eller: We didn't ask for the building since individuals wanting other sites might have blocked it. The request listed pros and cons for each. The building we wanted had fewest cons. Also the commandant of the yard, Rear Admiral W. K. Mendenhall Jr., endorsed our request strongly, favoring the building we wanted, the one we have now. This is the finest building possible, just like an 18th century one with flying buttresses. In fact, it goes back to the early part of the 19th century. After we got it, BuPers sent me the first commanding officer. The receiving station provided working parties who cleaned it up and we started in.

Paul Stillwell: Who was the first officer in charge?

Admiral Eller: Captain Jack Blandy. He didn't know a great deal about museums and wasn't very interested, but he was a good director in getting the building ready and starting displays, primarily outlined by me. Commander Keating, whose first name slips me, relieved him, a reserve officer who BuPers kept on for the job.

Paul Stillwell: What kind of shape was the building in when you took it over?

Admiral Eller: It was in perfect shape outside, but inside, on the old breechblock building it needed quite a bit of work cleaning it up. We didn't have time or money to do what has been done since. Admiral Kane, two or three years ago, closed it entirely and redid the decks and other work inside.[26] What we wanted to do first was to get it going. I participated almost daily, because the museum was one of my prime interests and objectives. We wanted to tell the story of the Navy from the very beginning up to the present. We have there a sequence of objects and graphics, as far as possible hands-on objects that you can manipulate, like a steering wheel. We

---

26. Rear Admiral John D. H. Kane, USN (Ret.), served as Director of Naval History from December 1976 to December 1985.

have a small bridge. Sometime later on we got 30 old periscopes from Admiral Pete Galantin, head of the Material Command, that were no longer useful for new submarines.[27] We put most of these on loan in museums across the country and installed two in our museum in a room, entered by a watertight hatch, which gives some feel of being in a control room of a submarine. I don't know whether you've been in it or not.

Paul Stillwell: Yes, I have. I also recall the 40-millimeter gun mount from the USS *South Dakota* is there that kids can climb up on.

Admiral Eller: Yes. Then outside we have the fairwater of a submarine. About this same time, of great benefit to us, we started scrapping a large number of World War II ships. We revised the scrapping directive and got it signed by SecNav. Instead of just taking two or three items, such as the bell, we took as much as we could, anything, small or large, we might use in the museum or loan for displays far and wide. These included in one case a whole bridge and huge anchors. One of the *Oklahoma City*'s anchors stands as a striking monument in the busy center of Oklahoma City through the efforts of Rear Admiral John Kirkpatrick of that city. We took all the surplus guns we could get, always on demand for displays.

Paul Stillwell: Where were they stored in the meantime?

Admiral Eller: We have a yard above Baltimore. Then there's one in Texas near Galveston. As ships came up for scrapping, we sent letters to namesake cities and states suggesting possible displays. Where appropriate we suggested preserving the whole ship. Some did. The first to run with the ball was North Carolina. The enthusiasm of a dedicated few can make a project succeed. One man started the drive to save the battleship *North Carolina*. He in turn interested Hugh Morton who had real estate holdings in Wilmington and the North Carolina mountains. Hugh directed the most remarkable job of preservation that I encountered. He organized the state, got the governor's backing, had somebody in charge in each county to raise money. (Agnes's brother in Winston-Salem had Forsyth County). In six months they raised money for the costly tow to Wilmington, and initial preparation of the ship. They now have half a million visitors a year. We worked closely

---

27. Admiral Ignatius J. Galantin, USN, served as Chief of Naval Material from 1 May 1965 to 30 June 1970.

with them, supplying materials, action reports, photographs, and anything else we could get, including guns that had been removed, the 40-millimeters and 20s.

Next Alabama got interested. Three able men in Mobile—Henri Aldridge, Steven Croom, and Robert Eddington—organized the drive, and soon we had the *Alabama* preserved. *Massachusetts* had a harder row. We couldn't get them stirred up. Many letters went to different people trying to encourage them. Reasons abounded why they couldn't raise enough money. Then finally they got started, and now they have the biggest fleet of all. Besides the *Massachusetts* they have one submarine, a destroyer, two PT boats and a PT boat museum.

The PT boats are an example of one individual doing "the impossible." J. M. "Boats" Newberry was a young boatswain's mate of a PT boat in the Guadalcanal campaign. Postwar he had developed a business that involved trucking and was prospering. He wanted to get a PT boat and start a museum in Memphis on the Mississippi. This was while President Kennedy was alive.[28] He came to Washington about '62 and got Justice White (Whizzer White to PT boaters), Rear Admiral John Bulkeley, retired Rear Admiral John Harllee from South Carolina, and myself, in a conference.[29] With assurance of the cooperation of my office, they decided to start the PT Boat Association.[30]

Boats was the power that made it succeed. Under his tireless drive it grew and grew and now has 7,500 members. In fact, I still work on it with him. A whirlwind, he wrote letters, organized meetings, traveled all over. In the Solomons he found a wrecked PT boat, got a battered-up one in Korea, discovered a modified one in Florida. He got his compatriots in the organization to refurbish two of the boats and provide about $400,000 for each for materials. Unable to get the museum under way in Memphis, he moved it to Massachusetts. He once wrote me that I got him "into a lifetime job, 26 hours a day, eight days a week." Dying of cancer he still works day and night for the future of the organization.

---

28. John F. Kennedy served as President of the United States from 20 January 1961 until he was assassinated on 22 November 1963.
29. Byron R. White served as an Associate Justice of the U.S. Supreme Court from 16 April 1962 to 28 June 1993. He served as an intelligence officer with the Navy in World War II. Rear Admiral John D. Bulkeley, USN, had commanded a PT boat squadron in the Philippines at the outset of World War II. Rear Admiral John Harllee, USN (Ret.) commanded a PT boat squadron in World War II and in 1947–48 served as Navy liaison to Representative John F. Kennedy.
30. James N. Newberry was the founder of P.T. Boats, Inc., which was chartered in 1967 as a nonprofit organization.

Paul Stillwell: It's a shame that the effort was not successful to preserve the *Enterprise*.[31]

Admiral Eller: It is. That failed very early in the game. Admiral Halsey headed the drive, but somehow it didn't make headway and the Navy Department held her until up against the stop for passing on the name to the eighth *Enterprise*, the world's first nuclear-powered carrier whose keel was about to be laid.[32] We did save much from her, including the bridge and whole bulkheads for cutting into pieces for different museums and communities who were interested.

Paul Stillwell: Was that mainly a matter of not being able to get any money raised?

Admiral Eller: Yes, and nobody in civilian life in New York really wanted it badly enough to push it through. If somebody had wanted it badly enough, it would have been done; for example, take the *Constellation*. Almost the day I came to the office, her preservation started being a problem and remained a problem almost throughout my tour. The Navy had kept the *Constellation* for 160 years. In the 1950s, about '53 or '54, the Department decided to scrap her, which is amazing. The Navy had decided to scrap the *Constitution* more than 100 years earlier. Then she had been saved by Oliver Wendell Holmes, his poem. But here we had kept the *Constellation* as a historic ship and now were letting her go. Happily the Flag House Association in Baltimore decided they would try to preserve her, a Baltimore-built ship. They formed a *Constellation* Committee, raised $50,000 or $100,000 to tow her to Baltimore and thought they were on their way.

Then people started saying it wasn't the true *Constellation*. Howard Chapelle led the objectors.[33] Committee members told me that Chapelle wanted to be on the committee; they fell out with him. He then started stating that she was a sloop built in the 1850s rather than the *Constellation*, the old frigate. That became quite a controversy. The ship deteriorated. She was moored at an out-of-the-way dock in the harbor, almost a derelict. They were in bad straits.

---

31. The aircraft carrier *Enterprise* (CV-6) served with distinction throughout the war in the Pacific. See Edward P. Stafford, *The Big E: the Story of the USS Enterprise* (New York: Random House, 1962).
32. Fleet Admiral William F. Halsey, USN (Ret.), used the *Enterprise* as his flagship during the early months of World War II.
33. Howard I. Chapelle was the author of many books, including *The Constellation Question* (Washington, D.C.: Smithsonian Institution Press, 1970).

William Bell Clark, who became editor of our *Naval Documents*, didn't trust Chapelle. He said he made errors. And I found that out myself in checking on a couple of ships. He was an expert on sailing ships of earlier days, and was very good, but did err at times. He either then or soon went to the Smithsonian and did a good job there, I think. He insisted she wasn't the original, and the comptroller in Baltimore wanted to take her out and sink her. He came to the National Archives, made some cursory investigations, and he reached the same conclusion as Chapelle—which you can *if you want to*, of course. So I looked into everything we had on her. Other files turned up in the National Archives, though President Roosevelt had sent most of the material on the *Constellation* to Newport, and the building containing it burned during the war. But we did find other material there over the years; and in Boston a naval constructor (I believe his name was Cushing) had been enamored of the *Constellation* and had saved some documents.

Then I had two senior naval constructors, Admirals A. H. Van Keuren and Schuyler Pyne, examine the records and the ship. They both came to the same conclusion that, of course, she had once been modified to a sloop, and greatly repaired over the years (timbers rot), but she still was as much an original as—or even more so than—the *Constitution*. In the course of restoration we found in her copper spikes with early 1800 dates. So it became clear to me that she was rebuilt in the 1850s as a sloop, but she still retained as much of the original material as possible, and she was ultimately changed back to frigate configuration. She's as much the same ship as my cruiser, the *Albany*, which was converted into a guided missile ship, but is still the cruiser *Albany*.

This was a long struggle. The *Constellation* Committee had monthly meetings, always considering means to get donations of funds and materials. Copper coins, with some copper from the ship, raised large sums, especially in the Navy. We sent a notice to all ships and stations, and placed groups of them consigned to me throughout the Navy Department. Admiral Rickover's neglect to pay caused my only substantial loss. Very soon they put me on the committee. I was intimate with the *Constellation* all the time I was in the job and worked with the committee years after I retired. Now, of course, she's the centerpiece of the Inner Harbor in Baltimore. Some of those deserving credit for their devotion and persistence are Charles Scarlett, Bob Michel, Gordon Stick, and Herbert Wirz. And Charles Stewart, long a devoted keeper of the ship in her difficult days.

Paul Stillwell: That's a magnificent area up there.

Admiral Eller: It is, and the *Constellation* pays her way. So the ships' scrapping program was very beneficial to us in that respect, and in may other ways. When we couldn't get a ship preserved, or as for an inland state like Indiana, we collected all the relics and anything we could from the ship and made them available to the communities. In states where naval commands took an interest and helped, we had special success. At the training command in Memphis, Admiral Fitzhugh Lee, an associate from academy days, did an especially effective job, getting material from the USS *Memphis* all over the state.[34] Every state had displays. At one time we had about 1,000 different schools and public buildings in Indiana with our material; and Indiana laid out an outline of the ship with her lifelines.

Paul Stillwell: I think that was South Dakota.

Admiral Eller: South Dakota. You're right. Indiana did something large besides the many small displays.

Paul Stillwell: They took her mast, I think, at a football stadium.

Admiral Eller: That's right. You remember better than I do. Now we have a total of some 30 restored ships, counting those little fleets as in Massachusetts and then the one in Charleston, that what's-his- name—

Paul Stillwell: Patriots Point, Clark Reynolds.[35]

Admiral Eller: Clark Reynolds, yes; an excellent project. And then the *Intrepid*; finally we have a carrier in New York.

---

34. Vice Admiral Fitzhugh Lee, USN, Commander Naval Air Technical Training Command.
35. Professor Clark G. Reynolds taught history at several universities, including the Merchant Marine Academy and the Naval Academy. In the 1970s and 1980s he was part-time historian and curator at the Patriots Point naval museum in Charleston. Among the ships there is the aircraft carrier *Yorktown* (CVS-10).

Paul Stillwell: They have up at Buffalo the cruiser *Little Rock* and destroyer *The Sullivans*.

Admiral Eller: Yes. Those are after I left. Interest kept growing; also in museums. Look at the naval memorial being built right at the National Archives in Washington.[36] And then the Undersea Warfare Museum.[37] Have you heard of that?

Paul Stillwell: No, I haven't.

Admiral Eller: Here are a couple of brochures you can have. You can join it. Development of it just started last year.

Paul Stillwell: There was one that preceded you; that was the USS *Texas*.

Admiral Eller: Yes.

Paul Stillwell: What hand did you have in that?

Admiral Eller: None. Texans jumped on the ball to preserve her when she came up for scrapping in the late '40s, soon after the war.

Paul Stillwell: Yes.

Admiral Eller: We kept contact with them and tried to help them. She looked pretty bad for a time, but I think they were not paying attention to her and didn't have anybody really interested other than a ship keeper. That was corrected in time.

Paul Stillwell: Was there an organization within your Naval History Division that saw to the maintenance and preservation of the ships?

---

36. The Navy Memorial in Washington, D.C., is across Pennsylvania Avenue from the National Archives. The memorial was dedicated on 13 October 1987, the Navy birthday.
37. The Naval Undersea Museum, Keyport, Washington, opened in 1995.

Admiral Eller: No, we couldn't do that, of course. We had no control over them. We would encourage and provide any material that we could. The curator section would do this. In its small staff, Henry Vadnais, a young officer just out of the Navy, developed into a tower of strength.[38] He did all things well.

Paul Stillwell: And he's still there.

Admiral Eller: Yes, happily.

Paul Stillwell: Doesn't the Navy have some mechanism, though, to make sure that those ships are kept up into shape so they don't embarrass the Navy?

Admiral Eller: That's the requirement when transferred, and if they really went down too badly, I guess it would ultimately be enforced. But I would have never done it if I could stir them up to do better.

Paul Stillwell: Right.

Admiral Eller: The *Olympia* was another almost constant problem.[39] An enthusiastic group in Philadelphia took her over about the same time the *Constellation* went to Baltimore. This group was made up of some who were really interested and others who wanted her from a political or prestige standpoint. She was saved and made into a good museum ship by a small group, a VFW chapter. Two key people led the way. Foremost was Edmund Crenshaw, class of '12 at the academy.[40] He got out after World War I and had apparently made quite a bit of money. A VFW member, he became interested and spent his whole time on her, a lot of money, too. When he couldn't get anything from us (they had little funding), he would provide it himself.

Paul Stillwell: I know the shipyard has been helping them out some too.

---

38. Captain Henry A. Vadnais Jr., USNR, headed the curator section of the Naval Historical Center
39. The cruiser *Olympia* (C-6) was commissioned 5 February 1895. During the Battle of Manila Bay, on 1 April 1898, she was the flagship of Commodore George Dewey, USN. The ship is now a memorial in Philadelphia.

Admiral Eller: Yes. We encouraged the district commandant to help in any way possible, including stirring up wider support in Philadelphia. The other hard worker was a Filipino steward, either he or his father had been Dewey's steward, and I think it must have been him. He and Crenshaw were on board working constantly. Every time I visited the *Olympia*, they were there working. Both of them loved the ship. They did everything they could for her. The Filipino said he could never do enough for America for what it had given him. They both gave themselves unselfishly, whereas some of the others were in it for politics or prestige—and this was one of the problems Crenshaw had with them. He was hard working, dedicated and devoted, but he was also crusty. He came to me often with his problems and I would try to soothe him. Finally they got her in good shape as a museum; and though moored like the *Constellation* in an out-of-the-way pier, got 50,000 visitors a year. Now, as you know, she's near Independence Hall on the waterfront.

Paul Stillwell: Penn's Landing, it's called.

Admiral Eller: Penn's Landing. To come back to the Navy Memorial Museum a little bit, we steadily made headway and began to acquire donations. For example, Admiral Richard Byrd became a friend when I was in Public Information.[41] When he died, I kept communicating with Mrs. Byrd and their son, trying to get his Arctic material; he was a packrat and had kept everything. They wanted to start a museum in the Boston area. That made no headway. Then they wanted to be sure that enough of it was displayed, and several museums, including the Smithsonian, sought to get the collection. By then we had the display center well under way, so I assured them we would display his hut and lots of other material. Finally it started coming by freight carloads. We have a large polar display built around his hut, containing the spartan equipment that sustained him through the winter. Then Admiral George Dufek, a classmate and friend, conducted operations after the war in the Antarctic, as did various other naval friends, including Admiral Dave Tyree, also a classmate.[42]

---

40. Captain Edmund A. Crenshaw, USNR (Ret.).
41. Commander Richard E. Byrd, Jr., USN (Ret.), explored Antarctica in 1928, 1933, 1939, 1947, 1955. He was retired for physical disability in 1916 but continued to be promoted, eventually becoming a rear admiral in 1929. He died 11 March 1957.
42. Rear Admiral George J. Dufek, USN; Rear Admiral David M. Tyree, USN.

Paul Stillwell: He just died two months back.

Admiral Eller: Yes. We kept asking the leaders for photographs and memorabilia and reports. Hence we have probably the best 20th century Antarctic material that can be found, both on display and in reserve storage.

When BuPers sent us Captain Slade Cutter we made real progress. Slade knew little about museums, but he knew how to get things done and did them. He carried out my suggestions with drive and effectiveness, just as he did in submarine warfare against the Japanese. He effectively followed my Museum Introduction Number 1, drafted about this time, that set forth with broad sweep the museum's scope and purpose. Slade was a joy; you should interview him.[43] I was sad when his wife's health forced him to go to a dry climate. BuPers sent a splendid relief. Roy Smith did an outstanding and imaginative job, as he did in transforming *Shipmate* into the best alumni magazine in the country.[44]

More and more people became interested. Before President Kennedy was assassinated, the family sent down his ship models and other things. When they got the museum going up Boston, they took them back, along with some of our collection. About '64, we began to have functions at the museum. I had the Civil War Round Table of Washington, D.C., earlier than that, one of their evening meetings. This group was a prime mover in the Civil War centennial. They were enthusiastic about the museum. As more people learned of it they began to donate. Everyone has something squirreled away that he wants preserved, that he knows his children won't keep, and he wants to be sure it has a good home.

Paul Stillwell: You get kind of an embarrassment of riches there, don't you? You can't possibly display all the good things you have.

Admiral Eller: No, that's not an embarrassment. They get preserved, rotate on display, and go out on loans.

I mentioned the Civil War Centennial. We were going along well, up to high speed on all fronts, and about that time the Civil War Centennial came along. Foreseeing it, we started

---

43. See the Naval Institute oral history of Captain Slade D. Cutter, USN (Ret.).
44. Captain Roy C. Smith III, USNR (Ret.), was editor of the Naval Academy alumni magazine *Shipmate*, 1971–83.

a chronology—that on first try didn't pan out very well, from my viewpoint. It wasn't detailed enough and there wasn't enough in it to show what the Navy did, what sea power really meant to victory. So we started over again and started putting it out by years. I guess you know it.

Paul Stillwell: I have a copy of the volume.

Admiral Eller: Of the hard bound one?

Paul Stillwell: Yes.

Admiral Eller: First we put it out by years in soft cover. In each of those, I have a little essay as the introduction in which I tried to point up what sea power meant that year. I remember one of my speeches (I had to make about a speech a week, often major ones, many short). I spoke before the Civil War Round Table of D.C. on the operations in the Mississippi. General Grant, a member of the Round Table, came up to me afterwards and said he couldn't believe the speech. So I broke out all the documents showing that Grant was also a very good sea strategist, although he operated on the rivers, and that Grant was saved two times, maybe three, by the operations of gunboats and of other warships.[45] So I think we got the Civil War Round Table pretty well indoctrinated into the need for the Navy in operations.

Paul Stillwell: Who was the general that was skeptical?

Admiral Eller: General U.S. Grant III.[46]

Paul Stillwell: Oh, I see. His grandson.

Admiral Eller: Yes. In fact, when the centennial was coming up, President Eisenhower appointed him head of the National Centennial Committee to plan for national observances

---

45. General Ulysses S. Grant was in command of the Union Army at the end of the Civil War and accepted General Robert E. Lee's surrender in April 1865. Grant later served as President of the United States from 1869 to 1877.
46. Major General Ulysses S. Grant III, USA (Ret.)

and to help the states plan for the local ones.[47] I worked on it with him; his offices were right above the White House near Decatur House. We filled his office with our naval hero series relating to the Civil War, objects and photos. One of his staff was Pat Jones, an excellent writer, who became a friend. He wanted to write something on the Civil War at sea and we finally developed a multivolume history. *The Civil War at Sea*. We worked on it constantly with him. I read the manuscripts and wrote forewords for each volume. He said that until he started research he believed if Lee had won at Gettysburg that the South would have been separated; but now understood that it couldn't be because of the blockade (which includes capture of ports, especially New Orleans) and the river forces. More and more people came to that correct view, including many other authors we helped. I think we got a number of them straightened out.

At the end of the centennial, we were going so fast that in 1966 we had to put out a separate edition for 1866, mostly of special studies by different individuals who as a hobby had become expert in a special field, such as naval ordnance in the Civil War. This included also our study (though we put it in the *Dictionary of Fighting Ships* first) listing all the Confederate combatants, something never done before. This took a tremendous amount of research. Miss Alma Lawrence, in our early archives research section, had started on this independently before she retired. Afterwards she worked with us still until she died. Then the Lord sent us a civilian volunteer, Jesse Thomas, who was devoted to Confederate ships. Several on our staff and other outsiders joined in.

I haven't said much about the *Dictionary of American Naval Fighting Ships.* It made slow headway, but within a couple of years we were going at pretty good speed.

Paul Stillwell: How much had been done under Admiral Heffernan?

Admiral Eller: He started it, but very little had been accomplished because there wasn't anybody there to do it.

Paul Stillwell: Was he the one that had the conception, the idea, the format and so forth?

---

47. Grant served as chairman of the Civil War Centennial Commission from 1957 to 1961.

Admiral Eller: He had the idea of the dictionary. As for the format, that evolved. Both format and content steadily developed and it improved as we went along. After much pressure, frequent changes, and participation of many in the division outside ships' history, and that of reserves and contract workers, we finally completed the first volume in late 1959. It had launched when we perceived needed improvements, though we had sent parts of the manuscripts to a host of naval commands and civilian experts. It didn't have illustrations, obviously a deficiency. The histories were generally too short and didn't bring out the ships' achievements. I wanted the histories to show, as pointed out in my preface to volume I, that each ship in large or small part has helped shape the destiny of the United States—a long and noble line from the tiny sailing craft of the American Revolution to the great battleships and carriers of our time, and now the atomic revolution. I wanted them to bring out how a ship becomes part of a man, how it fills him with pride. They improved as we went along, and certainly by the time we got up to the third volume they were reaching pretty good quality.

Paul Stillwell: How much did you do personally on that series?

Admiral Eller: I would read, or at least skim, most manuscripts, modify many, consult on inclusion of material. I wrote prefaces or introductions to each volume, trying to give an overall viewpoint. I was with the *Dictionary* almost daily, especially seeking to get completeness, inspiration, and significance into the histories. I worked with new authors, like young Sam Morison, or Dave Rosenberg.[48] I would talk to them to encourage them, and show them what might be useful.

Speaking of Dave, one day Miss Mertz came to me and said, "There's a couple wants to see you, and I think you should see them." So they came in, a Jewish couple. They said that their son craved to get into writing naval history, his love; would we let him work with us just for the experience. I called him in, talked with him and said sure. He was coming to American Washington University for his freshman year. He worked on the *Dictionary of Fighting Ships* without compensation just to get a chance to work in naval history. Later, through purchase

---

48. Dr. David A. Rosenberg is a military historian who has taught at a number of universities, including the Naval Academy. He is noted for his biographical work on Admiral Arleigh A. Burke, USN (Ret.).

orders, we got a little pay for him. Then finally he got on the staff, didn't he?

Paul Stillwell: I didn't know that.

Admiral Eller: I think he did for a short time, then he got interested in working on Admiral Burke's biography.

Paul Stillwell: You must have had some augmentation, because the volumes started coming out faster there.

Admiral Eller: We put on more pressure. Also, as we got into the swing of it, perfected the format, and authors got inspired, we naturally built up speed. We didn't get any augmentation in staff per se, though volunteers and reservists for short periods were a type of augmentation.

Paul Stillwell: One other publication that was coming along during the late '50s was Admiral Furer's *Administrative History*.[49]

Admiral Eller: Yes. As part of a general government program, Commodore Knox initiated that project.[50] Professor Robert Albion, a fast talker with a bloated reputation, was hired during the war and paid a large sum to prepare an administrative history. When I was in Public Information, in '46 to '48, he still hadn't prepared anything and was getting desperate. So was John Heffernan in a way, since his office administered the project. At the last minute Albion produced some jumbled notes—afraid, he had just milked the department. John asked us to help out. What Albion submitted was worthless. There was a very capable commander with me in Public Information, Commander Sam Reed. He and I prepared a little volume; it was hardly a start. Then we finally got Albion out of the picture and John Heffernan off the hook.

Paul Stillwell: Why did you do that? Because he hadn't produced anything?

---

49. Julius Augustus Furer, *Administration of the Navy Department in World War II* (Washington, D.C.: U.S. Government Printing Office, 1959).
50. Captain Dudley W. Knox, USN (Ret.), while on active duty, served as officer in charge, Office of Naval Records and Library, also curator of the Navy Department, beginning in 1921. In World War II he was also Deputy Director of Naval History. He remained on active duty until 1946, when he was promoted to commodore on the retired list.

Admiral Eller: Yes, he hadn't produced anything, and I think it was embarrassing to the Navy Department that they hadn't checked on him to get something produced; other contracts had been prepared and delivered. Now John got the right one to pick up the pieces. Admiral Furer was able, a distinguished naval architect, naval constructor, very wise and hard working. He tirelessly sought the facts and revised often, seeking to make the truth interesting. He labored on it for eight years or so, and I did get into that quite a bit. As with everything we published, I read and commented on the manuscript in its developing stages. We had a few differences, but always came to an agreement. When it came out, we sent it to the normal places you would send it for review. Also, in Public Information I got to know several hundred in the journalistic world, editors, publishers, columnists, top reporters. Usually if we had anything especially worthwhile, we would send it to them, as we did this fine volume. Walter Millis said that this was the finest administrative history ever written; and it is accurate and interesting.

Paul Stillwell: He was the one who worked with Forrestal on his diary, or edited the diary.[51]

Admiral Eller: Yes. John also had under way on contract command studies of Admiral Stark and Admiral Richardson.[52] These were well along when I came to the office. Admiral Richardson's study, by Admiral George Dyer, was a good job, although Richardson wouldn't talk freely about his relief from command in the Pacific by the President.[53] He never would. Admiral Vincent Murphy, a former staff officer of his and a good friend, got him to come in the office with me several times, just the three of us, to talk about it, but he never would talk.[54] He would get up to the point and then stop, as he did when talking to George. That study came out admirably, with little input from me. George knew what he was doing and did it well.

That of Admiral Stark's was different. He was one of the finest gentlemen I've known. He came to the office frequently. Intelligent, kind, gentle, wise, and pleasant, he was always eager to help, but he was troubled about the study. Captain John Dingwell

---

51. Walter Millis editor, in collaboration with E. S. Duffield *The Forrestal Diaries* (New York: Viking Press, 1951).
52. Admiral Harold R. Stark, USN, served as Chief of Naval Operations from 1 August 1939 to 26 March 1942.
53. Admiral James O. Richardson, USN (Ret.), and Vice Admiral George C. Dyer, USN (Ret.), *On the Treadmill to Pearl Harbor: The Memoirs of Admiral James O. Richardson, USN (Retired)* (Washington, D.C.: Naval History Division, Department of the Navy, 1973).
54. Vice Admiral Vincent R. Murphy, USN (Ret.).

was indefatigable and a thorough researcher.[55] For example, he indexed the 40 volumes of the Pearl Harbor hearings to locate easily anything relating to Admiral Stark.[56] Time after time he modified the manuscripts to meet Admiral Stark's desires—and there would again be something wrong. Much troubled, John kept coming to me. Finally he did get a manuscript approved, but then the admiral said he wanted to send it to his son-in-law, a lawyer in Philadelphia who had caused rejection of the other drafts. Dingwell called him "that damned Philadelphia lawyer." This time the son-in-law made certain statements that caused John to feel he was going to be sued for libel. I told him then to keep all of his notes and drafts and give them to me (which I put in classified archives) and complete a draft that Admiral Stark would approve. Then I would sign him off on the contract and take the responsibility myself. So we got the draft, but I'm sure it's not the full story of Admiral Stark.

Late in '55, or early '56, Walter Whitehill, Allan Nevins, father of oral history, and myself were appointed by SecNav to survey some differences between the Naval History Division and Public Information. It was after our report that responsibility for ship histories was transferred from Public Information to Naval History, and certain activities of the history division to Public Information. Our committee also recommended that there be a permanent Secretary of the Navy Advisory Committee on Naval History. There had been ad hoc committees since the war, but we recommended a permanent one. When I relieved in September '56, John Heffernan had formed the committee, and they were to meet in November. That was too fast for me because I hadn't got my teeth into the job. So I deferred it until next spring. Another reason was I had a very important speech in New York for the annual meeting of the National Foreign Trade Council, on "The United States and the Middle East," the importance of the Middle East to our future. And this was scheduled for almost the same date as the committee.

Next spring, we did meet. The committee was made up of these two, Whitehill and Nevins, plus other notable men like Dr. James Baxter Phinney, president of Dartmouth College and very knowledgeable in science and technology.

---

55. Captain John E. Dingwell, USN (Ret.).
56. Admiral Harold R. Stark, USN, served as Chief of Naval Operations from 1 August 1939 to 26 March 1942.

Paul Stillwell: He wrote a book.

Admiral Eller: *Scientists Against Time*, yes.[57] I was much interested in our getting more into the history of the Navy's leadership in science and technology; he was a natural one for that. Then we had Samuel Flagg Bemis, author and past president of the American Historical Association, without question the dean of historians on American foreign policy and diplomacy. He was also one of the few authors with clear perception of the interrelation of sea power and foreign policy. Among others we had the dean of archivists, Waldo Leland. Later when our American Revolution project got under way I added Julian Boyd, editor of the Jefferson Papers at Princeton, Leonard Labaree, editor of the Franklin Papers at Yale, and Lyman Butterfield, editor of the Adams Papers in Boston—three internationally known projects.

When we met in 1957, I brought up the question of publishing the naval documents of the American Revolution. Looking ahead to our bicentennial in the 1970s, I had been interested in doing something that would help educate writers and Americans in general on the decisive influence of sea power in helping us win independence. But it was a job felt to be almost impossible because the records were scattered all over in this country and oversea, and many of them gone. Besides, we had no staff. All the committee said it would be a good idea but they didn't think it could be done, except Walter Whitehill. He had an encyclopedic mind, knew everything, it seemed, about what was going on in the study of history of the United States. He was director of the Boston Athenaeum, secretary of the Massachusetts Historical Society, editor of *The American Neptune* and seemed to be able to do everything effortlessly, including being the most superb speaker. You could sit enthralled listening.

Walter said, "Well, if you can do it, there's one man you need to make it go, William Bell Clark." He had just retired to North Carolina from N. W. Ayer advertising agency as a vice president. All his life he had been writing on the Navy. His books are definitive studies, as on John Barry, and the one on John Young, and the first *Saratoga.* They were superbly researched, capably written; not brilliant, but interesting and accurate.

So I took some leave. I was going to North Carolina, anyhow, that summer to show our younger son, John, some colleges. He wanted to go to the Naval Academy, but his eyes were marginal. We drove, and though we had no funds, nor approval of the project, I started

---

57. James Baxter Phinney, *Scientists Against Time* (Cambridge: Massachusetts Institute of Technology Press, 1968).

researching right away. At the University of Virginia, I selected some very good documents and got them to be microfilmed and sent to us, planning to pay the cost myself if approval didn't come through. Then on to Brevard, North Carolina, to see Clark, whom I had written in advance. He received me in a large study about the size of this. All the bulkheads were lined from deck to overhead with cabinets and shelves filled with transcripts of documents of the American Revolution. He and I both, as we talked about it, thought that here and in the Navy's Record Group 45 at the National Archives, we had 90% of everything we needed. The project looked all the more promising to me after that. So I asked him if he would be the editor, told him we didn't have any money, that we would handle the mechanics in the office and I'd try to get enough money to pay him for clerical help and travel for research, if he needed to do any more. It turned out we did these thick volumes for $5,000 a volume.

Paul Stillwell: He was donating his time, then.

Admiral Eller: He was donating his time and his experience. You couldn't have bought what he did for $100,000 a year. He didn't want to do it; he thought he was too old, and had other plans. However he agreed to talk it over with his wife that night before turning me down. In his twilight years, he didn't want to start such a large task, but was, I think, enthralled with the idea that his life's work would be put into print in a usable form that would always be the basic source for the understanding of sea power's influence in the American Revolution. The next day he agreed to do it, though I didn't have funds or contract in sight.

We hurried on to Winston-Salem, my wife's home, where she and John remained. After some research in the Moravian archives, which I knew pretty well from Moravian books I'd written, I went to the University of North Carolina by bus and selected material for filming. It's a very good library, with good archives. I think it has the Southern Historical Collection, which is one of the finest in the country, with quite a bit on the Revolution. There I also inspected the NROTC Armory and told the commanding officer that we needed to send him some of the Naval Heroes series, and objects or displays to inspire and instruct his midshipmen in the background of a great Navy. (We got many ROTCs to set up displays.)

Paul Stillwell: Was that at Chapel Hill?

Admiral Eller: Chapel Hill. And from there to Raleigh, where the State Archives has a tremendously fine collection. I started in and happily developed a system of research there that continued throughout the years. This was to skim through a collection (I could cover 30 or 40 in a couple of hours). When I saw anything that mentioned the sea, I tabbed that document and went to the next one. If a fair percent of the first documents got tabbed, I read no further and took the whole collection for microfilming. Filming didn't cost very many dollars. We could do the selection in the office. We had nobody to go around doing research but me (though Bill Morgan made a few short trips,) and I did it only when I was making a speech or going to a launching or other duty.

It would take several trips to complete the state archives. After a few hours there I went to see Jonathan Daniels, son of Josephus.[58] He was a casual friend.

Paul Stillwell: He was a newspaper editor, wasn't he?

Admiral Eller: Yes, of the *Raleigh News and Observer*. He called connections in Edenton to help me. From Raleigh, I went to Duke University a few miles away, and got the little there in short order. Then on to Edenton, which was a port like Annapolis in the Revolutionary period. The courthouse and the historical society didn't have much, but nearby was a superb private collection at the Hayes Plantation. It had a great deal we needed. Happily, microfilm had been sent to Chapel Hill, and I was able to get copies from there without further ado.

At a field near Edenton, I caught a Marine plane flying to Norfolk, and then a Navy plane to Washington, both on regular runs. Thus in about four days, I had practically covered North Carolina, everything except the state archives, which I got to about once a year, stopping by for a few hours on business trips to the South, finishing in 1966.

We wangled $20,000 from the money people for the first four volumes of the naval documents, persuaded SecNav to sign the contract, and got started. Morgan and his small staff stretched themselves to handle our part of the editorial work.[59] We had pertinent parts of the microfilm blown up, and sent copies to Clark for editing. As we got more and more material,

---

58. Josephus Daniels served as Secretary of the Navy from 5 March 1913 to 5 March 1921, during both of President Woodrow Wilson's terms.
59. Clark was the editor of the first four volumes of *Naval Documents of the American Revolution*, published 1959–64.

we found that Clark had only a fraction on his shelves and almost all he had were hand transcripts, which are subject to error. We were getting the verbatim, of course, in microfilm.

A wealth of material awaited us in Washington at the Library of Congress and the National Archives in the Navy's early operational files, particularly Record Group 45, transferred there in the 1930s. As time permitted over the years our staff filmed documents, starting with those of the early years of the Revolution. Attending most of the monthly *Constellation* meetings, I spent a few hours each time in the Maryland State Archives at Annapolis or the Maryland Historical Society in Baltimore. Each had extensive collections requiring visits almost to the time of my retirement.

My next important trip came in 1958. The one in my job received invitations to all launchings and ship commissionings. I couldn't go to many of them, but the carrier *Independence* was being launched at Brooklyn Navy Yard in early June 1958. So I drove up a day early, taking Agnes along. In a few hours I completed the Morgan Library, which had some valuable materials, and the New York State Historical Society, which has the old Naval History Society collections, that also contained much of value. I didn't cover that archives completely, but got them interested in selecting other material. Last came the fabulous New York Public Library. It contains so much I could only start on the collections, but got the staff interested in helping. It took us a number of years to finish these, mostly by mail.

After the launch we went to Bethlehem, Pennsylvania, where the Moravian College was giving me an honorary degree for one of my books on Moravian history. And I guess this was also lining me up for a speech later on when I spoke at an international commemoration on John Amos Comenius, the great Moravian Bishop and educator. We returned by Morristown, New Jersey, where I had heard of a private collection in the custody of the National Parks Service that might have documents we needed. Morristown is a lovely little place. You probably know it. I had never been there. Instead of the few documents expected, this proved to be a goldmine. Frances Ronald, the director, a fine gentleman, helped with the research, so that we finished quickly.

Soon after we got back, Agnes and I went to England. I had a speech scheduled at Chatham House, the Royal Institute of International Affairs, on "Sea Power and the Western Allies" and another at Greenwich at the Royal Naval Staff College, "Sea Power and the Future." While there I went to the Public Records Office, which has, of course, a vast amount of material from the British side. I just went to get acquainted and explain our project. There wasn't time to do any real research. Coming out, whom should I meet on the steps but Allan Nevins going in? We had sent him to the Sixth Fleet, to get him interested in writing a history of the Sixth Fleet. On his way home, between planes, he was researching; always working.

Then we went on to Holland, France, Germany, and Italy to get naval historical staffs and other interested in our project, and to find someone in each country to go ahead with the research, usually for very little or nothing. In England one man selected illustrations and Commander W.E. May, Royal Navy (Retired), for just a pittance, selected whatever we asked him to get in manuscripts. If we wanted information for 1778, for example, we would send him the list of ships off our coast and ask him to get the logs and any communications he thought pertinent. In Holland, two museums had quite a bit for us but the state archives had little, nor the Navy. The museum directors helpfully selected what we needed.

France didn't produce a researcher then, despite much help from the Navy, but we got the word around, and later got a jewel in Mme. Ulane Bonnel, American wife of a French medical officer—you may know Ulane; she has spoken at the academy's history symposium. A WAVE during the war, she had continued in the Naval Reserve. A superb researcher, she got a contract with the Library of Congress for other material on the Revolution, and ran ours in with it on the same contract, by agreement with the library. We had her called to active reserve duty at one time, which she wanted, for a special research project. So she got us a great deal from France at no cost to us. Professor Bernard LeBeau of the Academy's French Department translated most of the French documents for a modest fee, so at little cost we multiplied what Clark had, and Record Group 45, many times.

We started working on Volume I right away in '57. Clark promptly sent in a batch of documents for the first months covering operational events in the northern colonies where his research and most of the early sea operations took place. He had not grasped the full scope of what we should cover. Besides naval operations it seemed necessary to include selected documents on diplomacy, foreign affairs, merchant marine, privateering. All played a role. However, he readily accepted the broader reach when he came to Washington for the first of several conferences at which we developed editorial policy and format. We early decided to include contemporary illustrations. Charts, maps, port scenes, went to the Library; other illustrations went to the Curator Section as a separate group in our expanding photo collection. My introduction to Volume I speaks to the broad sweep of our research, touches on the large number of repositories, public and private contributing, and names, many of the last who assisted, usually eagerly.

Only a few people raised real difficulty. Surprisingly Annapolis produced two of these. One was Professor Vernon Tate, Naval Academy librarian. Early on I asked him to film documents and graphics there that included a group on John Paul Jones. Months passed; nothing came. Letters and telephone calls got no answer. Finally he wrote he had no money for film. We offered to send that. Many months passed, and this time he had no help. Excuse followed excuse for two or three years. Nothing ever came.

Meanwhile, one day when our research was well under way, a friend said, "Captain Jack Stone here in Annapolis has some documents." Later I met Jack and asked about them.

"Oh," he said. "They don't amount to anything." Months later, while showing a friend through the chapel crypt, I saw some priceless letters loaned by him. I told Jack we had to film his collection. "We'll see about it," he said. Repeats of this rigmarole went on for months. So one weekend we called on the Stones at their home across from the Alumni House and talked him into showing me part of the collection. His first wife had inherited the papers of John Langdon, marine agent for New England during the Revolution. I repeatedly asked to borrow them for filming and got the standard answer, "We'll see about it."

Request after request got the same answer. Having exhausted efforts with Tate, we at least set a date with Captain Wade DeWeese at the museum and brought portable filming equipment to the academy. I asked Jack to borrow his manuscripts to film there and got, "We'll see about it." With Bill Morgan and one of his hands to work the equipment we began filming in the museum, and I telephoned Jack a final time asking for the manuscripts with the same "We'll see about it" results.

In desperation I said, "We'll come to your house and film there." And again the same "We'll see about it."

Finishing at the museum about 1630, we went to Jack's place. He answered the bell. "We've come to do the filming," I said. For a long minute I thought he would throw us out. In a quite frigid environment we started in for what I thought would be an hour of filming, from the folders of manuscripts he had shown me. But the collection turned out to be probably the largest of its type in the country. Two hours later, I left, not being able to help anymore. Bill and his helper didn't finish for another two hours.

By 1960 we could begin sending groups of documents to the printer for galley. By mid–1963 we had corrected galley proofs for Volume I in hand. By this time, also, our museum had begun to make a name for itself, and the expanding displays included a number of items, including ship models from President Kennedy's collection. We had further connection with him through furnishing his office with fine painting from the Naval Academy Museum. In addition he had held a sit-down luncheon at the White House for some 20 editors of major publications that included Clark and me and several of my committees. Allan sat at his right. On another occasion he spoke to a larger group at the Library of Congress. Hence it seemed logical to ask him for a foreword. Working directly through his naval aide, we got agreement. Against doubts of some up the line, we sent the galley proofs through channels with a suggested foreword. Instead we got a powerful one, showing his input, signed on 4 July, a day forever marking a milestone on the road to freedom. A few months later he was shot. We got forewords from presidents for succeeding volumes, except number IV. Secretary Chafee signed it, apparently for prestige, while I was on a fortnight's leave.[60]

Volume I completed the other steps in bookmaking to launch in late 1964. A giant of 451 pages (we packed in as much as possible on the $5,000 contract—money was hard to get). Rave reviews greeted it—"a monumental work," "a great historical enterprise," and many other across the country. The next three volumes followed at two-year intervals. Before this we got a contract for four more, and a few years later, for four more. Clark finished his part of eight volumes as well as some on the next four. (There was always more to do in the office.) Then working through the last day of his life, died in his sleep 31 October 1968, a great loss to us. Bill Morgan took over and brought out the next four, Volume VIII in 1980. Volume IX made slow headway. That December I had a small stroke, less than two months after Clark's death, and decided it was time to turn over the watch. So a year later, I did, actually, on my birthday, 23 January 1970. Throughout much of 1969 I looked for a talented relief who would stay on the job and work hard for years. Several wanted the job but didn't appeal to me. Vice Admiral Ed Hooper had always shown a real interest in his reports relating to Vietnam and in our classified summaries (more on

---

60. John H. Chafee served as Secretary of the Navy from 31 January 1969 to 4 May 1972.

Vietnam later).⁶¹ After months of persuasion he agreed, but couldn't come until June of 1970. My stalwart deputy and classmate, Kent Loomis, agreed to keep the ship on course until then.

Meantime, I've skipped over various things. One is atomic energy, obviously a great revolution of history, especially in its effect upon sea power. So I started right away in 1956 to get the original documents, and immediately ran into Rickover's great vanity. He had determined, although it's never been stated that way, that the credit for nuclear-powered submarines was to come to Rickover, nobody else. Of course, he didn't know anything about atomic energy until it was well under way, nor did anybody else in the Navy, except a handful, nor did the concept for its employment in submarines originate with him.

In the late 1930s scientists in Europe fissioned uranium. This was brought to the attention of the Navy Department in March 1939. Foreseeing the possibilities for nuclear propulsion, the department, through ONR, invested a few thousand dollars in research, the first U.S. government action. Outline of a submarine nuclear reactor, much like that which went into the USS *Nautilus* 15 years later, spurred our research.⁶² Under Drs. Ross Gunn and Philip Abelson we developed a thermal diffusion process for separating the key elements in uranium and made good progress at the plant we set up in Philadelphia. Later the Manhattan Project got under way at Oak Ridge on a massive scale, and the Navy's effort was merged into it under General Leslie Groves.⁶³ Only a small number in the Navy connected with these developments knew anything about what was going on.

Not making headway with Rickover, we started right away getting around him. Admiral Lewis Strauss, head of the Atomic Energy Commission, a wartime friend, uncovered a very valuable document and some others, As did his successor, another friend. BuShips and NRL had some files not in Rickover's hands. Meanwhile, we located Gunn and Abelson, both now out of government service. They gave me leads which brought in other documents. This was a slow project. Several years later, in '62, I got a nuclear physicist in for a short tour of reserve duty. It happened to be our son. Lieutenant Peter McN. Eller. He had just finished a three-year tour teaching nuclear

---

61. Vice Admiral Edwin B. Hooper, USN (Ret.), was Director of Naval History from August 1970 to November 1976.
62. Commander Eugene P. Wilkinson, USN, became the first commanding officer of the USS *Nautilus* (SSN-571), when she was commissioned as the world's first nuclear-powered submarine on 30 September 1954. The oral history of Wilkinson, who retired as a vice admiral, is in the Naval Institute collection.
63. Manhattan District derived from an Army Corps of Engineers term connected with the U.S. program to create an atomic bomb in World War II. The overall effort is often referred to as the Manhattan Project. Major General Leslie R. Groves, USA, was head of the Manhattan Project.

physics and chemistry at the Submarine School. Able, conscientious, and through, he researched in the National Archives, Atomic Energy Commission, and various sections of the Navy Department, and we collected quite a good bit of material. Rickover has valuable documents we never did get, but we do have a pretty solid background file in our classified archives.

Paul Stillwell: So you were looking mainly for primary documents?

Admiral Eller: Primary documents.

Paul Stillwell: Not for publishing.

Admiral Eller: No, I knew we didn't have the talent to do anything like that, and it wasn't necessary. The general story is well and accurately covered in various books like Phinney's *Scientists Against Time* and Lewis Strauss's excellent *Men and Decisions*.[64] Later in the '60s, as part of our effort to get commands to produce sound histories, I did get a reliable historian (who had worked for me in public information) to write NRL's history with emphasis on its part in the development of nuclear power. NRL, of course, funded and oversaw the project.

My experience with Rickover and nuclear propulsion ends on another sad note. Later on in the 1960s, the Department reached the point of awarding a medal to Abelson for his general concept of the nuclear submarine power plant and his early development work. As I remember, this had reached the point of setting a date for the ceremony and I planned to be present. Then Rickover somehow blocked it.

Vietnam, I mentioned. It began to build up in the '60s, right in the middle of our great involvement with the Civil War Centennial, our several large public projects, and other tasks, such as building up at the Naval Historical Display Center, which by '64 had become so well established we could call it the Naval Memorial Museum, the planned designation all along.

We began writing fleet and unit commanders involved in Vietnam asking for action reports, photos, objects, and detailed information. This was about the same time that the

---

64. Lewis L. Strauss, *Men and Decisions* (Garden City, NY: Doubleday, 1962).

torpedo boats attacked our destroyers in Tonkin Gulf, in '64.[65] After this I talked to CNO and we issued the same requirement for action reports developed in my section for the Pacific in World War II. A little later we set up a requirement for a monthly history from all command units involved; not every ship, but every command unit, like the River Force and the Coastal Force. This required another directive, of course. We often had to prepare directives for CNO's or SecNav's signature. For these we would always follow the same process as in getting the museum: send roughs to the different sections involved. Hence we usually had no trouble getting anything signed.

Meanwhile, in Dean Allard's shop we started a classified history of Vietnam, our involvement there from after V-J Day up to the current time. We had been involved one way or the other most of that time. The monthly history from commands became very useful to us. We soon started a monthly classified summary, which we issued to all commands in the Navy. We got a naval reservist from ONI as added manpower to work with us on it. After we landed the first Marines and the war escalated, we got authorization to bring in a few reservists to assign to different commands to write their histories and to get war reports. I talked with CNO and told him that we should have this arrangement, as we were in the middle of a real war; he agreed, of course.[66]

We soon had this set-up going. It became quite valuable to the Navy, providing irreplaceable source material for study of developments and lessons learned. As the war expanded, many officers from the Pentagon ordered to Vietnam came to us for study of our classified summaries and the reports from the field. And when possible, I got returnees in to learn from them. As a sad note, we lost one of our own field staff in combat. Assigned to the riverine force, he was properly participating in an operation better to report it. In addition to reports, after operations of importance, a letter went to the commander asking for material that could be used in our memorial museum or placed elsewhere on loan, citing types desired. Quantities arrived.

---

65. On 2 August 1964, North Vietnamese patrol boats in the Tonkin Gulf attacked the destroyer *Maddox* (DD-731) in international waters during daytime. On the night of 4 August the *Maddox* and the destroyer *Turner Joy* (DD-951) reported being attacked by North Vietnamese craft. The question of whether the second attack occurred has never been completely resolved, but it is unlikely that it happened. The reports of the two attacks led to the congressional Gulf of Tonkin Resolution, which provided the legal basis for the commitment of U.S. armed forces in Vietnam.

66. Admiral David L. McDonald, USN, served as Chief of Naval Operations from 1 August 1963 to 1 August 1967. His oral history is in the Naval Institute collection.

In the middle of all else, the Cuban crisis erupted in '62.[67] Admiral Bob Dennison, another friend, was SACLant-CinCLant.[68] He agreed that this was going to be a great historic event that should be well documented. So we sent Dean Allard down to help his staff organize and record it. That's one of our most valuable sets of documents, top secret, and closed for years.

I think I ought to finish up shortly. I've skipped around, but I might mention Polaris. We got everything we wanted in documents and objects from Red Raborn, who headed up Polaris.[69] And in some ways, it seems to me that was a more spectacular development than turning nuclear energy into motive power for ships. He was very cooperative and an entirely different kind of leader. Do you know him?

Paul Stillwell: No. I certainly know of his work.

Admiral Eller: He had an aggressive, positive, pleasant attitude. He led by inspiration more than anything else. I had known him in the Pacific. He had gunnery training, part of my overall field, for AirPac at Kaneohe.

We lost the Vietnam War because first the Whiz Kids tried to run it out of McNamara's office.[70] Second, because the President always hampered. We were cutting off the dog's tail a little bit at a time. Every time we had them on the ropes, we would seek to end the war. They gladly accepted the reprieve and just took the time to build up again.

Another reason was the abominable press. Many of the press reports from there were written in barrooms, unhappily; they always told about any damage Americans did to the civilian population, but very little about the brutalities of the Viet Cong. These sadists would cut off a child's arm, or tell the leader of the village they were going to do that to his child if he didn't come in accord with them—cut off children's arms or

---

67. The Cuban Missile Crisis was triggered in mid–October 1962, when a U.S. reconnaissance plane photographed a Soviet nuclear missile site in Cuba and the presence of Soviet bombers. On 22 October President John F. Kennedy went on national television to announce a naval quarantine of Cuba, to be implemented on 24 October. On 28 October Premier Nikita Khrushchev of the Soviet Union notified President Kennedy that he was ordering the withdrawal of Soviet bombers and missiles from Cuba.
68. Admiral Robert L. Dennison, USN, served as Supreme Allied Commander Atlantic, Commander in Chief Atlantic, and Commander in Chief Atlantic Fleet from 28 February 1960 to 30 April 1963. His oral history is in the Naval Institute collection.
69. Rear Admiral William F. Raborn, Jr., USN, was director of the Special Projects Office, which developed the Polaris submarine-launched ballistic missile system. He held the post from 1955 to 1962, being promoted to vice admiral in 1960. His Polaris oral history is in the Naval Institute collection.
70. Robert S. McNamara served as Secretary of Defense from 21 January 1961 to 29 February 1968. "Whiz Kids" was the nickname for the group of young civilian officials whom McNamara appointed to key positions in the Department of Defense hierarchy.

abduct them, and throw people down wells and seal them off. I learned this from the reports, from our officers who had served there, and from General Greene, who became head of the Marine Corps, starting in '64. A superb leader, he visited Vietnam and took the deepest interest in his Marines. Both the Marines and the Navy had high morale. They knew they were helping peace-loving citizens who needed them. Were you out there at any time in that period?

Paul Stillwell: Oh, yes. I was out there from '66 to '68, off and on.

Admiral Eller: You were right in the hot period.

Paul Stillwell: Oh, yes.

Admiral Eller: Wally went to the front lines, pushed civic action, which was splendid, by both Marines and the Navy. Then when he came back, he tried to correct some of these horrible exaggerations on TV and in the press. I was at his office one morning for breakfast with him (which he always started with a prayer). Then we reviewed TV from the night before. Each day he had clips cut of all TV that referred to Vietnam and the operations of Marines, and the film shown to him early the next morning. Then he had the film flown to the troops in Vietnam and shown to the troops and reporters who had sent it in. Soon the reports got a little better because much was so slanted and so exaggerated that it was obviously untrue, the total picture was untrue.

I am sure if we had tried to win the war, we could have. Several times we had them completely on the ropes, and all we had to do was continue the blockade that President Nixon finally sent in.[71] The mine blockade was just what was needed for a start, plus the riverine force, which was admirably handled. One of our best brochures briefly covered our Navy's early participation in riverine war, then went into detail on operations in Vietnam that were on the point of cleaning out the water rats when we gave

---

71. In May 1972, confronted by North Vietnamese intransigence at the Paris peace talks and a North Vietnamese spring offensive against South Vietnam, President Richard M. Nixon ordered the Navy to carry out existing plans for mining the harbors of North Vietnam. On 9 May, A-6 Intruders from U.S. carriers sowed mines at Haiphong, Hon Gai, Cam Pha, Thanh Hoa, Vinh, Quan Khe, and Dong Hoi. The flow of seaborne supplies into North Vietnam ceased immediately.

up. Much of the credit goes to Captain Salzer, who impressed me greatly.[72] Zumwalt did a good job, too. He was a good ship captain and a good field operator in the rivers, but he should have stopped there.[73]

Paul Stillwell: Who was your boss while you were Director of Naval History?

Admiral Eller: Nominally the Naval History Division came under OP-09, which came under the Vice Chief. In my other hat as curator I came directly under SecNav. But nobody really bothered us. In fact, the only thing 09 did was to help us to get money and men, what little we could get in men. But really there was no one who supervised.

Paul Stillwell: So you ran a pretty autonomous show, then.

Admiral Eller: Yes. In fact, as mentioned, largely on our own we got Kennedy's agreement for a foreword to Volume I of *Naval Documents* without going through channels. Now I think it's time to cease fire, leaving other matters to rest in peace.

Paul Stillwell: Well, Admiral, I certainly would like you to talk about the origins of the naval oral history program.

Admiral Eller: Oh, I left it out accidentally. In '57, at our first Advisory Committee meeting, Allan Nevins hesitantly suggested, "Why don't you do oral histories?" His program hadn't developed greatly then at Columbia, I don't think, and I didn't know much about it.
    I said, "I'd like to, but we don't have any money." Nobody else seemed interested, and I was swamped with other new projects, so nothing was done.
    In '58 we met in the autumn just after Agnes and I got back from Europe. I had sent Allan to the Sixth Fleet, having prepared the way with letters to Com6th Fleet, then

---

72. Rear Admiral Robert S. Salzer, USN, who had previously commanded the riverine forces as a captain, served as Commander Naval Forces Vietnam/Chief of Naval Advisory Group Vietnam from 5 April 1971 to 30 June 1972. The oral history of Salzer, who retired as a vice admiral, is in the Naval Institute collection.
73. Vice Admiral Elmo R. Zumwalt, Jr., USN, served as Commander Naval Forces Vietnam/Chief of Naval Advisory Group Vietnam from 30 September 1968 to 14 May 1970. His oral history is in the Naval Institute collection.

my old shipmate, Admiral C. R. Brown, Cat Brown.[74] He gave Allan the royal treatment. Trustworthy, charming, and a tireless researcher, Allan had been given full access and had collected a great deal for a projected history of the Sixth Fleet. The material he collected went in our classified archives. Now at the '58 meeting, he said positively, "I'd like to help you start oral history. We'll absorb the administrative cost if you can get a few hundred dollars for the expenses of the interviewer." I managed to get some $300.00. Dr. Shaughnessy of Columbia would do the interview. I had great trouble persuading anybody to do the first interview despite assurance it would be kept privileged. They were all reticent. They didn't want to hurt anybody's feelings, or they didn't want to look as if they were vain tooting their own horns. Those that did want to talk had already got somebody to write something on them, like Halsey.[75]

Seeking the top leaders first, all of whom knew me well, I tried Nimitz and Spruance and Turner, and Admiral Hewitt, who already had somebody working on a partial oral history. Finally I got reluctant Admiral Conolly, and it took a year for him to work out details so that he would do it. He was also very reticent, but his acceptance helped to break the ice. As I remember the interviewing had just about got under way when our advisory committee met in 1960. Allan had returned from his second tour with the Sixth Fleet. This time he said, "I'd like to give the royalties of my book on Kennedy's speeches for the oral history program." Then he told us about Jack Mason, who had been in the Navy, as you know, during the war, was now a minister, discreet, very genial and pleasant to deal with and very knowledgeable.[76] He was superb for the job, as his many splendid interviews attest. Soon we started with Jack. I can't remember whom he first interviewed. Still Spruance and Turner and Nimitz wouldn't talk.[77]

At the same time I was working on them to do command histories, like Stark and Richardson; no, they wouldn't do that. Finally Turner agreed when we got the right man. He said if George Dyer would do it, "He's a mean enough S.O.B. that he'll say it just the way I want to say it." He wanted to be known exactly as he was. George got sick just as he got started.

---

74. Vice Admiral Charles R. Brown, USN, commanded the Sixth Fleet from 4 August 1956 to 30 September 1958.
75. William F. Halsey Jr., with J. Bryan III, *Admiral Halsey's Story* (New York: Whittlesey House, 1947).
76. John T. Mason Jr. was an Episcopal minister. As a civilian he had worked in the Office of Naval Intelligence during World War II.
77. Admiral Raymond A. Spruance, USN (Ret.); Admiral Richmond Kelly Turner, USN (Ret.). Turner died 12 February 1961. Spruance died 13 December 1969).

When he recovered, he had only one interview, I think, before Turner died.[78] I'd been working on Admiral Spruance all the time too. Turner's death may have shaken him. He finally agreed if we could get the right man. After much persuasion we got him, his operations officer, with whom I had often worked during the war.

Paul Stillwell: Savvy Forrestel.[79]

Admiral Eller: Savvy Forrestel. He made me agree to participate fully. He had trouble figuring out how to do it. But after many partial drafts for my kibitzing he finally did a brilliant job, as I point out in my introduction, which is one of the best essays on leadership I've written.

Admiral Nimitz wouldn't give in. He wanted to save his biography for his children. Chester Jr. retired in August 1957. The admiral hoped he would write the biography, and I corresponded with Chester about getting his father's papers to Washington. But young Chester got a job in industry that led to success as head of a fine old manufacturing company in Connecticut.

Admiring the admiral, we did as much as possible for him, also hoping as a byproduct to get his papers for preservation. Early on we collected all photographs we could relating to him, including those from him to copy. We got him to sign photographs of all ships in which he had served and used them as illustrations in the appropriate volumes of the *Dictionary*, and in displays developed for museums and schools. He was especially pleased when after a long search in the U.S. and overseas we uncovered a dim photo of the *Panay*, an ex-Spanish gunboat he commanded in the Philippines.

We got him to send uniforms and other memorabilia for the Memorial Museum. Several schools were named for him. We sent them selected photos, speeches, action reports (especially Midway, which I wrote with his modifications), selections from our "Hall of Naval Heroes" series, offered relics, and sent suggestions on developing displays (part of our larger program of developing displays with all naval name schools). The San Antonio Nimitz School, as I remember, took a number of relics, including a mast, and held morning colors. Admiral Charlie Duncan entered into the spirit at the

---

78. George C. Dyer did undertake the project, though not as an oral history. It was a book titled *The Amphibians Came to Conquer* (Washington: U.S. Government Printing Office, 1972). Admiral Eller wrote the foreword.
79. Vice Admiral Emmet P. Forrestel, USN (Ret.), *Admiral Raymond A. Spruance, USN: a Study in Command* (Washington, D.C.: U.S. Government Printing Office, 1966).

school on Oahu and developed excellent displays. Admiral Nimitz appreciated all this. Whenever he came to Washington he stopped by to talk. Each time, and in frequent letters (he always answered in longhand; a sizable collection is with my papers in Dean's shop), I kept pressing him to send his papers. Turner's death also affected him. He began to send unclassified ones. At intervals other groups came, including low classification. By then current CNOs were sending us their highly classified ones, and he sent even higher ones.

Early in the '60s a movement got under way in Fredericksburg, Texas, to establish a repository for his papers. We helped to expand this in scope to a major museum established in and around his grandfather's "Ship Hotel."[80] This consumed an increasing amount of my time, more than the *Constellation* or the *Olympia* or Pemberton House. Several factors, including politics, caused it to nearly shipwreck. Even Governor Connally, whom I had known as SecNav and wrote several times, would do nothing.[81] President Johnson, whose ranch was nearby, seemed cool. We helped in fund drives, provided quantities of World War II relics, wrote letters and articles. Happily a dedicated few in Fredericksburg held on. In time they got Douglass Hubbard from the Park Service as a director, who worked hard and well. I visited the struggling museum in 1966. Later President Johnson began to show interest (I think Mrs. Johnson prodded him). Tom Moorer, then CNO, and I flew down one Sunday in his high-speed jet, landed at the Air Force base near San Antonio, rode the President's waiting helicopter to his ranch (where Mrs. Johnson welcomed us), entered waiting autos for the museum, had a short visit in the museum, lunch, and then back to Washington before dusk.[82] In the 1970s after retiring, I went a third time with Arleigh and Tom (now retired from the Joint Chiefs). I continued to work with Hubbard through the '70s. He has built the museum into one of the greats in the U.S. The Texas Park Service has now taken it under its wing, so it should live as long as Texas.

A year or so before his death the admiral sent his most secret papers. This major breakthrough was followed by another. We got Allan Nevins interested in writing the admiral's biography, if possible putting the Sixth Fleet history on hold, and arranged for a visit. Allan made such a good impression that Admiral Nimitz accepted. Allen had a capable researcher on the West Coast who started in and had developed a sizable body of

---

80. Originally known as the Admiral Nimitz Museum, it is now called the National Museum of the Pacific War.
81. John B. Connally Jr., served as Secretary of the Navy from 25 January 1961 to 20 December 1961.
82. Admiral Thomas H. Moorer, USN, served as Chief of Naval Operations from 1 August 1967 to 1 July 1970. His oral history is in the Naval Institute collection.

notes when Admiral Nimitz died. Unhappily Allan began to fail, but we had all the papers in Dean's shop, where they well served Ned Potter.[83]

Admiral Nimitz got special pleasure from our submarine brochure. We got him to sign the foreword, which summarizes the steps taken during his tour as CNO to develop nuclear power for submarines. It was one of the few screeds I wrote for him that he accepted without changing a word. We put out eight or ten brochures on different facets of the Navy.

Paul Stillwell: I'd like to have you talk about those, if you would, please.

Admiral Eller: These were our first publications. Being shorter, they were the easiest to do. Responsibility for a brochure went to one section, with the other kibitzing. The library, of course, drew bibliographies; the first was a few pages; and now the last edition is over an inch thick. Dean Allard's shop prepared naval sources for research; that started out small, too, and grew into quite a book. The library also prepared *Naval Honors to George Washington*. Every time the *Sequoia*, the Secretary's yacht, passed Mount Vernon, it fired a salute. So we prepared a lovely little brochure in blue and gold, on the background of the custom, printed in the Navy Department. Most of the others were printed by GPO.

We assigned one to the curator shop to try to stimulate displays in ships and stations that would inspire and develop pride. Much of the preservation section was written by Commander Mendel Peterson of the Smithsonian during periods of reserve duty. Ships' history prepared one on ships' christening, launching, and commissioning. These all had a fundamental reason to help develop morale within the Navy; another was to reduce our research for correspondence, because often we could answer queries with flyers or brochures. (We had one or two-page flyers to answer popular queries.) All had good sales; those on destroyers and submarines went like hot cakes. We did others that were simply historical, like one on sailing ships on the line. That was a hobby of Reilly's. Do you know him, John Reilly?[84]

Paul Stillwell: Yes.

---

83. E. B. Potter, *Nimitz* (Annapolis: Naval Institute Press, 1976).
84. John C. Reilly Jr. headed the ships' history branch from 1984 until his retirement in 2001. All told, he was with the Naval History Division/Naval Historical Center for 34 years.

Admiral Eller: Yes. That was John's hobby, and, I think, he probably did most of it at night.

Paul Stillwell: There was a fellow named Thaddeus Tuleaja came in and worked on the battleships, I know.

Admiral Eller: Yes, he worked on it during reserve duty, and he also wrote one of the best books on Midway.[85]

To come back to oral history, after we got started on this, we finally built up steam. To stretch out Allard's funding we persuaded those of means to contribute $1,000 towards the costs—such as Admiral Tommy Hart (who also provided a portrait and other paintings for our project to accumulate them), Admiral Jimmy Fife, and my dear friend Eugene E. Wilson, '08, pioneer in naval aviation, who became head of United Aircraft after resigning as a commander.[86] We had somewhere between 30 or 40 histories, didn't we, when Jack left to come to the Institute?[87]

Paul Stillwell: I would say right at that number, yes.

Admiral Eller: We were running low on funds, and about this time, (again, this shows how the Lord takes care of us) the Naval Institute decided to start an oral history program and asked me who I'd recommend to conduct it. I replied that Jack Mason was the best man in the country, and I believe he was.[88] He certainly was from the Navy's standpoint. He knew so much by then, of course, having talked to all these people and read up on them a great deal. I was delighted to see this because though we would miss him, I knew the Naval Institute would carry on, and when Jack left, would get another superb interviewer.

Paul Stillwell: Thank you very much.

Admiral Eller: You have done a splendid job in his footsteps.

---

85. Thaddeus V. Tuleja, *Climax at Midway* (New York: W. W. Norton, 1960).
86. Admiral Thomas C. Hart, USN (Ret.); Admiral James Fife, USN (Ret.).
87. In 1969 Dr. Mason inaugurated the oral history program at the Naval Institute.
88. Dr. John T. Mason Jr. headed the Naval Institute's oral history program from 1969 to 1982. He did the bulk of the interviews for Admiral Eller's oral history.

Paul Stillwell: I'm curious, why was the Marine Corps able to get its own program funded and the Navy wasn't?

Admiral Eller: They started after we did, I think, didn't they?

Paul Stillwell: Yes.

Admiral Eller: I believe Wally Greene was responsible. He was deeply interested in all things historical that strengthen our ties to the best of the past.[89] At my invitation he came to see our Navy Memorial Museum when it was well along. Meanwhile, he had started a small one at Quantico, like our museum to instruct and inspire. John Magruder, a reserve officer of great artistic talents developed it into a jewel. Wally also helped me get a Marine for a time in the Naval Memorial Museum to insure Marines were not neglected. I got a Coast Guard officer also for a couple of years and occasionally from a bureau came to help work up a particular display.

To conclude oral history, I was delighted to see Jack go to the Naval Institute. I probably could have got funds to continue with Columbia, but what would happen later? We didn't need two Navy programs, and the Naval Institute has the money. I hope this fine work will now go on forever.

Paul Stillwell: I do, too.

Admiral Eller: How many have you done now?

Paul Stillwell: I just couldn't have a number because they're all in various stages of completion.

Admiral Eller: I know it. That's the way they work out. Well, is there anything else?

Paul Stillwell: I wonder if you had laid the keel for that series on Vietnam that is coming out.

---

89. General Wallace M. Greene Jr., USMC, served as Commandant of the Marine Corps from 1 January 1964 to 31 December 1967.

Admiral Eller: We collected the documents in Dean's archives to be available for a full-length study and worked on a classified account besides our classified monthly studies. Besides these we prepared a brochure on riverine warfare, one of the best. Several sections collaborated. After a brief summary of our long involvement in inland water combat, most of it dealt with the bold achievements in Vietnam. Drafts had the input of veterans there. I spent an especially long time on it. My introduction ended with the noble words of Lieutenant William Roark, U.S. Navy, written to his wife not long before he flew off his carrier into the blue vasts never to return: "I don't want my son to fight a war I should have fought...1 will not live under a totalitarian society and I don't want you to either. I believe in God and will resist any force that attempts to remove God from society...This is what we all must do if we believe in what the Founding Fathers stood for."[90]

Paul Stillwell: There was another booklet on the monitors and one on CNO's house.

Admiral Eller: Yes, we got the latter out early because of CNO interest. While with us, Lieutenant Weber fell in love with monitors, and continued working with them in civil life. He finished the brochure during short periods of reserve duty with us, a sound and thoroughly reliable work. Among others, I like especially those on "Keeping the Peace" and a short history, "The U.S. Navy."

Paul Stillwell: I'm curious why the publication program has lost a good deal of momentum there.

Admiral Eller: I don't know. Probably because of a shortage of talented reservists and others in civil life ready to help just for the love of it. Also perhaps because they weren't needed as much. The Civil War chronology was finished. We had collected most of the material for the *Documents of the Revolution*. Bill Clark had sent in his part for several volumes ahead, so Bill Morgan continued to push them out relatively fast. Our other multivolume work—under the able hand of Jim Mooney, the *Dictionary* did get finished, of course. We

---

90. Lieutenant William M. Roark, USN, was killed on 7 April 1965 while flying an A-4 Skyhawk on a bombing mission over North Vietnam. He was a member of Attack Squadron 153 (VA-153). The destroyer escort *Roark* (DE-1053) was named in his honor.

celebrated that in the Memorial Museum two or three years ago, with me as a participating guest. This required climbing the *Constitution*'s fighting top. We had obtained it in the '60s when the mast had to be replaced. In the renovation of the building, Jack Kane installed it.

Besides the loss of Clark, publication of the *Naval Documents* slowed down when Morgan retired. Bill Dudley, his relief, is doing a good job, but he's working more on publishing 1812 documents. We also had this project in mind for later on. Frequently in research trips for documents of the Revolution we would run across some on the War of 1812 or the Civil War or any other period, and we'd have them microfilmed along with the documents of the Revolution.

Before we close. I'll mention a few other projects we started. One was a scientific and technological chronology. This is a valuable project somebody could take on. The Navy has led the nation in many scientific/technical fields such as oceanography, radio communication, nuclear energy, computers, radar. This facet of the Navy had long interested me. It grew when we prepared a speech for Secretary Gates to deliver to the Newcomen Society. The speech, dealing with some highlights, appeared as a Newcomen publication. One of our brochures mentioned these and others, but we need a full-length study. Much was done when I left. An interested worker could go with it.

Another unfinished project ready for an author is a chronology and calendar of the Navy from 1775 to date. Under contract, John Heffernan worked years on this. His final draft was an admirable one from certain standpoints, but after several tries, he still couldn't get technical and scientific highlights. So we never did print it. And then I wanted a good history of the growing power of the sea against the land. If you follow this from sailing ship days to steam and atomic power you begin to realize that the power of sea against land has multiplied. No longer do tide and wind have the same adverse effects, and today we have nuclear-powered carriers and Trident subs with Poseidon missiles. I summarized these new elements in an introduction to one of our Civil War chronologies and elsewhere, but we needed a full-length study starting with the age of oars.

We got Professor Richard West, Civil War historian, under contract to undertake this with my kibitzing. He did a good job up to the World Wars of our century, when he got beyond his depth. I worked with him to put in significant points. When we got into World War II, he just couldn't grasp it completely. That period especially went through many drafts. These went out to the field, as with other pertinent manuscripts, to leaders who were participants. It was coming along in good shape, but still needed work. Then he finally got sick and tired of it because I kept hounding him, and he asked to finish up. So in the late '60s we accepted the finished manuscript, but it's not ready yet. If somebody with the right perception of the overall significance and the overall influence of sea power could get into it, it would be an excellent book.

This book had hardly cleared the ways when a group talked me into editing a volume on the upcoming American Revolution bicentennial. It appealed because I could bring out the controlling effect of the sea, neglected by most historians. I took the first and last chapters. Fifteen others prepared those between. Besides my chapters, all but a couple of the others ate up my time on rewriting. Work on *The Chesapeake Bay in the American Revolution* took as many years as the Revolution, but it came out a handsome and well-received book. My concluding chapter on George Washington's sea strategy, "the pivot on which everything turned," met my goal.

Returning to the manuscripts bringing out the growing power of sea against land, if you find anybody that would be interested in finishing this, stimulate him.

Paul Stillwell: All right.

Admiral Eller: It would be a fine book. I'd like to take it myself but I just can't. Then during that time, we did get a number of published works out besides those we've mentioned, such as Wainwright, the forerunner of CNO, and, of course, the Spruance and Turner books, Turner's is finally out.

Paul Stillwell: And there was one on Admiral Pratt that came out not too long after you left there.[91]

Admiral Eller: I don't remember our doing that.

Paul Stillwell: Jerry Wheeler did that one.

---

91. Gerald E. Wheeler, *Admiral William Veazie Pratt, U.S. Navy: a Sailor's Life* (Washington: Naval History Division, 1974).

Admiral Eller: Yes. He wrote that on his own.

Paul Stillwell: You may have had, though, a mechanism to publish works like this. Maybe that's worth discussing.

Admiral Eller: We published anything worthwhile developed in house at GPO, and occasionally we would publish something we liked that others had prepared. GPO made considerable money on some of our work. The *Dictionary of Naval Fighting Ships* became a best seller right away; so did the Civil War chronology as each year's issue came out. In fact, we got several awards for it from different Civil War groups, including a gold medal. Various other works were well received, especially certain brochures, and then the *Naval Documents*. Of course, there's just nothing like it.

Paul Stillwell: On that *Naval Documents* how did you decide what to put in and what not?

Admiral Eller: In the first volume, we put in virtually anything that referred to the sea. As I noted, Clark's initial draft for the early months was skimpy, largely material that he knew about in Pennsylvania and New England. He left out opening events in the South, the diplomatic field, and the merchant marine. It seemed important to cover all facets in any way relating to the sea, so as to get a true picture of the total effect of the sea on the war. We went through several drafts for these early months before reaching agreement. Small events, as well as great, went into Volume I. We could then begin leaving out lesser ones except those that obviously had a significant effect.

Early on we started collecting illustrations, which enhance any book. We have, I believe, the best and newest complete collection available. In illustrative charts of the Revolution, for example, the Library of Congress has a superb group of originals, but we have these and others all in film. Also we have probably the biggest collection of photos of sea-related objects of the Revolution. In Greenwich, for example, I got the director, Frank Carr, interested, and we got there a vast amount of photographs of 18th century materials. Additional ones came from other museums in Europe and the United States, from several private collections, including a large one of weapons in France, and from old books. Then there's a fine encyclopedia, *Diderot's Encyclopedia*, beautifully illustrated.

We selected from it and other early books. Abundant illustrations helped swell the size of *Naval Documents* but added greatly to their value. We made them large to pack in as much as we could since money didn't come easily. Those volumes would be two or three volumes of an ordinary documentary study.

Paul Stillwell: Yes, they would.

Admiral Eller: The museums interested me. I've always felt that anything you could see and touch was more valuable in seeking truth than anything written about an object. Next most valuable are original documents if used with caution. However books like the *Naval Documents* are read by scholars, mostly. If you illustrate heavily, like our Civil War chronology, then the buffs also will read. Even popular history reaches only a small percent of citizens. Most Americans don't read anything worthwhile very much, especially history.

Hence developing museums interested me as much as our publications. We now have, as I mentioned, museums or major maritime displays spread across the country. Most are new like the great Naval Aviation Museum at Pensacola and the fine Submarine Museum at Groton. That was a small display run by the Electric Boat Company originally, then turned over to the sub base. I don't think the base took much interest in it for a time. Then after the Aviation Museum and the Memorial Museum grew, they got interested. I haven't seen it for years. Have you been there?

Paul Stillwell: Yes. I think you should certainly go if you haven't.

Would you say that the creation of museums was the greatest satisfaction you had in your tour as Director of Naval History?

Admiral Eller: No, I wouldn't say that, but it was one of the greatest.

Paul Stillwell: Is there anything you could single out?

Admiral Eller: No, I'd say it was a culmination of these projects—the publishing, the museums, the historic ships, especially the *Constellation, Olympia,* and the battleships, the superb collection of photographs for current operations as well as past, the archives, oral history. In fact, practically all the projects I've mentioned, plus others not mentioned, would line up almost at the front line—and not for me only, but also for the fine staff who pulled the oars and brought us safe to port.

Paul Stillwell: It would be like trying to pick a favorite child, then; you just couldn't do it.

Admiral Eller: It would. Then I had this mild stroke and decided to retire. As retirement neared, Cowles Publishing Company in New York asked me to write something on Soviet sea power. As quick as I left the office, I started working on it full time. Pertinent portions of the manuscripts went to appropriate bureaus and operations in the department who would know anything about the subject, such as weapons, for example. I got help from all. I would do it, but before I retired Cowles Publishing Company asked me to do something on the Soviets' mad rush to win the sea, on which I had written and spoken for years, including an article in the Institute *Proceedings* in 1955. My book. *The Soviet Sea Challenge* took a couple of years and came out in '71.[92] I forecasted ahead as much as I could, although the weapons are not exactly the same any more. The challenge is far worse than I could forecast because both Republican and Democrat administrations failed to fund the Navy we needed, despite the furious Soviet buildup. The book received excellent reviews from coast to coast, though *The Washington Post* and *The New York Times* blacklisted it. Hanson Baldwin could not get one in the *Times*.[93] Despite the many good reviews, sales were modest. Jaundiced by Vietnam, readers didn't want to read anything about future danger.

Hardly had the book appeared when friends asked me to help them get started on a book on the Chesapeake in the Revolution for the forthcoming bicentennial. I agreed to advise, and pretty soon ended up being the editor and writing part of *Chesapeake Bay in the American Revolution*; that ate up some eight years.[94] I did that largely because I wanted to show Washington's clear understanding that sea power was, in his words, "the pivot upon which everything turned." I had started writing on the decisive influence of the sea

---

92. Ernest M. Eller, *The Soviet Sea Challenge* (Chicago: Cowles Book Co., 1971).
93. Hanson W. Baldwin was a 1924 graduate of the Naval Academy. Following several years of naval service, Baldwin began a distinguished career as a newspaperman, culminating as military editor of *The New York Times*. His oral history is in the Naval Institute collection.
94. Ernest M. Eller, *Chesapeake Bay in the American Revolution* (Centreville, MD: Tidewater Publishers, 1981).

in the American Revolution with an article for the *Proceedings* in the '30. To put the sea's importance in broad perspective, I wrote the first and last chapters. Editing the other 12 was a much harder job. Most of them required constant checking against original sources and revision; two required change of authors. The author of one of the two chapters that needed only minor editing now lives in Annapolis, Canon Pierce Middleton, an Episcopal minister, like Jack Mason. Before he went in the ministry he published a book on Chesapeake Bay shipping in colonial times, so we got him to take one of the chapters. He'd be an interesting man for you to interview. Also, have you interviewed Gene Fluckey?[95]

Paul Stillwell: No, I haven't. I hope to.

Admiral Eller: When he became CNO, Admiral Nimitz chose Gene as his personal aide.[96] He's an excellent talker and can give you much on his boss, as well as his own exploits. He may have been a factor in helping me finally to get all of the admiral's papers, after ten years of trying. One time after attending a submarine reunion in New York with Lockwood and other top commanders of the Pacific, Admiral Nimitz wrote me and said the finest speech made there was by Gene Fluckey, apparently a very stirring one.

Paul Stillwell: He wrote some very stirring patrol reports also.

Admiral Eller: Yes. And got the Medal of Honor. Now it seems fitting to close with a summary of my reaction to 14 years in Naval History. It was not a job I sought, wanted, or ever expected to hold. My thoughts turned elsewhere; but looking back over this tour I am convinced that going back to academy days, the Lord time after time blocked other roads and steered me to this job. Whatever contributions I may have made in other duty, as in antiaircraft training and development prior to World War II, and on Admiral Nimitz's staff, all are dwarfed by this last duty. In it I carried out my primary service to the Navy, the country, and to freedom that depends upon the sea to exist. Our two score books, many

95. During World War II, Commander Eugene B. Fluckey, USN, earned the Medal of Honor for his service as commanding officer of the submarine *Barb* (SS-220). He described his experiences in the book *Thunder Below!: the USS Barb Revolutionizes Submarine Warfare in World War II* (Urbana: University of Illinois Press, 1992).
96. For Admiral Fluckey's amusing account of his time with Admiral Nimitz and the trip to Richmond, Virginia, in the spring of 1946, see "The Nimitzes Call," *Naval History*, Spring 1988, pages 18-19.

filled with facts hard to locate, some widely read, some enduring reference works, and those of numerous authors we helped, demonstrate the crucial importance of strength at sea to the survival of our nation and of liberty. So do the naval displays in every state, and the great new museums devoted to sea power. So do more than a score of World War II warships, majestic memorials of victory at sea that made overall victory possible—and the defeat of totalitarianism that ever seeks to return man to slavery. Surely the Lord put me where I could be most useful. Now I think we might call down the watch, unless you have some questions.

Paul Stillwell: No, I think you've pretty well covered it. I am grateful to you, on behalf of the Naval Institute, for all the effort I know you've put into this oral history, and indeed, for being a sponsor of the program itself and helping bring that into being.

Admiral Eller: I was lucky on that, having the right man who advocated it and the right man to do it. I was delighted to do this oral history, and delighted to finish it up with you, Paul.

Paul Stillwell: Thank you very much, sir.

Index to the Oral History of
Rear Admiral Ernest M. Eller, U.S. Navy (Retired)

Abelson, Dr. Philip H.
Work in the late 1940s in developing nuclear power for the U.S. Navy, 841, 1099–1100

Air Force, U.S.
Was an opponent of the Navy in defense unification in 1949, 853–864

Albany, **USS (CA-123)**
Midshipman training cruise to Europe in the summer of 1951, 983–995
Deployment to the Sixth Fleet in 1951 and return home, 995–1008
Recovery of pilots from the aircraft carrier *Franklin D. Roosevelt* (CVB-42) in 1951, 995
In 1952 participated in cold-weather operational tests near Greenland, 1008–1014
Ship handling, 1005, 1012, 1015–1016
Training of officers and crew in 1951–52, 1014–1016
Relationship with the city of Albany, New York, 1016–1017

Albion, Dr. Robert G.
Harvard professor who served from 1943 to 1950 as Assistant Director of Naval History, 1055, 1089–1090

Algeria
Algiers visited by the heavy cruiser *Albany* (CA-123) in 1951, 1005–1006

Allard, Dr. Dean C.
In the 1960s and 1970s headed the operational archives section of the Naval History Division/Naval Historical Center, 903, 1060–1061, 1070, 1101, 1111

American Ordnance Association
An outgrowth of the Army Ordnance Association, it embraced the Navy shortly after World War II, 843

Anderson, Eugenie
Served 1949–53 as U.S. Ambassador to Denmark, 989

Antarctica
In the late 1950s Rear Admiral Richard Byrd's family donated his Antarctica material to the Naval History Division, 1084

Antiair Warfare
The training ship *Utah* (AG-16) participated in a war game against the Army Air Corps in 1937, 864–865

Antiaircraft practice by heavy cruiser *Albany* (CA-123) in the summer of 1951, 983, 988, 991–992

ARAMCO (Arabian American Oil Company)
Role in Saudi Arabia in the early 1950s, 888, 900, 905, 931, 933–938, 944–947, 959, 962

Army Air Corps, U.S.
Participated in a war game against the Navy in 1937, 864–865

Austin, Rear Admiral Bernard L., USN (USNA, 1924)
Served from 1952 to 1954 as director of the International Affairs Division of the Office of the Chief of Naval Operations, 1019, 1024, 1027

Austria
Part of 1949 planning for the establishment of the military part of the North Atlantic Treaty Organization, 872

Bahrain
Operation of the Bahrain Petroleum Company in 1950, 884, 888, 900
In the late 1940s–early 1950s served as a base for the Middle East Force flagship, 905, 934–935, 941, 954, 962, 966–967
Local sheikhs in 1950, 906–907, 941–943

Barnard, Rear Admiral Geoffrey, Royal Navy
In 1950 commanded the Indian Navy, 891

Bayer, Colonel William L., USA (USMA, 1926)
In 1949 was part of a U.S. delegation that went to Europe to plan the military organization for the North Atlantic Treaty Organization, 869, 872, 875

Beirut, Lebanon
Site of a 1951 meeting concerning the Trans-Arabian Pipeline, 968–969

Blandy, Admiral William H. P., USN (USNA, 1913)
Contender to be Chief of Naval Operations in 1947 but not selected, 845–846, 871–872

Bolger, Rear Admiral Joseph F., USN (USNA, 1921)
In 1951, as CinCNELM chief of staff, accompanied Admiral Robert Carney on a tour of the Middle East, 962, 966, 980

Bombay, India
Local living conditions in 1950, 890–892

Boone, Rear Admiral Walter F., USN (USNA, 1921)
  In the early 1950s was chief of staff to CinCNELM, 980
  Served 1954–56 as Superintendent of the Naval Academy, 1046–47

Bradley, General of the Army Omar N., USA (USMA, 1915)
  As Army Chief of Staff, 1947–49, 848, 852, 867, 870–871, 873
  Served as Chairman of the Joint Chiefs of Staff, 1949–53, 876–877

Briner, Captain Richard R., USN (USNA, 1930)
  Commanded the seaplane tender *Greenwich Bay* (AVP-41), 1949–50, 892–893, 908, 929

Brown, Vice Admiral Charles R., USN (USNA, 1921)
  As Sixth Fleet Commander in the 1950s welcomed historian Allan Nevins, 1104–1105

Brown, John Nicholas
  Served as Assistant Secretary of the Navy for Air shortly after World War II, 840

Buchanan, Captain Charles A., USN (USNA, 1926)
  In 1951 accompanied Admiral Robert Carney on a tour of the Middle East, 962–963, 966

Bucknell University, Lewisburg, Pennsylvania
  Eller's role in the mid–1950s in working with the engineering department, 1052–1058

Burke, Rear Admiral Arleigh A., USN (USNA, 1923)
  In the early 1950s participated in negotiations to end the Korean War, 1020–1022
  As Chief of Naval Operations in the 1950s strongly supported the establishment of a Navy museum in Washington, 1074

Byrd, Rear Admiral Richard E., USN (Ret.) (USNA, 1912)
In the late 1950s his family donated his Antarctica material to the Naval History Division, 1084

Canada
  U.S. Navy ships visited Halifax, Nova Scotia, in early 1952, 1011–1012

Cannes, France
  The heavy cruiser *Albany* (CA-123) visited in 1951, 999–1000

Caribbean Command, U.S.
  Based in Panama, in the late 1940s, under Lieutenant General Matthew Ridgway, USA, 861

Carney, Admiral Robert B., USN (USNA, 1916)

As CinCNELM toured the Middle East in 1951, 961–967, 981

Served 1951–53 as Commander in Chief Allied Forces Southern Europe (CinCSouth), 999

Ceylon

In 1951 Colombo was the site of a conference on South Asia and Southeast Asia affairs, 971

Local landscape and population in 1951, 971–975, 977–978

Trincomalee was the base in 1951 for the British East India Force, 977–978

Chapelle, Howard I.

Author who argued that the relic ship *Constellation* in Baltimore was no longer a frigate, 1079–1080

Chiang Kai-shek

For many years was the leader of Nationalist China, which was ousted from the mainland in 1949, 856–859

China

Communist takeover of the mainland in 1949, leading to the establishment of the Republic of China on Taiwan, 856–859

Civil War

Activities in the 1950s–60s on the part of Naval History Division in observance of the war's centennial, 1085–1086

Clark, William Bell

Editor of the series *Naval Documents of the American Revolution,* 1080, 1092–1098, 1111, 1114

Codd, Colonel Leo A., USA

Involvement with the American Ordnance Association in the late 1940s, 843

Cold-Weather Operations

In 1952 the heavy cruiser *Albany* (CA-123) participated in operational tests near Greenland, 1008–1014

Collisions

In January 1952 the attack transport *Mellette* (APA-56) collided with the attack cargo ship *Vermillion* (AKA-107), 1010–1011

Colombo, Ceylon

In 1951 was the site of a conference on South Asia and Southeast Asia affairs, 971-975

Communism

Involvement in U.S. labor unions during the 1940s, 859–860

The 1947 Truman Doctrine was designed to support nations threatened by Communism, 851

Takeover of mainland China in 1949, leading to the establishment of the Republic of China on Taiwan, 856–859

In the late 1940s Eller wrote papers on the Soviet Union and Communism for the National War College, 860–861

Negotiating tactics during the Korean War, 1020–1021

Congress, U.S.

Held hearings in 1949 on unification of the services, 877

Conolly, Admiral Richard L., USN (USNA, 1914)

Served in the late 1940s as CinCNELM, 875–876, 882, 903, 905, 930

In the 1960s did an oral history with Columbia University, 1105

Constellation, USS (IX-20)

Arguments in 1950s about her legitimacy as a frigate, 1079–1081

Crenshaw, Captain Edmund A., USNR (Ret.) (USNA, 1912)

Supported the preservation of the cruiser *Olympia* at Philadelphia as a museum ship, 1083–1084

Crete

Visited by the heavy cruiser *Albany* (CA-123) in 1951, 1002–1004

Crommelin, Captain John G. Jr., USN (USNA, 1923)

As a student at the National War College in the late 1940s was concerned about the future of naval aviation, 863

Cutter, Captain Slade D., USN (USNA, 1935)

In the late 1950s headed the Navy Museum in Washington, 1085

Defense Department

Creation of the department in 1947 led to ensuing attempts to curtail naval aviation and the Marine Corps, 844, 852–853, 863, 880

Restructuring of the department in the early 1950s increased bureaucracy, 1024–1027

Denfeld, Admiral Louis E., USN (USNA, 1912)

Served as Chief of Naval Operations, 1947–49, 845, 867–877

Personality, 869–871

Denmark

Visited by the heavy cruiser *Albany* (CA-123) in the summer of 1951, 987–989, 991

Dingwell, Captain John E., USN (Ret.)
Frustrated biographer of Admiral Harold R. Stark, 1090–1091

Drones
Flown from the heavy cruiser *Albany* (CA-123) in the summer of 1951 for antiaircraft practice, 983, 991–992

Duncan, Admiral Donald B., USN (USNA, 1917)
As Vice Chief of Naval Operations in the early 1950s developed a plan for Defense Department reorganization, 1025–1026
Role in enabling Eller to become Director of Naval History in 1956, 1058, 1060

***Duxbury Bay,* USS (AVP-38)**
In early 1951 became flagship of the U.S. Middle East Force, 967–968, 971

Dyer, Vice Admiral George C., USN (Ret.) (USNA, 1919)
Wrote biographical books on Admiral James O. Richardson and Admiral Richmond Kelly Turner, 1105–1106

Eckberg, Captain Herbert F., USN (Ret.) (USNA, 1927)
Upon retirement from active duty in 1956, joined the faculty of Bucknell University, 1057

Egypt
Landscape, people, and importance of the Nile River in 1950, 884–886, 928
Resentment in 1950 of British control, 886

Eisenhower, President Dwight D. (USMA, 1915)
Served 1951–52 as NATO Supreme Allied Commander Europe, 874, 999

***Elkomin,* USS (AO-55)**
Fleet oiler that made transatlantic crossing in 1951, 992, 1007

Eller, Rear Admiral Ernest M., USN (Ret.) (USNA, 1925)
Wife Agnes, 837, 864, 880–882, 982, 995, 1051–1052, 1059, 1093, 1095, 1104
Sons, 880, 995, 1059, 1092, 1099–1100
Suffered for years from chronic back pain and eventually retired on disability, 878-879, 1024, 1034–1038, 1059
Served 1946–48 an the Navy's Director of Public Information, 832–844, 861
In 1948–49 was a student at the National War College, 846–867
Served 1949–50 in the strategic plans division on the Joint Staff of the Joint Chiefs of Staff, 867–881
Commanded the Middle East Force, 1950–51, 883–981
In 1951–52 commanded the heavy cruiser *Albany* (CA-123), 982–1018

From 1952 to 1954 served as the Assistant Director, International Affairs Division of OpNav, 1019–1030
Retirement from active duty in 1954 for medical reasons, 1035
Prolific as a writer and speaker following his 1954 retirement, 1037–1052, 1113, 1116–1117
Role at Bucknell University in the mid–1950s, 1046, 1052–1058
Served from 1956 to 1970 as Director of Naval History, 1059–1118

Enterprise, USS (CV-6)
Scrapped in the 1950s, despite Admiral William Halsey's efforts to save her, 1079

Eritrea
Strategic importance in the early 1950s, 928–931

Ethiopia
Relationship with Eritrea in the early 1950s, 929–931

Evans, Major General Vernon, USA (USMA, 1915)
Chief of the U.S. Military Mission with the Iranian Army, 1948 to 1951, 912

Felt, Captain Harry D., USN (USNA, 1923)
In the early 1950s served as Commander Middle East Force, 980–981

Fluckey, Commander Eugene B., USN (USNA, 1935)
Medal of honor submariner who served after World War II as aide to Fleet Admiral Chester Nimitz, 1117

Forrestal, James V.
Role as Secretary of the Navy in the post-World War II period, 835, 837–838, 841, 844
Secretary of Defense from 1947 to 1949, 844, 853, 866, 1027

France
Part of 1949 planning for the establishment of the military part of the North Atlantic Treaty Organization, 872
The heavy cruiser *Albany* (CA-123) visited Cannes in 1951, 999–1000

Franklin D. Roosevelt, USS (CVB-42/CVA-42)
Two of the ship's pilots were rescued at sea in 1951 by a helicopter from the heavy cruiser *Albany* (CA-123), 995

Furer, Rear Admiral Julius A., USN (Ret.) (USNA, 1901)
In the 1950s wrote a book on the administrative history of the Navy in World War II, 1089

Germany
Berlin blockade, 1948–49, 856
Part of 1949 planning for the establishment of the military part of the North Atlantic Treaty Organization, 873
U.S. occupation forces in 1949, 873–874

Gibraltar
Visited by the heavy cruiser *Albany* (CA-123) in 1951, 1006–1007

Grady, Henry F.
Served as U.S. Ambassador to Iran, 1950–51, 894, 913–914, 922, 935, 960–961

Grant, Major General Ulysses S. III, USA (Ret.) (USMA, 1903)
From 1957 to 1961 headed the Civil War Centennial Commission, 1086–1087

Great Britain
Involvement with Palestine/Israel over the years, 854–855
Part of 1949 planning for the establishment of the military part of the North Atlantic Treaty Organization, 870, 872
Cooperation between the Royal Navy and Foreign Office in maintaining the British Empire over the years, 1033–1034

Greece
Visited by the battleship *Missouri* (BB-63) in 1946, 851
Piraeus visited by the heavy cruiser *Albany* (CA-123) in 1951, 1000–1001, 1005

Greene, General Wallace M., Jr., USMC (USNA, 1930)
Served as Commandant of the Marine Corps, 1964–67, 1103, 1110

Greenland
In 1951 the heavy cruiser *Albany* (CA-123) participated in operational tests near Greenland, 1008–1014

Greenwich Bay, USS (AVP-41)
In 1950 served as flagship of the Middle East Force, 888–889, 892–893, 905–908, 928–930

Gruenther, Major General Alfred M., USA (USMA, 1917)
In the later 1940s was Deputy Commandant of the National War College and later Director of the Joint Staff, 846–847, 867–869, 871, 875–876
Served as NATO Supreme Allied Commander Europe, 871

Guadalcanal
CNO Chester Nimitz's proclamation on the invasion's fifth anniversary in 1947, 839

Gunnery-Naval
    Antiaircraft practice by heavy cruiser *Albany* (CA-123) in the summer of 1951, 983, 988, 991–992
    Shore bombardment of Corsica and Algeria by the *Albany* in 1951, 999–1000

Halifax, Nova Scotia
    Visited by U.S. Navy ships in early 1952, 1011–1012

Hart, Parker T.
    In 1950 was consul general in Dharan, Saudi Arabia, later served as ambassador, 887–888, 906–907. 927

Headden, Captain William R., USN (USNA, 1925)
    U.S. naval attaché in Egypt in 1950, 884–885

Heffernan, Rear Admiral John B., USN (Ret.) (USNA, 1917)
    Served as Director of Naval History from 1946 to 1956, 1055, 1059, 1064, 1087–1088–1090, 1112

Henderson, Loy
    Foreign service officer who was U.S. ambassador to India, 1948–51, 889, 894, 972

Hensel, The Hon. Struve
    Role in the early 1950s in reorganization of the Defense Department, 1025–1027

Hill, Vice Admiral Harry W., USN (USNA, 1911)
    As Commandant of the National War College, 1946–49, 846–847

Holloway, Vice Admiral James L. Jr., USN (USNA, 1919)
    In 1947 was a guest on board the yacht *Sea Cloud,* former IX-99 in the Navy, 837
    Served 1950–53 as Commander Battleship-Cruiser Force Atlantic Fleet, 983, 987, 989, 991–992, 995, 1012, 1017–1018

Hooper, Vice Admiral Edwin B., USN (USNA, 1931)
    Served 1970–76 as Director of Naval History, 1098–1099

Huie, William Bradford
    Author who wrote biased articles against the Navy for *The Reader's Digest* in 1949, 863–866

Ibn Saud, King
    As ruler Saudi Arabia in the late 1940s–early 1950s, 883, 905–906, 932–933, 946, 963–967

India
    Contact in 1950 between U.S. officials and those of India, 889–890, 897, 901–903
    Local living conditions in 1950, 890–892, 975–980

Indian Navy still commanded by British officers in 1950s, 891

Iran
Spheres of influence for various nations in the late 1940s, 849–850, 855, 922
U.S. military mission to the country in the late 1940s–early 1950s, 850, 912–914
Strategic importance in 1950, 883–884, 922, 925–926, 960–961
Description of the landscape/seascape and inhabitants in 1950, 903–904, 911–926, 935–937, 954, 956–960
Prime Minister Razmara served from 1950 until his assassination in 1951, 921–923, 961, 980
Concern in the mid–1950s about the supply of oil from Iran, 1038–1040

Iraq
Strategic importance in 1950, 883–884
Description of the landscape and inhabitants in 1950, 925, 954–958

Israel
Established as a nation in 1948 and immediately recognized by the United States, 854–855

Istanbul, Turkey
Visited by the battleship *Missouri* (BB-63) in 1946, 850–851
Site of a 1951 conference on defenses in the Middle East and Mediterranean, 967-968
Visited by the heavy cruiser *Albany* (CA-123) in 1951, 1003–1004

Italy
In 1950 Rome was the site of a State Department conference concerning possible evacuation of Americans from the Middle East, 926–928
Naples visited by the heavy cruiser *Albany* (CA-123) in 1951, 997–999

Jackson, Captain Paul, USN (USNA, 1923)
In the early 1950s served as U.S. naval attaché in Pakistan, 894

Jefford, Rear Admiral James W., Royal Navy
In 1950 commanded the Pakistani Navy, 895

Johnson, Louis A.
As Secretary of Defense in 1949–50 pursued an anti-Navy and anti-Marine Corps agenda, 853, 866, 870–871, 880

Joint Chiefs of Staff
Planning in 1949–50 for the military organization of the North Atlantic Treaty Organization, 868–876

Joint Research and Development Board
Involvement in development work in the late 1940s, 839–843

Jones, John Paul
Revolutionary War hero whose 200th birthday the Navy celebrated in 1947, 836
In the 1950s the Naval History Division published a popular lithograph of Jones, 1071

Joy, Vice Admiral C. Turner, USN (USNA, 1916)
In the early 1950s participated in negotiations to end the Korean War, 1020

Khalifa, Salman bin Hamad Al
Ruler of Bahrain from 1941 until his death in 1961. 941–943

Khan, Liaquat Ali
As Prime Minister of Pakistan, 1951–53, 895–899, 901–903, 923

Knox, Commodore Dudley W., USN (Ret.) (USNA, 1896)
Long-time naval historian and curator, 1089

Korean War
Began in 1950 with invasion of South Korea, 880–881
Persian Gulf oil supported U.S. Navy ships operating off Korea in the early 1950s, 900, 905, 908, 935
Soviet and Red China participation, 947–948, 1021–1022
Negotiations that led to the armistice in July 1953, 1019–1020

Kuwait
Description of the landscape and inhabitants in 1950, 938–940

Labor Unions
Communist involvement in U.S. unions in the 1940s, 859–860

Leahy, Fleet Admiral William D., USN (USNA, 1897)
In 1947 influenced the selection of Admiral Louis Denfeld as Chief of Naval Operations, 845, 872

Leave and Liberty
For the crew of the Middle East Force flagship in the early 1950s, 941, 977
For the crew of the heavy cruiser *Albany* (CA-123) in 1951–52, 989, 996, 999–1000, 1011–1012

Lebanon
Beirut was the site of a 1951 meeting concerning the Trans-Arabian Pipeline, 968–969

Lee, Vice Admiral Fitzhugh, USN (USNA, 1926)
Commanded the aircraft carrier *Franklin D. Roosevelt* (CVB-42), 1951–52, 995, 1003–1004
In the 1950s helped round up historical on the cruiser *Memphis,* 1081

LeMay, Major General Curtis E., USAF
In the late 1940s served as the Air Force's Deputy Chief of Staff for Research and Development, 840

Lemnitzer, General Lyman L., USA (USMA, 1921)
Deputy Commandant of the National War College, 1947–49, 846–847

Lisbon, Portugal
Visited by the heavy cruiser *Albany* (CA-123) in 1951, 996

Loon Missiles
Former German V-1 rockets were used as Loon missiles by the U.S. Navy in the late 1940s, 832

Lovett, Robert A.
As Secretary of Defense in the early 1950s favored reorganization of the Defense Department, 1025

MacVeagh, Lincoln
U.S. Ambassador to Portugal from 1948 to 1952, 996

Mansour bin Abdulazia Al Saud
Served as Saudi Arabia's Minister of Defense from 1943 to 1951, 930–933

Mao Tse-tung
Leader of the People's Republic of China, which ousted the Republic of China from the mainland in 1949, 857–858

Marine Corps, U.S.
The creation of the Defense Department in 1947 led to ensuing attempts to curtail the Marine Corps, 852–853

Marshall, General of the Army George C., USA
Special U.S. envoy to China shortly after the end of World War II, 856–858

Mason, Dr. John T. Jr.
In the 1960s began doing naval oral histories for Columbia University, 1105
Later moved to the Naval Institute, 1109–1110, 1117

Maury, USS (AGS-16)
    Surveying ship that operated in the Persian Gulf in the early 1950s, 908, 943–944, 948

McKnew, Thomas W.
    As Secretary of the National Geographic Society in 1951, visited the heavy cruiser *Albany* (CA-123), 1006–1008, 1041

Medical Problems
    Eller suffered for years from chronic back pain and eventually retired on disability, 878–879, 1034–1038, 1059

Mediterranean Sea
    In 1946 the battleship *Missouri* (BB-63) visited various Mediterranean nations, 850
    Exercises and port visits involving the heavy cruiser *Albany* (CA-123) in 1951, 996–1007
    In the early 1950s Eller spoke in Washington, D.C., about the history of naval operations in the Mediterranean, 1030–1033

Mellette, USS (APA-56)
    In January 1952 collided with the attack cargo ship *Vermillion* (AKA-107), 1010–1011

Middle East Force, U.S.
    Contact in the early 1950s with India, 889–892, 901–903, 961, 975–980
    Contact in the early 1950s with Pakistan, 894–903, 974
    Contact in the early 1950s with Saudi Arabia, 900, 906–911, 930–940, 961–967
    Contact in the early 1950s with Iran, 850, 883–884, 903–904, 908–909, 911–926, 935–937, 954, 956–961
    Contact in the early 1950s with Iraq, 925, 954–958, 961
    Contact in the early 1950s with Eritrea, 928–929
    Contact in the early 1950s with Kuwait, 938–940
    Contact in the early 1950s with Muscat, 948–950
    Contact in the early 1950s with Syria, 968–970
    Contact in the early 1950s with Ceylon, 971–977
    Persian Gulf oil supported U.S. Navy ships operating off Korea in the early 1950s, 900, 905, 908, 935

Midway, USS (CVB-41)
    Firing of V-2 rocket from the aircraft carrier in 1947, 836–837

Mills, Vice Admiral Earle W., USN (USNA, 1918)
    As Chief of the Bureau of Ships after World War II, was involved in the development of nuclear power, 841

Milne, Cecil P.
As Assistant Secretary of the Navy in the late 1950s lent support to a naval museum in Washington, 1075–1076

Missiles
Loon was the first U.S. submarine-launched missile in 1947, 832
Testing of the Regulus I in the 1950s, 832–833
Firing of V-2 rocket from the aircraft carrier *Midway* (CVB-41) in 1947, 836–837
Development of the Terrier surface-to-air missile in the late 1940s, 842–843

Missouri, USS (BB-63)
In 1946 visited various Mediterranean nations, 850

Morgan, Dr. William J.
Historian who was involved in compiling the *Naval Documents of the American Revolution* series, 1062, 1091–1092, 1098, 1111

Morison, Rear Admiral Samuel Eliot, USNR (Ret.)
Wrote a multi-volume *History of United States Naval Operations in World War II*, 1065–1066

Morison, Samuel L.
Ship specialist who worked in the Naval History Division in 1960s–70s, later arrested in 1994, 1073, 1088

Mosaddegh, Mohammed
Served as Prime Minister of Iran from 1951 until he was ousted by coup in 1953, 980, 1039

Mullins, Captain Henry Jr., USN (USNA, 1931)
Commanded the fleet oiler *Elkomin* (AO-55), 1951–52, 1007

Muscat
Visited in 1950 by Commander Middle East Force, 948–950

Naples, Italy
Visited by the heavy cruiser *Albany* (CA-123) in 1951, 997–999

National Geographic Society
Thomas W. McKnew, Secretary of the National Geographic Society, visited the heavy cruiser *Albany* (CA-123) in 1951, 1006–1008

National Security Act
The law, enacted in 1947, created what became the Defense Department, 844
Amendment in 1949 created the post of Chairman of the Joint Chiefs of Staff, 871

National War College, Washington, D.C.
    Leadership personnel involved in the 1948–49 class, 846–847
    Program of study in the late 1940s, 847–861
    Field trip for students to visit Panama in the late 1940s, 861
    In the mid–1950s Eller spoke in at the college on the importance of sea power, 1037–1038

Naval History Division/Naval Historical Center
    Unrest in the division in the mid–1950s, 1055
    Varied activities from 1956 to 1970, 1059–1118
    Staffing in the 1950s and 1960s, 1059–1062, 1065, 1067–1074
    Ship naming in the 1950s–1970s, 1062–1064
    Washington-area naval museums, 1064–1065, 1071, 1074–1077
    Dictionary of American Naval Fighting Ships series began in the 1950s, 1064, 1073, 1087–1088, 1111–1114
    Samuel Eliot Morison series on World War II, 1065–1066
    Collection of artifacts and preservation of ships as museums, 1064, 1076–1083, 1115–1116
    Research and publication of the series *Naval Documents of the American Revolution,* 1080, 1090–1098, 1104, 1111, 1114–1115
    Activities in the 1950s–60s in observance of the Civil War Centennial, 1085–1087, 1111
    Coverage of the Vietnam War, 1100–1103, 1110–1111
    Involvement with oral history, 1104–1007
    Publication of booklets on various topics, 1108, 1111

Naval Research Laboratory
    Began working on nuclear power shortly after the end of World War II, 841

Naval Reserve, U.S.
    Recruiting of members in 1946–48, 833–835
    Flew prominent civilians to shipboard orientation cruises in the late 1940s, 838
    Value of reservists in the Korean War, 834
    Reservists beefed up manpower in the 1950s–1960s for the Naval History Division, 1071–1072, 1075, 1101–1102, 1109

Nehru, Jawaharlal
    Served as India's first Prime Minister from August 1947 to May 1964, 897, 902–903

Netherlands
    Visited by the heavy cruiser *Albany* (CA-123) in the summer of 1951, 990–991

Nevins, Professor J. Allan
    Pioneer at Columbia University in the field of oral history, 1940s–50s, 1054–1055, 1091, 1104–1005

Research visit to the Sixth Fleet, 1104–1005, 1107
For a time gathered material for a biography of Fleet Admiral Chester Nimitz, 1107–1108

Newberry, James N.
In the 1960s established P.T. Boats, Inc., 1078

News Media
Coverage of a 1947 Chesapeake cruise of the former Navy yacht *Sea Cloud* (IX-99), 837–838
Author William Bradford Huie wrote biased articles against the Navy for *The Reader's Digest* in 1949, 863–866
The heavy cruiser *Albany* (CA-123) hosted civilian newspapermen during her 1951 midshipman training cruise, 994–995
Opinion on the value of sea power expressed by the editor of the *Arizona Daily Star* in the 1950s, 1034
Coverage of the Vietnam War, 1101–1104

Nimitz, Fleet Admiral Chester W., USN (USNA, 1905)
Size of his staff while commanding the Pacific Fleet in World War II, 1066–1067
Served as Chief of Naval Operations, 1945–47, 839, 841, 844–845, 851–852
In 1953 wrote a letter to the selection board on Eller's behalf, 1028–1029
Declined to participate in an oral history but donated historical materials, 1106–1107
Development of the Nimitz Museum in Fredericksburg, Texas, 1107
Subject of a biography by E. B. Potter, 1107–1108

Noble, Rear Admiral Albert G., USN (USNA, 1917)
Served 1947–50 as Chief of the Bureau of Ordnance, 842–843

Norstad, Major General Lauris, USAF (USMA, 1930)
Involved in the post-World War II planning on unification of the services, 877

North Atlantic Treaty Organization (NATO)
Planning in 1949–50 for the military organization of NATO, 868–876

Nuclear Power Program
The U.S. Navy began working on nuclear power shortly after the end of World War II, 841, 1099–1100

Nuclear Weapons
U.S. use against Japan in 1945, 842
Effect on U.S. strategy and attitudes in the late 1940s, 833–834, 848–849, 852
The Soviet Union tested its first atomic bomb in 1949, 848
Training in 1950 on U.S. capabilities, 880

Oil

Granting of rights in Iran in the late 1940s, 850, 855

Persian Gulf oil supported U.S. Navy ships operating off Korea in the early 1950s, 900, 905, 908, 935

Role of ARAMCO in Saudi Arabia in the early 1950s, 888, 900, 905, 931, 933–938, 944–947, 959

Concern in 1950–51 on countering a Soviet attempt to control Middle East oilfields, 945, 947–948, 960, 964

Concern in the mid–1950s about the supply of oil from Iran, 1038–1039

Oliver, Vice Admiral Geoffrey, Royal Navy

In the early 1950s commanded the British East India Force, based in Ceylon, 977-978

Olympia, USS (C-6)

Preserved as a museum ship at Philadelphia, 1083–1084

Pahlavi, Mohammed Reza

As Shah of Iran, late 1940s–early 1950s, 850, 913–914, 922–925, 935, 959–960, 1039–1040

Pakistan

Local conditions in 1950, 893–900

Political leadership in the late 1940s–early 1950s, 895–903

A Pakistani destroyer visited Saudi Arabia in 1950, 932

Military assets in the early 1950s, 974

Panama

Lieutenant General Matthew B. Ridgway served as Commander in Chief Caribbean Command, based in Panama in the late 1940s, 861

Life in the country in 1949, 861–863

Pastorius, Dr. Johann

Prussian-born individual who came to the United States in the 1890s, served in the Spanish-American War, and later practiced medicine, 1035–1036

Peet, Commander Raymond E., USN (USNA, 1943)

In the 1950s served as aide to CNO Admiral Arleigh Burke, 1074

Persia

See Iran

Persian Gulf

Persian Gulf oil supported U.S. Navy ships operating off Korea in the early 1950s, 900, 905, 908

View of the surroundings from the Middle East Force flagship in 1950, 903–904

Pierce, Colonel James R., USA (USMA, 1922)
In 1950 was involved with training Iranian gendarmes, 912–913

Planning
Role of the strategic plans division of the Joint Staff in 1949–50, 867–868
Planning in 1949–50 for the military organization of the North Atlantic Treaty Organization, 868–876
Concern in 1950 on countering a Soviet attempt to control Middle East oilfields, 945, 947–948, 960, 964
U.S. strategy in the early 1950s concerning South Asia, 972–974

Portugal
Lisbon visited by the heavy cruiser *Albany* (CA-123) in 1951, 996

Post, Marjorie Merriweather
In 1947, while married to Ambassador Joseph Davies, hosted a cruise on board her yacht *Sea Cloud,* formerly IX-99 in the Navy, 837–838, 840

PT Boats
Establishment of P.T. Boats, Inc., in the 1960s, 1078

Public Relations
Role of the Navy Office of Information, 1946–48, 833–844, 861

Qatar
U.S. contact with local officials in 1950, 940
Description of the landscape in the early 1950s, 941

Radford, Admiral Arthur W., USN (USNA, 1916)
As Vice Chief of Naval Operations in 1949, testified to Congress on unification of the services, 877–878
Worked on his memoir while his papers were stored at the Naval History Division, 1070

Ramsey, Admiral Dewitt C., USN (USNA, 1912)
Contender to be Chief of Naval Operations in 1947, 845

Rassieur, Captain William T., USN (USNA, 1923)
Commanded the Middle East Force in 1950, 883, 888, 892

Razmara, Haji Ali
Iran's Prime Minister from June 1950 until his assassination in March 1951, 921–923, 961

Reader's Digest
    Author William Bradford Huie wrote biased articles against the Navy for the magazine in 1949, 863–866

Recruiting
    For the Naval Reserve in 1946–48, 833–835

Reeves, Vice Admiral John W., Jr. USN (USNA, 1911)
    In the late 1940s commanded the Naval Air Transport Service, 840–841

Regulus Missiles
    Testing of by the U.S. Navy in the 1950s, 832–833

Remón, José Antonio (Cantera)
    Head of the National Guard in Panama in the late 1940s, essentially ran the country, 861–862

Rhee, Syngman
    Served as President of the Republic of Korea during the Korean War, 1020–1021

Richardson, Admiral James O., USN (Ret.) (USNA, 1902)
    Worked with Vice Admiral George Dyer on Richardson's memoir, 1090

Rickover, Captain Hyman G., USN (USNA, 1922)
    In the late 1940s got involved in the Navy's nuclear power program, 841–842, 1099–1100

Ridgway, Lieutenant General Matthew B., USA (USMA, 1917)
    Army officer who was Commander in Chief Caribbean Command, based in Panama, in the late 1940s, 861

Roark, Lieutenant William M., USN (USNA, 1960)
    Sent a patriotic letter to his wife before being killed over North Vietnam in 1965, 1111

Rome, Italy
    In 1950 was the site of a State Department conference concerning possible evacuation of Americans from the Middle East, 926–928

Rosenberg, Dr. David A.
    Burke biographer who worked in the 1960s writing entries for the *Dictionary of American Naval Fighting Ships,* 1088–1089

Royal Navy
    In the early 1950s Royal Navy officers commanded the navies of India and Pakistan, 891, 895

British Force in the Far East in the early 1950s, 977–978
Cooperation between the Royal Navy and Foreign Office in maintaining the British Empire over the years, 1033–1034

Satterthwaite, Joseph C.
Served as U.S. Ambassador to Ceylon from 1949 to 1953, 973, 977–978

Saudi Arabia
Visited by Admiral Richard Conolly in 1946, 883
Landscape/seascape description in 1950, 886–887, 900, 903–904, 931–934
Role of ARAMCO (Arabian American Oil Company) in the early 1950s, 888, 900, 909–911, 931, 933–940, 944–947, 959
U.S. contact with local leaders, 887–888, 906–910, 930–933, 946–947, 961–967
Construction of the Trans-Arabian Pipeline in the early 1950s, 909–911, 968–970

Sea Cloud, ex-USS (IX-99)
In 1947, while married to Ambassador Joseph Davies, Marjorie Merriweather Post, hosted a cruise on board her yacht formerly IX-99 in the Navy, 837–838

Selection Boards
In 1952 passed over Eller for rear admiral, 1027–1028
In 1953 Fleet Admiral Chester Nimitz wrote a letter to the selection board on Eller's behalf, 1028–1029

Shah of Iran
See: Pahlavi, Mohammed Reza

Shahin, Vice Admiral Havibollah, Iranian Navy
As the Navy's Chief of Staff, visited the United States in the late 1950s, 958

Sherman, Admiral Forrest P., USN (USNA, 1918)
As DCNO (Operations) shortly after World War II, 841–842, 851, 877–878
In 1948–49, served as Commander Sixth Task Fleet in the Mediterranean, 851, 875-876
Served 1949 as Chief of Naval Operations, 878–880, 982, 1015, 1027
Death of in July 1951, 1015

Ship Handling
In the heavy cruiser *Albany* (CA-123) in 1951–52, 1005, 1012, 1015–1016

Sicily
Visited by the heavy cruiser *Albany* (CA-123) in 1951, 997

Sides, Captain John H., USN (USNA, 1925)
In 1950–51 commanded the heavy cruiser *Albany* (CA-123), 982

Sixth Fleet, U.S.
    Exercises and port visits involving the heavy cruiser *Albany* (CA-123) in 1951, 996–1007
    Role in supporting population around the Mediterranean in the 1950s, 1031
    Visited by historian Allen Nevins in the mid–1950s, 1104–1105

Soviet Union
    Tested its first atomic bomb in 1949, 848
    Efforts in the late 1940s–early 1950s to extend the reach of Communism, 849–851, 896, 922, 925–926, 974, 981
    Support for Arabs in the late 1940s, 855
    Berlin blockade, 1948–49, 856
    In the late 1940s Eller wrote papers on the Soviet Union and Communism for the National War College, 860–861
    Support for North Korea in the early 1950s, 881, 947–948, 1023
    Concern in 1950–51 on countering a Soviet attempt to control Middle East oilfields, 945, 947–948, 960, 964
    Change of power with the death of dictator Joseph Stalin in 1953, 1024
    Efforts in the 1950s to spread its influence, 1032, 1039–1040
    In 1971 Eller published a book titled *The Soviet Sea Challenge,* 1116

Spruance, Admiral Raymond A., USN (Ret.) (USNA, 1907)
    Subject of a command study/biography by Vice Admiral Emmet Forrestel, 1105–1106

Stark, Admiral Harold R., USN (Ret.) (USNA, 1903)
    Hesitant about cooperation on his biography, 1090–1091

State Department
    Its personnel participated in National War College programs in the late 1940s, 847, 857–858
    In 1950 Rome was the site of a State Department conference concerning possible evacuation of Americans from the Middle East, 926–928

Stilwell, Lieutenant General Joseph Warren, USA (USMA, 1904)
    Service in China in World War II, 857–858

Stroh, Captain Robert J., USN (USNA, 1930)
    Commanded the small seaplane tender *Valcour* (AVP-55) in 1950–51, 928, 951, 1037–1038

Sullivan, John L.
    Served 1947–49 as Secretary of the Navy, 837–838, 844

Syria
    Construction of a portion of the Trans-Arabian Pipeline in the early 1950s, 969–970

Terrier Missile
Development work at Inyokern in the late 1940s, 842–843

Trans-Arabian Pipeline
Construction of in the early 1950s, 909–911, 968–970

Trincomalee, Ceylon
Base in 1951 for the British East India Force, 977–978

Truman, President Harry S.
Involvement in defense matters in the late 1940s, 848–853, 866, 869–872, 877–878, 880
Friendly, outgoing personality, 851–853
The Truman Doctrine in 1947 was designed to support nations threatened by Communism, 851, 868
Recognition of the nation of Israel in 1948, 854
Spoofed at the Gridiron Club in Washington in 1951, 982

Turkey
Visited by the battleship *Missouri* (BB-63) in 1946, 850–851
Istanbul was the site of a 1951 conference on defenses in the Middle East and Mediterranean, 967–968
Visited by the heavy cruiser *Albany* (CA-123) in 1951, 1003–1004

Turner, Admiral Richmond K., USN (Ret.) (USNA, 1908)
Subject of a biography by Vice Admiral George Dyer, 1105–1106

Unification
Creation of the Defense Department in 1947 and ensuing attempts to curtail naval aviation and the Marine Corps, 852–853, 863–864, 877–880
Restructuring of the Defense Department in the early 1950s increased bureaucracy, 1024–1027

Utah, **USS (AG-16)**
Participated in a war game against the Army Air Corps in 1937, 864–865

V-2 Rocket
Firing of from the aircraft carrier *Midway* (CVB-41) in 1947, 836–837

Valcour, **USS (AVP-55)**
Served as flagship of the U.S. Middle East Force in 1950, 928–930, 934, 950–953

Vandenberg, General Hoyt S., USAF (USMA, 1923)
Served 1948 to 1953 as Air Force Chief of Staff, 843, 867, 870, 875

Vedel, Vice Admiral Aage Helgesen
    Served as Commander in Chief Royal Danish Navy in the early 1950s, 988, 990

***Vermilion*, USS (AKA-107)**
    In January 1952 collided with the attack transport *Mellette* (APA-56), 1010–1011

Vienna, Austria
    Rundown postwar condition in 1949, 875–876

Vietnam War
    Coverage of the war by the Naval History Division, 1100–1104, 1110–1111

Walsh, Colonel James L., USA (USMA, 1909)
    Involvement with the American Ordnance Association in the late 1940s, 843

Warren, Avra M.
    U.S. Ambassador to Pakistan, 1950–52, 894, 901, 972

Washington Navy Yard
    In the late 1950s became the home of the Navy Museum, 1075–1077

Weather
    A storm struck the French Riviera and the heavy cruiser *Albany* (CA-123) in 1951, 1000
    In 1952 the *Albany* participated in cold-weather operational tests near Greenland, 1008–1014

Whitehill, Walter M.
    Historian who assisted the Navy in compiling the *Naval Documents of the American Revolution* series, 1091–1092

***Wild Goose*, HMS**
    Flagship of the British Persian Gulf Force in 1951, 980

Winnecker, Rudolph A.
    Taught at the National War College before becoming Chief Historian of the Office of the Secretary of Defense in 1949, 862

Yeager, Captain Howard A., USN (USNA, 1927)
    In the late 1940s served as senior aide to Chief of Naval Operations Louis Denfeld, 869, 871

Launched in 1969, the U.S. Naval Institute's award-winning oral history program is among the oldest in the country. Used in combination with documentary sources, oral histories offer a richer understanding of naval history through candid recollections and explanations rarely entered into contemporary records. In addition, they help depict the atmosphere of a particular event or era in a manner not available in official documents.

The nonprofit Naval Institute accomplishes its history projects through contributed funds and gratefully accepts tax-deductible gifts of all sizes for this purpose. This support allows the Institute to preserve the life experiences of today's service men and women so they may enlighten and inspire future generations.

For information about opportunities to underwrite Naval Institute oral history projects, please contact the Naval Institute Foundation at 291 Wood Road, Annapolis, Maryland 21402; by phone at (410) 295-1054; or by e-mail at foundation@usni.org.

www.ingramcontent.com/pod-product-compliance
Lightning Source LLC
Chambersburg PA
CBHW082150070526
44585CB00020B/2157